1982

The Philosophy of Man

THE PHILOSOPHY OF MAN

A New Introduction to Some Perennial Issues

HOWARD P. KAINZ

THE UNIVERSITY OF ALABAMA PRESS
University, Alabama

Library of Congress Cataloging in Publication Data

Kainz, Howard P
  The philosophy of man.

  Bibliography: p.
  Includes index.
  1. Philosophical anthropology.   I. Title.
BD450.K28   128   79-14716
ISBN 0-8173-0019-8
ISBN 0-8173-0066-X (pbk.)

Contents

ACKNOWLEDGMENTS   vi

FOREWORD BY GERALD F. KREYCHÉ   vii

INTRODUCTION   1

1. HOW IS MAN DISTINCT FROM THE OTHER ANIMALS?   9

2. WHAT EVER HAPPENED TO INSTINCT IN MAN?   17

3. THE ENVIRONMENT-HEREDITY CONTROVERSY: WHAT IS BEHIND IT AND CAN IT BE RESOLVED?   29

4. MEN AND WOMEN: WHAT IS THE DIFFERENCE, REALLY?   41

5. WHAT IS THE FUTURE OF HUMAN EVOLUTION?   48

6. IS MAN A UNITY OR A DUALITY?   57

7. WHAT IS FREEDOM?   68

8. HOW DOES CONSCIOUSNESS DEVELOP?   77

9. WHAT IS MATURITY?   87

10. WHAT IS LOVE?   93

11. PARANORMAL PHENOMENA: DO THEY EXIST, AND IF SO, WHAT ARE THEIR PHILOSOPHICAL IMPLICATIONS?   102

12. IS THERE SURVIVAL AFTER DEATH?   113

EPILOGUE: A RETURN TO THE BEGINNING—WHAT IS MAN?   135

NOTES   136

GLOSSARY OF NAMES   154

GLOSSARY OF TERMS   163

BIBLIOGRAPHICAL EXCURSUS   173

INDEXES   186

Acknowledgments

I would like to thank Mr. Lowell Herr and Mr. Kerry Walters for valuable help researching several sections of this book; Dr. Bernard Boelen of DePaul University for theoretical and methodological ideas that eventually led to the development of Chapters 8 and 9 in their present form; Dr. Brian Lewis, a zoologist at the City of London Polytechnic, for suggestions relating to Chapters 1 and 2; Mr. Mark Schersten for assistance in preparing the Glossary of Names; Professor Gerald F. Kreyché for contributing the Foreword; and Mr. F. P. Squibb, Senior Editor of The University of Alabama Press, for help in the development of the final version of this book.

Finally, I wish to thank the many hundreds of students whose enthusiastic responses to earlier versions of this work have encouraged me to finish it, and whose many constructive criticisms, freely offered and gratefully accepted, have helped make this a better book than it otherwise would have been.

For such imperfections as may still remain, I bear sole responsibility.

Foreword

Those of us who have been teaching in college these past twenty-five years have witnessed some rather harried curricular changes in philosophy and the other humanistic studies. I myself have played a small role in giving birth to such innovation. (However, I am not sure I would recognize, much less own up to, some of the resultant offspring!)

The first such major change occurred in the fifties, largely in response to the burgeoning enrollment of ex-GI's, anxious to catch up on their years lost in service. Responding to this inrush, philosophy departments, while still staving off egalitarianism, were constrained to mitigate their traditional elitism.

A second major change occurred in the turbulent sixties. It might be dubbed, "the quest for relevancy."

In our own time, curricular changes are once more in the offing. These are pressured because of a changing college clientele. Populating institutions of higher learning today are not only the white middle-class majority, but Blacks, Spanish-speaking peoples, vocationally oriented women and, in general, the housewife who wants to see what she may have missed during all those years when she was busy raising a family.

Sometimes leading, sometimes following, but always associated with curricular change, is the introduction of new textbooks. These help consolidate new courses or programs of studies. The current new genre of textbook demands less dogmatism from a college student who, fortunately, is more prepared to challenge, rather than passively accept, ideas foreign to his own experience. The new situation in the classroom demands an approach that is *fundamentally* interdisciplinary, because of the need for integration and a renewed emphasis on general education. It demands an ability to get the student to think for himself, for this is the age of involvement.

Howard P. Kainz' *The Philosophy of Man: A New Introduction to Some Perennial Issues* scores well on all of the above points. It is not only a challenging textbook, but also a genuine contribution to the literature, as well. As any long-standing academic can testify, this is a rare combination indeed! It could be achieved only by one who is a scholar, an experienced teacher, and a professional writer.

This is not to deny that there were and still are some good standard texts in *The Philosophy of Man*. Faithfully, they still lead students through the darkness of Plato's Cave, the ambiguities of Hegel's dialectic, and the bleakness of Sartre's desert of despair. However, when one examines these texts carefully, one sees that they are generally launched from a positional viewpoint, and one whose presuppositions seldom surface. Then, too, one can search these texts in vain for any hint of the problems of everyday living and what touches upon this, e.g., love, maturity, and the differences of man and woman. It is to just such issues that Kainz addresses himself. His "position," if it can be called such, is *critical,* in the best sense of this term. That is, he outlines the problem and then sets forth the main strengths and weaknesses of conflicting points of view. When possible, he shows how these can be ameliorated. He leads, he encourages, but he never insists on having the last word, recognizing that it is the reader's right to make that judgment. Kainz' avoidance of "pat answers" is especially appreciated by the long-suffering teacher, who often is embarrassed by texts in sharp disagreement with his own views. Nonetheless, if philosophy is more an activity than a body of facts, there can be no question that Howard Kainz is "doing" philosophy. And he is setting a good example for others to follow in his honesty, his openness, and in his refusal to succumb to the temptation of simplistic answers.

Lastly, the book has balance. Neither the contemporary nor the traditional is emphasized at the expense of the other. Both are given a fair hearing. While the text makes no claims to present the history of philosophy, the reader will be rewarded by learning something of that history, *en passant.* I am sure that the author would agree with my quoting Santayana on this point: "Those who cannot remember the past are condemned to repeat it."

Welcome, then, to a useful text and an absorbing book.

DePaul University   Gerald F. Kreyché
1980

The Philosophy of Man

Introduction

The twelve issues we will be considering in this book are not new or novel, but have been confronted now and again throughout the history of philosophy, from a variety of philosophical vantage points. Thus it should be illuminating at the outset to examine briefly the "lineage" or historical antecedents of these issues, in order to indicate in a preliminary way how, if at all, the debatable points have changed over the years, and what, if any, contextual changes of relative importance or significance they have undergone; and in order to prepare ourselves to gauge, eventually, how congruent, if at all, the approaches to their solution have been, both now and in antiquity.

(1) *The Specific Differences Between Man and the Other Animals.* This topic, usually stated in the form of a question, has been considered by many philosophers (Aristotle, Thomas Aquinas, Hegel, Marx, Nietzsche, Dewey, et al.) and it seems that virtually every one of them has come up with his own distinctive solution. In our day, studies in anthropology and animal psychology seem to challenge some of the answers that have enjoyed wide acceptance. We need to take a new look at the evidence.

(2) *Human Instincts.* In ancient Greek philosophy, Socrates and Plato spoke about a "divine instinct" in man, and the medieval scholastics, following Aristotle, speculated about the existence of some human instinct (*vis cogitativa*) analogous to animal instinct (*vis aestimativa*). At present there is considerable disagreement about whether there are any specifically human instincts, and, if so, what they might be. In a culture such as ours, which emphasizes cerebration, education, and conscious control, the emphasis on learned behavior may be so extreme as to force important questions about unlearned behavior into the background.

(3) *Environment vs. Heredity.* Plato explicitly broaches the nature-nurture (or heredity-environment) problem in his *Timaeus,* and in the *Republic* and elsewhere gives much attention to the effect of education and other "conditioning" factors on human character, vice, and aberration. In our day we frequently tend toward an "environmentalist" solution to the problem, but now and then apparently hereditarian facts emerge to challenge our environmentalist presuppositions.

(4) *The Differences between Man and Woman.* In the *Republic,* Plato proffers a particularly bold proposal for the equality of the sexes, and in the *Symposium* he speculates at length about the origin and nature of sex differences. Aristotle, Schopenhauer, Hegel, Kierkegaard, and many others have tried to pinpoint some basic "ontological" difference or differences between the sexes, although they have done this at times with overtones that we in our day might consider biased or "chauvinistic." Their chauvinism aside, however, the philosophical problem they raise seems to be a real and important one.

(5) *The "Highest Stages" of Evolution.* Although primitive but interest-ing theories of the evolution of man from "lower" animals were posed by Anaximander, Anaximines, and Democritus in ancient times, the question about "the future of evolution," as some have pointed out, is in continuity not so much with these primitive theories as with the ancient concept (in Plato, Aristotle, Plotinus, et al.) of a "Great Chain of Being" extending hierarchically and in gradual steps from the lowest to the highest orders. The contemporary questions raised by Henri Bergson, Julian Huxley, Pierre Teilhard de Chardin, and others about the "future of evolution" are simply reformulations, in consonance with evolutionary theory and with specific emphasis on *temporality*, of the notion of a hierarchical de-velopment in the progress of existence, life, and consciousness.

(6) *Dualism vs. Monism in Anthropology.* Ever since Aristotle tried with only moderate success to bridge the yawning gap between soul and body that is found in Platonic philosophy, philosophers in the Western world have been oscillating between dualistic views of man (e.g., René Descartes, Immanuel Kant) and monistic views (e.g., Benedict Spinoza and the existentialists). Is a solution to be found in the one camp or the other? Or somewhere in between? Or—disconcerting thought—at all?

(7) *Freedom.* The question of the "freedom" of man is found only in a seminal way in ancient philosophy, e.g., in Plato's question in the *Meno* about how a man who really knew what was good could do evil, and in Aristotle's attempts to distinguish between voluntary and involuntary acts in his *Nichomachean Ethics.* This question, including its interpersonal and political ramifications, has been explicated as a central philosophical prob-lem in modern philosophy from extremely divergent viewpoints, i.e., by Thomas Hobbes and John Locke, Immanuel Kant and John Stuart Mill, Jean-Paul Sartre and Bertrand Russell, and many others.

(8) *The Development of Consciousness.* Plato and Aristotle both had theories about the relationship of the various stages of life to a corre-sponding perfection of intellect or consciousness, and philosophers such as G.W.F. Hegel and J.G. Fichte have considered the analysis of the sequential development of various stages of consciousness in the human individual to be an important part of, or introduction to, their philosophi-cal systems. Contemporary developmental psychology corroborates the validity of some of the questions they were asking.

(9) *The Concept of Human Maturity.* Philosophers such as Aristotle, Plato, Hegel, and Friedrich Nietzsche have speculated about and tried to determine the highest perfection of existence attainable by individual men—a question that, in contemporary parlance, boils down to the ques-tion of the meaning of "maturity." Can philosophical analysis throw any light on this concept, which is a central but often vague presupposition in much contemporary psychological literature?

(10) *Love.* In ancient Western philosophy, Heraclitus speculated that love resulted from a conflict of opposites, Empedocles supposed that love

was the product of the attraction of similars for similars, and philosophers ever since have been oscillating between these two extremes. If we knew once and for all what love is, perhaps loving would become easier. Or perhaps not.

(11) *The Paranormal.* Aristotle in his treatises on dreams and divination, Thomas Aquinas in his discussions of the occult, and Hegel in the discussions of hypnotism, clairvoyance, telepathy, and precognition in his *Philosophy of Mind* have prepared the way for discussion of the philosophical significance of the data now available concerning parapsychological phenomena.

(12) *Immortality.* And finally, ever since Plato's *Phaedo* (if not before) philosophers have been debating the possibility of individual survival after death. Perhaps they have been asking the wrong questions, or the right questions in the wrong way. Can we reformulate the basic question so as to make it answerable?

Our overall purpose in the discussions that follow will be to take a fresh look at some of these "old" questions about man, to reformulate them and update them as may be necessary, to analyze their contemporary relevance, and to bring new evidence and insight to bear on them, wherever possible.

Any philosopher who treats of man (and anyone who reads such a philosopher) should be aware, however, of the potentially wide-ranging effects on objectivity of what may seem to be innocuous initial presuppositions or respectable world views. One's basic conceptions of what man is will eventually affect the methodology one uses to treat of man, and indirectly (if certain types of conclusions tend to follow from certain types of methodologies) the conclusions one reaches. For instance, the Platonist who views man as essentially an eternal and indestructible soul imprisoned in a body and only temporarily dependent on the mere shadows of reality ("matter") will tend to disparage shadowy "empirical" evidence in trying to solve philosophical questions about man and will appeal primarily to rationalistic thought-forms and a priori principles and procedures. The kind of Christian who is particularly sensitive and committed to the notion of the original "sinfulness" of man and the disorderliness of man's sensual and sensory faculties will also tend to a kind of rationalism and dogmatism when it comes to philosophizing about man in order to bolster, to some extent, fallible human perceptions by an appeal to principles derived from the better parts of man (natural reason and reason illuminated by, and subordinated to, faith); this tendency is perhaps best exemplified in the "rational psychology" of medieval scholasticism, which began with Aristotelian psychology as the purest representative of natural reason and proceeded to correct and redirect the Aristotelian insights and render them serviceable to the "higher" inspirations of Christian revelation.

On the other hand, the materialistic reductionist who interprets all prima facie psychic or mental phenomena as "merely" physical processes and is made distinctly uncomfortable by any suggestion of the existence of an independent "subjectivity" will admit only those questions about man that are susceptible of exact empirical analysis and, for those few questions that are thus admitted, will tend to rule out any approach that seems subjective, holistic, or unverifiable according to standard and publicly recognized procedures.

An awareness of the significance of such presuppositions, coupled with a desire to avoid both rationalistic and materialistic extremes, led in Renaissance times to what later came to be known as "philosophical anthropology." This movement has taken so many different directions over the centuries that it is virtually impossible to define. However, the following generalization would express the character of the most representative expressions of the movement: it unites a commitment to human freedom with a determination to understand the material forces, including cultural conditions, affecting man; and it tempers an acceptance of, and enthusiasm for, science with a resolution to maintain a humanistic understanding of, and control over, the copious data that science produces.

The multiple forms that philosophical anthropology has taken may perhaps best be accounted for by a consideration of the multiple connotations of the term *empirical*. For some philosophical anthropologists, e.g., Montaigne and Shaftesbury, the "empirical" study of man was a study in which there was primary and constant reference to ordinary human experience. For certain others, e.g., John Locke and David Hume, it meant primarily ordinary experience subjected to philosophical analysis. For others, e.g., Denis Diderot, Henri Bergson, and Pierre Teilhard de Chardin, it has meant drawing extensively on science to illuminate the human condition or to correlate the findings of various sciences in a humanistic fashion. For still others, e.g., Edmund Husserl, Martin Heidegger, and Jean-Paul Sartre, it has connoted a direct introspective analysis of the basic structures of human consciousness as related to the world and social structures.

It is this last interpretation of *empirical* that is emphasized in the contemporary movement that explicitly lays claim to the label "philosophical anthropology." This movement, mostly European in inspiration and representation, includes a loosely knit assemblage of phenomenologists, existentialists, existential psychologists (e.g., Rollo May and Erich Fromm), anthropologists (e.g., Arnold Gehlen), and theologians (e.g., Martin Buber and Dietrich Bonhoeffer) who have subscribed to existential phenomenology. (It should be noted, however, that both Heidegger and Karl Jaspers, whose works have to some extent inspired the contemporary movement, have disclaimed any direct association with it.)

We might be justified in multiplying the meanings of *empirical* even further. Is not the examination of language and semantical structures, for instance, which receives so much attention in Anglo-Saxon philosophy today, an empirical pursuit in the strictest sense? If it is, then the branch of philosophy that is currently called "philosophy of mind" and that characteristically places great emphasis on linguistic analysis would be a branch of "philosophical anthropology" in a very real sense, at least among those philosophers who utilize these methods from a humanistic rather than a predominately skeptical or exclusively materialistic vantage point. Then again, in the widest sense possible, *empirical* might congruently include explicitly "second-order" experience, i.e., the experience of concepts; in this case the "metaphysical" speculations about man that are veridically based on some fund of conceptual experience that we all share could be designated "empirical," and such "metaphysical" study would be a form of philosophical anthropology.

It should be noted, however, that it would hardly be practical or realistic to dub all or many of the above senses of *empirical* as valid and then in umbrella-fashion designate all the diverse schools of thought indicated as manifestations of philosophical anthropology. The fact is, each of the schools or movements designated would tend to dispute and deny the validity (i.e., the empirical solidity) of many of the others. Phenomenology and existentialism, for example, are suspicious of any direct use made of scientific data in philosophy; linguistic analysts tend to look upon all other approaches to philosophy as naïve or mystical and both unverifiable and unfalsifiable; and those who practice a philosophy of science sometimes view both phenomenology and linguistic analysis as species, albeit only covertly related, of "metaphysics."

In view of these empirically ascertainable disputes and the equivocity of the term *philosophical anthropology,* and because I do not wish to confine myself to the methodology of philosophical anthropology in the Renaissance or Enlightenment senses or in the contemporary existential-phenomenological sense, I will not designate the discussions that follow "philosophical anthropology." However, these discussions *are* inspired by what I take to be the essential spirit running throughout that philosophical movement—that is, the attempt to bring about a kind of synthesis of philosophical speculation about man with the experimental "givens" currently available.

The sequence of the chapters that follow was not dictated by any natural and necessary interrelationship among the topics discussed, but by pedagogical considerations. We begin Chapter 1 with the very basic philosophical question of the difference or differences between man and the other animals.

One of the more commonly accepted answers to this question is that man is ruled more by reason, the other animals more by instinct; this answer, which has far-reaching ramifications, is critically examined in Chapter 2. Any examination of instinct, however, must lead us to consider the distinction between innate or instinctive qualities, on the one hand, and acquired or environmentally induced qualities, on the other (Chapter 3). No doubt the paradigmatic area in which the heredity-environment (or innate-acquired) distinction has been applied and misapplied from ancient through modern times has been the area of male-female differentiation (Chapter 4). As we focus on the specific ways in which the idea of sexual differentiation has evolved (and is evolving), we cannot help but become aware of the way that evolution—and particularly sociocultural evolution—has affected "objective" human perspectives and values; an overview of the ways that human consciousness has been affected by evolution is attempted in Chapter 5. In considering the evolution of human consciousness, however, we find that the most significant evolutionary development so far has been the emergence of individual consciousness, especially since the seventeenth century. The accentuation of individual consciousness, in its turn, brings about a concomitant experience of an apparent dualism between mind and body. Various aspects of the dualism-monism controversy are examined in Chapter 6, and a synthesis of the opposing viewpoints is attempted.

Insofar as there is admitted to be some dualism between mind and body (or will and body), however, we must come face-to-face (Chapter 7) with the idea of freedom, which has been traditionally associated with the affirmation of the will as something independent or at least distinct from the body. But any philosophy of freedom would be one-sided if it ignored the very real determinisms that affect human life, especially the determinisms connected with natural "stages" of development and growth (Chapter 8). The consideration of developmental stages naturally leads to the question of whether these stages are teleological approximations to some final state of ultimately attainable perfection, or "maturity" (Chapter 9). The highest peak of maturity is often said to be the power and practice of love; thus it seems appropriate to devote the entire following section (Chapter 10) to a critical analysis of this basic intuition of love as a kind of perfection. No matter how sublime love may be, however, it is usually considered (rightly or wrongly) to be within the compass of the powers of the normal human being, whereas it is also possible (Chapter 11) that the highest stages of consciousness may be states thought to be "transcendent" (i.e., suprahuman or paranormal). Having considered the possibility of such "transcendence" of normal human existence, it is, finally, but one short step to considering (in Chapter 12) the possibility that man may in some way be able to transcend his natural condition, and even death itself, by entering into a "higher" state.

One should notice that there is some dependence of the latter chapters on the former. For example, if one were to absolutely deny any distinction between man and the other animals (Chapter 1), it would make no sense to raise any question about whether there is some "specifically" human instinct (Chapter 2), because there would be nothing specifically *human;* if one were to completely reject dualism (Chapter 6), one's treatment of freedom (Chapter 7) would have to be very esoteric indeed; if one were to reject the teleological development of consciousness (Chapter 8), it would make little sense to speak about a state of maturity ultimately attainable by consciousness (Chapter 9); and if one were to reject the possibility of transcending normal perceptual experience (Chapter 11), it would be much harder to make a case for the possibility of ultimately transcending all dependence on what now counts as ordinary human experience (Chapter 12).

The so-called empirical sciences that are utilized most liberally in the following discussions are psychology, anthropology, and parapsychology.

One might ask how we can use psychology as a springboard for philosophical investigation when psychology itself is at present a hotbed of so many different and often conflicting approaches and opinions—"analytic" psychologists (Freudians, Jungians, Adlerians), behaviorists, developmental psychologists, differential psychologists, existential psychologists, personalists, etc. From a philosophical point of view these differences present no problems and are even a source of philosophical interest. Some of the most interesting philosophical questions are those concerning topics on which the various schools of psychology differ. For example:

(a) is there an "unconscious" or subconscious?

(b) does the conditioning of behavior preclude the possibility of freedom?

(c) are "masculinity" and "femininity" inherited psychological traits or merely physical differences that have been influenced culturally in certain specific ways?

(d) what is the basis of the sense of self-identity that emerges in the mature person?

(e) what, for that matter, is maturity?

(f) how do we explain the emergence of the various psychological powers—memory, imagination, intellection, volition, etc.—and can we say anything about their relative priorities or interrelationships?

In anthropology there is more agreement and, for that matter, less of a tendency to splinter off into opposing "schools." However, there are a number of in-house disputes among anthropologists—whether, for instance, the former "missing link" in human evolution—*Australopithecus*—is really a hominid or just an ape, and whether it is an ancestor of man or a contemporary of Homo sapiens; whether physical evolution is still continuing in the human race; and whether heredity or environment is relatively more important in the development of human beings from conception to death (a problem that anthropologists have in common with psychologists).

Some anthropological problems that merit philosophical consideration are:

(a) what is the essential basis for the differentiation of Homo sapiens from his ancestors?

(b) can anything meaningfully be said about the teleology of man's evolution and its future directions?

(c) is the aspiration for an afterlife, which is an important element, in many forms, in the religions, myths, and folklores of many cultures, a possibility in some form, or is it self-contradictory?

(d) is there anything in man corresponding to the more complex animal instincts?

In the infant science of parapsychology, which is replete with uncertainties at the present time, (a) philosophical problems emerge with regard to the interpretation of data: e.g., if a researcher were able to demonstrate that the "spirits" during a séance with a medium had exact knowledge of intimate information that could not have been obtained from any external sources, how could the researcher be sure that this was the result of a bona fide contact with someone on the "other side" and not simply the result of mind-reading on the part of the medium? (b) Philosophical problems emerge also with regard to certain basic presuppositions germane to parapsychological research, e.g., is it logically consistent even to look for evidence of survival after death? Is it not logically self-contradictory to conceptualize the possibility of human existence outside time, outside the realm of ordinary experience accessible to our senses?

We will be considering these questions and certain others of the same type and tenor in the following pages. As science and philosophical attitudes progress and change, some or all of these questions may become irrelevant or dated, while others, perhaps more interesting and more important, will take their place. Our concern here is to focus on some selected problems that seem to be interesting and important right now.

1: How Is Man Distinct From the Other Animals?

Man is part of nature. He falls through space at the same rate that rocks and animals do, even when he thinks noble thoughts or has high aspirations. His body conforms to the laws that govern other bodies; like the animal he comes to a dusty end. But he is not a thing, not even a complicated one. Nor is he an animal, not even a very intelligent, talking animal. . . . Browning said that a man's reach should exceed his grasp. One must reply that it always does. It could not be otherwise. A man lives in part in terms of powers, meanings, values, compulsions and realities which do not have a natural place or a natural history. . . . A man has responsibilities and a possible career that no other thing, animals and no child can even approximate.—Paul Weiss, "What Is Man?" in *This Week* (Nov. 2, 1969)

> Man can be either more or less than an animal, but never an animal.—Max Scheler, *Man's Place in Nature*

How can we best define the difference between man and the other animals? This question has been discussed for a long time by philosophers and others, but the final answer, if indeed there is one, has always seemed to be "just around the corner." Let us start by giving some examples of attempts by some major philosophers to answer the question. Later we will see that their answers are not as solid as they may seem to be at first.

Aristotle, one of the first philosophers to devote much attention to this question, approached it from a number of different angles. First of all, considering the necessity of giving man his proper logical classification, Aristotle classified man as a "rational animal," i.e., as the only animal capable of forming general concepts through a process of "abstraction" and of deriving conclusions from these concepts syllogistically by following rules of inferential reasoning. More concretely, in *On Memory and Reminiscence,* Aristotle pointed to man's power of "reminiscence" as a trait that distinguished human beings from subhuman beasts. Animals have memory, but only humans have reminiscence, i.e., the power to search systematically through one's mind for a specific memory of something forgotten—for instance, mentally retracing one's steps until one recalls where one left one's coat. On a sociological level—although the word *sociology* had not yet been coined—Aristotle defined man as a "political animal," i.e., as the only animal capable of organizing into complex communities, cities, states. Finally, probably in a more whimsical mood, Aristotle offered some "less essential" definitions of man: man is the risible animal (the animal with a sense of humor); or man is a two-legged animal without feathers (here Aristotle was using a classification already suggested in Plato's *Statesman*).

G.W.F. Hegel, in his *Philosophy of Right*, distinguished man from the lower animals on the basis of needs. Animals have needs that are limited in number, while man has an ineluctable tendency to multiply his needs infinitely—a tendency of which advertising men, in our culture, seem to be very much aware.

Friedrich Nietzsche, in his *Genealogy of Morals*, taking an "existential" point of view, described man as the only being who can "make promises for the future," i.e., one who can commit himself to a certain line of action and stick to it responsibly.

Finally, Ernst Cassirer defined man as the animal who can make and use symbols, i.e., created meanings (as contrasted with the natural or instinctive signals and signs that animals are capable of giving to one another and to man).

All these definitions, once we reflect on them, begin to give us trouble.

If man is indeed a rational animal, for example, he also seems to have the power to dispense rather easily with reason. For if we maintained that reason rather than drives, passions, or instincts ruled man, it would become very difficult to explain things like the depredations of ruthless capitalism, two world wars culminating in Auschwitz and the Holocaust, terrorists who kill babies out of hatred for their parents, and other commonplaces of civilized living in the twentieth century. Of course, world wars cannot be waged and efficient death camps cannot be devised and administered without a very elaborate use of reasoning powers, and we might well call them signs of a myopic, restricted, or even perverted use of reason. Even so, it is questionable whether reason, normal or perverted, is something unique to man. William James mentions in his *Psychology* the case of a well-trained hunting dog that usually handled the birds he retrieved very skillfully, never biting them hard enough to kill. But one day when he had to bring in two birds, each still alive and kicking, he bit one of them hard enough to kill it, brought the other to his master, and then returned for the dead bird. It is possible to surmise—but not possible to prove—that the dog was making an exception to his usual rule of not biting hard enough to kill because a new situation had arisen in which he had to apply a more important general rule, i.e., that of not letting any birds get away.

Offhand, one might say that the ascription of "reminiscence" to man would be a very good way of differentiating him from the "lower" animals. It is hard to conceive of a dog or cat stopping in its tracks and retracing its memories in order to relocate a particular lost memory. On the other hand, there may be approximations to this process among at least some lower animals. A homing pigeon, for instance, in trying to find its way home, will veer first in one direction and then in another, looking for landmarks. Is this not fundamentally the same procedure as that followed by a man looking for his coat, who goes physically from one room to the next, while mentally running methodically through his memories, trying to get into the "vicinity" of the temporarily lapsed memory?

No one who knows anything of the history of mankind can doubt that man is the political animal par excellence. But can we say that animals do not have a degree of bona fide political organization? In most species of animals there are greater or lesser degrees of hierarchical organization involving leadership, sexual dominance, and property dominance (e.g., rights of territoriality, rights to certain pieces of property, rights respecting the appropriation of food); and, in general, a social system in which higher rank means "greater freedom of action, easier access to food, and a less strained style of living."[1] To be sure, this is not a picture of a democratic society, but it does seem to show a sense of order and organization approximate to that prevalent in some human arrangements that go by the name of "political system."

What about Hegel's "infinite multiplication of needs"? Man, so lacking in instincts and built-in equipage (fur, special teeth, claws, especially acute sense of smell, etc.), certainly has a greater need for outside supports than other animals, and he has exhibited an extraordinary versatility in seeking and finding new ways to satisfy his needs and to enjoy himself. But an *infinite* multiplication? Surely this is an exaggeration. (Following Hegel on this point, Karl Marx, in his *1844 Manuscripts,* limited the infinite multiplication of needs to "capitalist man"; for Marx, it was a perversion that would go by the way when temperate, unselfish "communist man" came upon the scene.)

As for Nietzsche's "promises for the future," animals cannot speak our language—or, if they can, they choose not to do so—but if the bird that enters into lifetime pair-bonding could but speak to us, mightn't it declare a lifelong commitment to its mate? And if the ever-faithful domesticated mammal (dog, monkey, etc.) could but speak, would it not say something about its sentiments of fidelity and obedience toward its master?

The use of symbols seems at first sight to be one of the most likely strictly human traits that an anthropologist could point out. But one thing prevents our making a blanket generalization about this matter—the example of the honeybee. H. Munroe Fox describes the behavior of bees in communicating the location of nectar or pollen:

> The dance of a bee on returning to the hive is all the more lively the richer the booty she has brought back. And the more sprightly the dance, the more numerous are the bees that fly out when the dance is over. There are various words or phrases in the bee language. The dance gives information that pollen or nectar is available and should be sought. The vigor of the dance says if the harvest will be rich or poor. But this is by no means the whole of

the bee language. The most amazing part of it comes next. The distance is announced by the number of turns per minute. For instance, for food that is 300 yards away the dancer makes twenty-eight turns per minute, if 3000 yards away she turns only eleven times in the minute. . . [The bee also does a "figure 8" dance]. If the figure of 8 lies on its side, thus ∞, and the straight run between the loops is made vertically upward on the comb, then the feeding place is in the same direction as the sun at the moment. If the run is downwards, the flowers are in the direction directly opposite to that of the sun. If the run is say sixty degrees to the left of the vertical, the flowers are in a direction sixty degrees to the left of a line from hive to sun. And so on for all other possible directions.[2]

One may object that all this is only instinctive behavior. Bees do not invent their own symbols and vary them to attain new goals. This may be a valid objection, but it also emphasizes the need to delimit one's definition of man, not in terms of symbol utilization (which man has in common with the bees), but in terms of symbol-*making*. One would also do well to consider whether man's continual variegation of symbols is not itself a manifestation of some instinct in the human species, i.e., of something that takes place outside man's conscious control as a consequence of the peculiar characteristics of *his* adaptation to *his* peculiar environment, both of which differ in some respects from those of all other animals.

As mentioned earlier, we are concerned for the moment with only a few representative samples of the sorts of answers that have been given to the "difference question." But to get an idea of the sheer multiplicity of answers that have been given by philosophers, consider the following partial list of specifically "human" attributes: (1) knowledge of "good and evil," and the feeling of shame (the book of Genesis), (2) the ability to formulate negative assertions (Hans Kunz), (3) the ability to weep (Helmut Plessner), (4) aiming intentionally for the future (Martin Buber), (5) awareness of the necessity for dying and the ability to commit suicide (Franz Rosenzweig and Rudolf Ehrenberg), (6) magnanimity (John Milton), (7) freedom of will (Rousseau), (8) the power of speech (Thomas Hobbes), (9) ambivalent oscillation between infinity and nothingness (Blaise Pascal), and (10) openness to the world beyond the immediate environment (Max Scheler). Without going into a detailed rebuttal of any of these contentions, I might simply point out that a reasonably astute observer who had noticed in animals: (a) glimmerings of conscience, (b) systematic and habitual refusals, (c) moisture welling up in the eyes of cocker spaniels, (d) apparently purposeful activity, (e) premonitions of death and even apparent suicide (e.g., among lemmings and some species of whales), (f) generosity, (g) rudimentary choice, (h) often-sophisticated communication, (i) an oscillation between ostentatious pride and groveling debasement, and (j) as much openness to the outer world as is found in some humans—this observer would have prima facie evidence against all the positions just enumerated.

Contemporary anthropologists and psychologists using empirical scientific methods have tried to come up with more certain determinations of the differentiating factors. They tell us that man is the only animal that has a difficult and painful childbirth. He is distinguished from other animals by his educability, by his playfulness, by his ability to subsist on diverse diets, by his freedom from specific breeding seasons, by his brain-size, by his ability to act on the basis of more remote considerations, by his religious and aesthetic orientations, by his ability to make tools, and so forth.

Some of these latter distinctions are obviously superficial. Difficult and painful childbirth certainly falls into this category (and it may even be false, if we are to believe the advocates of "natural childbirth"). And some of the distinctions are plainly differences only in degree—playfulness and the aesthetic sense, for instance. (Animals in their mating displays and other ritual acts often seem to manifest what we might call aesthetic appreciation and sensitivity.) On the other hand, some of these distinctions seem to indicate a sharper difference—a difference in kind, rather than merely of degree, e.g., the religious orientation, provided that we understand religion to mean something different from a sense of unity with the world, with nature, and with one's own species—qualities that, though not elaborately articulated, are certainly found to some degree in various animal species.

Mortimer Adler, in *The Difference of Man and the Difference it Makes*,[3] stresses the importance of pinpointing a difference in *kind*. Following Aristotle, he finds this difference in man's power to go beyond perceptions of particular objects and attributes, to form abstract concepts, and to utilize these concepts in thought and speech. He argues (a) negatively, that there is nothing in the behavior of animals that would lead us to believe that they can form concepts (as contrasted with mere perceptual abstractions), and (b) positively, that men do have such a capacity, which is manifested in their ability to use concepts in the absence of any perceived particulars to designate a class and to make statements about it. What about the hunting dog mentioned by William James? Adler would no doubt interpret the dog's behavior as an instance of mere perceptual abstraction; that is, the action of the dog could be interpreted as an instinctive reaction to a bird that was trying to get away. And Adler might well be right, although there *is* another possible interpretation of the dog's behavior. However, it would take a more clear-cut example than this to convince Mortimer Adler that animals are capable of anything like conceptual reasoning.

Such an example might be found in some remarkable experiments involving a chimpanzee named Lana.[4] As a result of special training under the direction of Dr. Duane Rumbaugh at the Yerkes Regional Primate Research Center in Atlanta, Georgia, Lana acquired a fairly respectable vocabulary and demonstrated the apparent ability—so it seemed to some—to use and rearrange the words she had learned to form sentences. Indicating each word in proper sequence by nudging the appropriate buttons on a computer, Lana asked for food, for comfort, for companionship, etc.—and she did so in complete sentences (e.g., "Please, John, give Lana banana," etc.). Sometimes she even rearranged sentences in grammatically different ways to ask for the same thing. At the age of four years, she learned to ask for the names of objects, to invent names for objects (e.g., "apple which is colored orange" as the name of an orange), and to use sentences including prepositional phrases. Given Lana's apparent accomplishments, which were made known to the world subsequent to the publication of Adler's 1967 book, one might well take issue with some of the statements in that book. For example:

> If by a verbal concept is meant a concept that is or can be expressed in words—not just in a name by itself, but in a sentence using that name—then it is at once clear that animals do not have verbal concepts. (p. 163)

> What can and must be said is that no signs which have designative significance, whether words or icons, function in the behavior of nonlinguistic (i.e., subhuman) animals. (p. 175)[5]

Lana the chimpanzee used names correctly in sentences and used words to designate real objects—all in defiance of Adler's dicta on the limitations of animal behavior.

As a matter of fact, Adler eventually retracted both of the above contentions in a later publication.[6] He now contended (in 1975) that the decisive difference lay in man's ability to learn words in the absence of the corresponding objects and to use conjunctions, disjunctions, prepositions, and definite and indefinite articles in formulating propositions.[7] We must wait for further experiments over the years to see if gifted primates like Lana can measure up to Adler's new and higher standards. If they do not, then perhaps one may be justified in concluding that there is a "difference in kind" between the conceptual thought of humans and the mental processes by which a chimpanzee can seemingly generate simple sentences.

At this point one may well pause to wonder whether a complicated series of arguments and subtle qualifications and continual tentative experimentation should really be necessary to establish a difference between man and the other animals! Is there no clear-cut distinction that, once understood, will make you open your eyes wide and say, "Aha, of course, this puts man in a completely different category"? [8]

Pierre Teilhard de Chardin seemed to think that he had found such a clear-cut distinction when he observed (in *The Phenomenon of Man*) that "animals know, but only man knows *that* he knows." Reflection and self-consciousness do seem to be definitely human attributes. We do not usually think of animals as having the power of reflection on self, especially if we take "reflection on self" to mean explicit thinking about ourselves and even about the act of thinking as such. For although one may find in animals approximations of "self-consciousness" in a wide sense of the term,[9] who would seriously maintain that a "lower" animal could sit down and concentrate on its self as an object? On the other hand, we do not have (and we probably never will have) definitive proof that animals do not do this, and someone in a pessimistic frame of mind might even question why this power of separating oneself from oneself as object—a power that presumably has some causal relationship to the high incidence of debilitating depression, mental disease, suicide, etc., among humans—should be considered a positive trait at all.

On the other hand, "self-reflection" is so general and so intangible that it almost seems to be different-in-kind from the other "differences-in-kind" that have been proposed (rationality, reminiscence, etc.), which were rather specific and capable of being publicly observed. It must be admitted, however, that if one is willing to accept these defects, self-consciousness shows great promise in being the "pivotal" difference, since it also seems to be the common source of many (if not all) of the other differences that have been pointed out: rationality, reminiscence, awareness of death, ability to commit suicide, religious aspirations, etc. In fact, the act of self-reflection may be synonymous, if not tautologous, with the act by which a man distinguishes himself from others. In other words, in the very act of turning back on myself, in making myself a center of reflection, I am withdrawing from my environment and from all others who happen to be in my environment (I am distinguishing myself from them). Hence, to say that "man's power of self-consciousness is the basic distinction between him and the animals" is to say that man's power of distinguishing himself is the reason he is distinguished from the other animals—and this is a tautology pure and simple.

One major problem that emerges out of discussions about differentiating characteristics of man is the apparent presupposition, held both by those who defend and by those who deny the radical difference of man, that man has a well-defined and stable "nature." Those who insist on the radical difference and superiority of man often presuppose that there are certain essential attributes that are associated with being born a man; and they make this presupposition with full knowledge of the fact that there is a significant minority of exceptional human beings who seem less able to adapt and function intelligently in their human environment than certain precocious "lower" mammals. On the other hand, those who deny that there is much real difference between man and the other animals often base their case on the same presupposition that there is a cluster of stable characteristics associated with being a "man," the only difference being that, in their view, none of these characteristics, taken singly or in unison with others, is extremely remarkable when compared with the characteristics of lower animals.

We might do better to avoid, if possible, the problematical presupposition of a stable human nature. We could do this, and also do justice to man's evolving nature,[10] by reading the question about the difference of man in a future tense: Even if man is not *now* radically different from the animals, is it not possible that he may *become* so, i.e., that he will establish himself as completely *sui generis* in the near or distant future? Conceive, if you will, a future state of society in which man has not only stopped making war with other members of his own species (animals, with very few exceptions, do not perpetrate organized violence on their own species); but has also overcome national, sectional, and racial rivalries; established a harmonious world order based on brotherhood rather than power; and finally, after much trial and error, found ways to utilize the 90 percent or so of the human brain that (scientists tell us) now goes unused, and ways also to reduce (by medicine, genetics, education, etc.) the incidence of subnormal intelligence in our midst. In such a state of affairs, it would be true to say that man was radically *distinct* from the lower animals because he would have radically *distinguished* himself. But strictly speaking, if we reached such a point, the question of man's difference from the other animals would probably be superfluous and meaningless, for the difference would be so obvious that no one would think of asking the question—unless, of course, the other animals had also advanced in the same ways and to the same extent. But that would be another problem altogether.

2: What Ever Happened to Instinct in Man?

[Socrates, speaking to Meno:] To sum up our enquiry—the result seems to be, if we are at all right in our view, that virtue is neither natural nor acquired, but an instinct given by God to the virtuous. Nor is the instinct accompanied by reason, unless there may be supposed to be among statesmen some one who is capable of educating [i.e., imparting knowledge of virtue to] statesmen [a type of education which Socrates and Meno have just concluded is impossible].—Plato, *Meno*

> The intuitive reason involved in practical reasonings grasps the last and variable fact, i.e., the minor premises. ... Of these [variable facts] we must have perception, and this perception is intuitive reason. This is why these states [of discriminating judgment] are thought to be natural endowments—why, while no one is thought to be a philosopher by nature, people are thought to have by nature judgment, understanding, and intuitive reason.—Aristotle, *Nicomachean Ethics*

Two things instruct man about his whole nature: instinct and convenience.—Pascal, *Pensées* (VI, 396)

> The primordial image (elsewhere also termed the "archetype") is always collective, i.e. it is at least common to entire nations or epochs ... it is an inherited organization of psychic energy, a rooted system, which is not only an expression of the energic process but also a possibility for its operation. In a sense, it characterizes the way in which the energic process from the earliest times has always run its unvarying course, while at the same time enabling a perpetual repetition of the law-determined course to take place. ... It is, therefore, the necessary counterpart of (animal) instinct.—Carl Jung, *Psychological Types*

It is sometimes argued that modern empiricism overcomes the limitations of the earlier tradition, but I think that this belief is seriously in error. Hume, for example, presented a substantive theory of "the secret springs and principles, by which the human mind is actuated in its operations." In his investigation of the foundations of knowledge, he suggested specific principles that constitute "a species of natural instincts." Modern empiricists who disparage Hume have simply replaced his theory by vacuous systems that preserve empiricist (or more narrowly, behaviorist) terminology while depriving traditional ideas of their substance. ... As Hume says, "the experimental reasoning itself, which we possess in common with beasts, and on which the whole conduct of life depends, is nothing but a species of instinct or mechanical power, that acts in us unknown to ourselves," undirected by our "intellectual facul-

ties." ... Throughout, Hume is offering substantive proposals about
questions that we surely regard as "scientific questions" (as he did too, it
seems clear). He is discussing the instinctive foundations of knowledge
(including unconscious and even innate knowledge), surely an empirical
matter, as he correctly understood the question. ... To the extent that S
[a scientist] succeeds in characterizing the innate properties of mind that
make possible the learning of grammar and common sense ... he would
now regard the properties of mind that underlie the acquisition of
language and common sense as biological properties of the organism, on
a par in this respect with those that enable a bird to build a nest or
reproduce a characteristic song.—Noam Chomsky, *Reflections on Language*

In Chapter 1 we were primarily concerned with the question whether
there is a difference-in-kind, as opposed to a mere difference-in-degree,
between man and animals. Among partisans on both sides of the question,
however, we could find rather general agreement that a basic difference
between man and animals is the absence (either relative or absolute) of
instinct in man, in contrast to the prevalence (either absolute or relative) of
instinct throughout the animal world. This presupposition calls for
further examination. Let us suppose that animals could think and speak
and communicate with us and that we asked them point-blank, "Do you
have instinct?" It is likely that they would answer in the negative, for an
instinct, by definition, is something that one does not have to think about,
that one does not have sophisticated control over, and that one usually
ascribes to children and primitive men. If we insisted on confronting
sophisticated disbelievers in instinct with evidence that they do certain
things that we designate "instinctive," we should not be surprised if they
succeed in quite human fashion in rationalizing what they did, showing it
was really the result of conscious decisions (in the same way that a hyp-
notized subject will try to rationalize the actions he or she performs in a
trance state). Therefore we should no doubt maintain a stance of healthy
skepticism when hearing man's disclaimers about his own instincts, and we
have good philosophical justification for trying to probe behind the appearances to see just how comparatively free of instinct man really is.

   Before approaching the subject of the prevalence or nonprevalence of
instinct in man, we should point out that the term *instinct* is sometimes
used equivocally. For instance, someone will say "I instinctively pulled my
hand back from the hot pan" to refer to what might best be described as a
reflex action (although the action might be indirectly related to the instinct
of self-preservation). Again, English Freudian psychologists speak of the
"life instinct" and the "death instinct"; in so doing, however, they are
translating the German word *Trieb* as "instinct," when "drive" would
certainly be a more literal translation.

Finally, there is some disagreement among psychologists about whether *instinct* should refer to the inner impulse that gives rise to what we call "instinctive behavior," or to the external behavior itself, which we interpret as being instinctive. Some psychologists insist that only one or the other usage is correct. A good compromise would be to allow both these usages of the word, in accord with what the philosophers call "the analogy of attribution," which involves taking one act, state, or quality as the primary reference point and then applying the term in a looser and secondary sense to things, acts, etc. that bear some resemblance to it. For example, *love* primarily means an internal affection; but we can also call various acts (e.g., sexual intercourse, kissing, hugging) "love" by the "analogy of attribution," because these are acts that are supposed to manifest love. In like manner, *instinct* refers to a special internal, psychophysical mechanism, completely unlearned, initiated ordinarily by certain external stimuli, or by chemical changes within an organism (we will call this Instinct$_1$); but we can also apply the term analogously to the *acts* that are set in motion by instincts (we will call this Instinct$_2$).

In considering the instinct of animals, we will be concerned primarily with Instinct$_2$, i.e., as referring to overt behavior. One good reason for this emphasis is that we have no first-hand knowledge of the inner impulses behind their acts but must simply infer or imagine them. In dealing with man, however, we do have first-hand experience and will be able to focus primarily on Instinct$_1$; but we will also raise questions about Instinct$_2$ in man, and questions about the interrelationship of Instinct$_1$ and Instinct$_2$ in man.

It is also important for our purposes to distinguish between simple and complex instincts. Examples of relatively simple Instincts$_2$ in animals would be: dogs burying their bones; dogs, even on a carpet, turning around several times before lying down, and depressing the carpet fibers with their paws as if flattening grass to make it more comfortable; kangaroos carrying their young in a pouch. A relatively simple Instinct$_2$ is also illustrated in a recent experiment with "processional" caterpillars. When searching for food, this kind of caterpillar instinctively marches with its head touching the tail of the caterpillar immediately in front of it. One experimenter deviously arranged the front caterpillar so that it was touching the tail of the last one. The caterpillars walked around in a circle for a week.

Some examples of more complex Instincts$_2$ would be: the instinct of salmon to fight their way upstream to spawn in the place where they spent their youth; the extraordinary concatenation of activities that takes place in the life-cycle of the worker bee;[1] and the spider's spinning of its web. It is difficult to say whether such activities would be best described as complex instincts or as complex chains of simple instincts. In any case, they are successive or serial concatenations of activities that are unlearned and much harder to explain (by reference to external stimuli, biochemical changes, neural discharges, etc.) than the simple instincts are.

Complex instincts seem to be less prevalent in mammals than in birds and insects. However, there are exceptions. A female cat, for example, will go through a somewhat complicated series of activities before, during, and after giving birth. She will look for a dark, isolated, and warm spot, to which she retires before labor begins. Having delivered her kittens, she removes the placental sac and eats it. She cleans off the kittens in order to keep the nest clean, she stays with the kittens continually, and she carries them by the nape of the neck to a better place if she notices too much noise or light in the "delivery room."

An even more striking exception to the comparative rarity of complex instincts in mammals is to be found in the behavior of beavers:

> Beavers accomplish most astonishing engineering works which give them safety from the attacks of carnivores and from frost. They fell trees and cut them into pieces by gnawing. They make canals for water transport of the logs. They jam up a post with logs carried into position by their forepaws. The dam is plastered with mud and homes are prepared with their entrance under water. Bark of trees is stored for food. All this work is communal.[2]

What about instincts in man? There seems to be almost universal agreement that there exist simple Instincts$_2$ in man, but there is some disagreement as to just what they are. Among those that have been suggested are: the sucking instinct of the newborn infant at the breast; following the leader; social status seeking; cleanliness; sexual pursuit (which does not necessarily include knowledge of how to copulate); maternal reactions (although many feminists deny that these are truly instinctive); reactions of self-defense; and acting in common with a crowd.

There is nothing in this list comparable to what we have called the "complex" Instincts$_2$—chains of activities or reactions following one another with unvarying precision in response to certain changes in the environment or the organism. Is it true to say that there are no complex Instincts$_2$ in man? Or are we in this case too close to the subject matter, so that we fail to notice what we were looking for, or we call it by the wrong name, or we even try to rationalize behavior that is really quite instinctive?

There is no denying the fact that, as we "ascend" the tree of evolution, there seems to be a general diminution in the prevalence of instincts. As we arrive at the mammals, the more complex Instincts$_2$ are scarcely to be found, with the notable exception of beaver-architecture and perhaps a few other more ambiguous cases. As we go even higher, to the primates (apes, chimpanzees, etc.) there seems to be, on this "higher" level, both a complete lack of complex Instincts$_2$ and a greater freedom from simple Instincts$_2$ than is found in "inferior" species. So, at least, many authorities tell us. The lesson of evolution, in their estimation, seems to be clear: instinct has all but disappeared by the time we reach Homo sapiens, and learned behavior has taken the place of unlearned behavior.

Some writers, however, think that we are looking in the wrong place for human instincts, whether simple or complex. All the human instincts suggested above are Instincts$_2$, which we have in common with other animals, e.g., infantile sucking, following the leader, etc. These writers would like us to raise our eyes to a higher level, so to speak, to catch sight of certain other Instincts$_1$ that are peculiar to man in the same way that nest-building, web-construction, the "homing instinct," etc. are peculiar to certain species of animals. They would have us focus on these special Instincts$_1$ as being "proper" to man, in order to appreciate really the importance of instinct in human intellectual and spiritual life.

Carl Jung, for example, hypothesizes that the most important instincts we have inherited from our ancestors are certain internal ways of reacting to our physical and social environment, which, when coupled in a minimum way with consciousness, produce certain unconscious inner images called "archetypes." There is a set of these images that seems to be universal throughout mankind, judging by the comparative analysis of myths, folklore, and religious beliefs. Examples of such inherited archetypal images are: the Shadow, i.e., the universal idea of the "enemy," or the "other"; the Anima, or the ideal female; the Animus, or the ideal masculine personality; the Wise Old Father, a symbol of authority; and the Self, a symbol of complete reconciliation of opposites, which is also identified with God and with various Christ-images. These archetypes are not Instincts$_2$. Rather, they are cognitive presuppositions that supply a context for *all* our behavior (Instinctive$_2$ as well as noninstinctive). They are modes of apprehension, ways of looking at the world that have been gradually built into the human race and passed on from generation to generation. Are Jung's archetypes "simple" or "complex," to use the terminology we introduced earlier in this chapter? Jung does not speak of them specifically with reference to the categories of "simplicity" vs. "complexity," but he does show how the numerous major archetypes have entered into an intricate web of interconnections in the formation of various historical and prehistorical world views. So in this sense they might be complex.

Henri Bergson, unlike Jung, locates the primary Instinctive$_1$ faculty in man not in the unconscious, but in a certain area of consciousness that Bergson calls "intuition." For Bergson, consciousness is subdivided into two major spheres: (1) the intellect, or abstract, conceptual reasoning; and (2) intuition, which is an extension of animal instinct and a raising of it to the nth degree of perfection. For the animal, Instinct$_2$ will point out this or that basic direction that it should follow in its life-activities; for man, the power of intuitive consciousness (an Instinct$_1$) will offer direct perception of the basic directions of life as a whole (not just the life-activities of the individual man or of his species). The man who is endowed with the power of intuition and creatively utilizes this power will find himself on the track of the secrets of the universe—without knowing how he got there. Once "on the track," he may proceed to follow up his intuitions with action or with intellectual cogitations. For example, a charismatic leader, who begins to act on the basis of an intuitive vision of future societal perfection, but without knowing how to get there, will then begin to organize and implement his plans (in an ethical way, it is hoped), and his initial faith will gradually begin to take on substance. Another example would be the scientist who, in spite of criticism or ridicule, follows up a "hunch" (an intuition) and finally gets to the point where he can present this hunch as a publicly demonstrable hypothesis. According to Bergson, such an intuitive process is at the basis of the major discoveries or break-throughs that we so often attribute (wrongly) to the "progress of *reason.*" It is this instinctive process of intuition that is also responsible, says Bergson, for religious faith and what is called "mystical experience."

Would intuition in the Bergsonian sense be a "simple" or "complex" instinct? Here again, Bergson himself does not utilize these two categories. If we tried to apply them in Bergson's case, we would run into something of a paradox. Intuitive consciousness is "simple" in the sense that it goes beyond all the particular intuitions that animals have and yields a simple, highly intensive intuition of the general drift of Life. On the other hand, it is also "complex'" in the sense that it descends to all the details of evolving life and is able to coordinate them and discover their interrelations. Perhaps Bergson's theory may be a good example of a "limiting case," i.e., a case that shows the limits of the viability of a principle or a categoriza-tion. When we get to the rather unusual and cosmic interpretation that Bergson gives to instinct in man, categories such as "simple" and "com-plex" may cease to be applicable.

According to William McDougall the primary Instincts$_1$ in man are expressed by certain primary emotions, which are woven into webs of "sentiment." For example, Instincts$_1$ that are devoted to perpetuating our national group become organized into the complex sentiment we call "patriotism"; the maternal Instinct$_1$, in combination with feelings of al-truism and egoism, becomes the "parental sentiment"; and the Instinct$_1$ for self-assertion or aggression, in combination with negative self-feeling, fear, and sympathy, becomes the "self-regarding sentiment." Thus McDougall's answer to the question of complex instincts in man would be that they do indeed exist, and that they are sublimated or hybrid forms of the more primitive Instinctive$_1$ impulses that (we presume) are also pres-ent in animals. (For example, the Instinct$_1$ of self-preservation is supposed to be the cause of various Instinctive$_2$ acts of self-defense or claims of territoriality in animals; this supposition is based on an analogy with our own experience.)

Most contemporary anthropologists hold to a different view. To their mind, the need for something like instinct throughout the evolutionary processes of "natural selection"[3] becomes less and less as the brain of vertebrates grows larger, and as cerebromammals, including man and apes, acquire a more generalized intelligence that enables them to devise a greater number of more appropriate or beneficial alternatives in adapting to their environment. To put it more succinctly, they have much less need for instinct (unlearned responses to the environment) because they have a greater capacity for learning. They also have a greater capacity for transmitting what they have learned to their progeny. Especially in man, learning, to a great extent, has taken the place of instinct.

Although the anthropologists sharply contrast learning and instinct, we might be able to read their answer as a covert attempt to suggest the existence of a special human $Instinct_1$. Learning itself is a primary (unlearned) reaction of man to his environment. According to this reading, $Instinct_1$ in man would be paradoxical, insofar as it would be an unlearned tendency to learn. Animals also are presumed to have an $Instinct_1$ to learn, but in man this $Instinct_1$ has become much more complex, involving such things as recollection, abstraction, categorization, analysis and synthesis, syllogistic reasoning, etc. By dint of these complex cognitive processes, man is able to handle his environment without much dependence upon $Instincts_2$. But humans don't have to be taught to learn, can't be taught to learn, and in fact must even learn (by themselves) to be taught, before teaching can have any effect on them.[4]

Mention should be made of two other possible solutions, both of which were proposed (historically) before the question we are considering here was formulated, that is, before the development of the modern science of anthropology. Thomas Aquinas and G.W.F. Hegel were not concerned specifically with the question "What happens to instinct when we get to man on the tree of evolution?," but they each proposed psychological constructs that seem to have a bearing on this problem.

Aquinas, in company with other medieval scholastics, builds upon certain suggestive ideas of Aristotle and infers the existence of a "cogitative power" in man, which corresponds to the "aestimative power" ($Instinct_1$) in animals. The function of the cogitative power in man is to go beyond what is actually perceived by the senses, to show a man what is good for *his individual organism*, without any special reasoning process being involved. It has a definite ethical bearing, since it would be impossible for a man to make prudent judgments without it; and in its ethical thrust it perhaps bears some resemblance to what Socrates, toward the end of Plato's dialogue, *Meno*, calls the "instinct for virtue."

Hegel, following certain theories about "intellectual intuition" that were in vogue in his day, focuses in his *Phenomenology* upon man's experience of subject-object differentiation as the starting point for all cognitive and intellectual progress. This insight corresponds with what is now a well-known assumption in developmental psychology: that the newborn infant is subject to "coenesthesis," a vague perceptual state in which there is no subject-object differentiation, and that the child begins to make progress in consciousness only when it comes to make distinctions between the ego and the world, the ego and various parts of the world, etc.

If we granted that Aquinas' "cogitative power" or Hegel's "intuition of subject-object differentiation" were human Instincts$_1$, would they be complex instincts? In each case, complexity is conceivable. The insights of the "cogitative power" about what is conducive to my well-being would be incorporated into an intricate network of practical, prudential decision-making. And although the initial differentiation of "subject and object" seems a simple automatic response, there is still required the further differentiation of the subject into various aspects (sensory aspects, intellectual, etc.) and of the object into its various aspects (size, properties, etc.), the differentiation of self from body, self from other bodies, self from other selves, associated selves ("we") from nonassociated or alien selves ("they"), and so on ad infinitum. Both of these "Instincts$_1$" would have life-long ramifications, although they had simple beginnings.

The six possibilities for human instinct that we have touched on—archetypes of the unconscious, creative intuition, sentiment, the ability to learn, the cogitative power, and the faculty for subject-object differentiation—are all examples of Instinct$_1$, i.e., internal ways of reacting to stimuli. It has already been suggested that these Instincts$_1$ may be considered "complex" insofar as they involve complex comprehension or complex organization of simple things that have been apprehended.

Are these Instincts$_1$ (simple or complex) necessarily related to any specific Instincts$_2$, i.e., overt behavior patterns that would be interpreted as their manifestations or effects? It would seem not. The archetypes in dreams or myths *may* result in congruent external responses in those who are influenced by them. Learning *may* result in certain changes of behavior. Creative intuition *may* result in practical activities concerned with justifying, perfecting, or propounding intuitively perceived hypotheses. And so forth. But in all such cases, the internal response does not have to result in any specifically congruent behavioral expression. It can remain within, as a purely "immanent" operation (to use a technical term employed by some philosophers).

If there are such complex "immanent" instincts in man, then the contrast with animals becomes especially sharp. We cannot speak with any certainty of complex Instincts$_1$ in animals. Even if we grant that, for example, the curiosity of certain animals amounts to a simple instinct to learn, the complex ramifications or results of this instinct are not described in terms of a final cognitive process, but in terms of a relatively complex serial activity, e.g., the hunting Instinct$_2$ or the playing Instinct$_2$—which we presume to be "caused" by some initial state of curiosity. As regards man, on the other hand, we have our own first-hand experience to testify that the primary result of initial curiosity, or the simple Instinct$_1$ to learn, is very often a complex state of cognition, which does not necessarily lead to any complex chain of external activities. Truth is sought, at least sometimes, for its own sake.

Thus far we have pointed out in man simple Instincts$_2$ (e.g., infantile sucking), simple Instincts$_1$ (e.g., self-preservation, curiosity), and some possibly complex Instincts$_1$ (e.g., the Jungian archetypes in their extensions and multiple interconnections). But complex Instincts$_2$ seem to be conspicuously absent in man.

We become more convinced of this absence of complex Instincts$_2$ in man if we try to place ourselves, in imagination, in the situation of an animal that is carrying out a complex Instinctive$_2$ operation such as nest-building, web-weaving, or dam-construction. All these operations have a certain definite sequence, dictated by nature. Each stage of the operation follows upon its antecedents with utmost rigidity, provided no obstacles are placed in the way of the ordinary completion of the operation. There is no variation in the way the operation is performed except for minor variations attributable to differences of material utilized in individual circumstances. What does an animal *feel* when weaving a web or building a nest? For one thing, we can be fairly sure there is no choice of alternatives or decision-making involved, since the same type of activity is carried out each time. For another, from the point of view of the animal, the operation must be experienced as something that he is "programmed" to do, rather than something that he does spontaneously. The bird building its nest does not, it would seem, start by surveying trees and building materials; and then think to itself, "I'd better find a good perch and build a nest there, because I'm pregnant and I'm going to have to settle down for a bit"; and then methodically plan the foundation, frame, and filling of the nest, etc. On the contrary, it must all of a sudden find itself overcome with an irresistable impulsion to start looking for this and that—an impulsion to which it submits passively and as if suspending its own normal workaday control over its behavior.

There *are* a few possibilities of such complex Instincts$_2$ in man, which are characterized (just as in animals) by passive abandonment and almost programmed activity. However, I have postponed speaking of these possibilities until now because the first two of them lack universal prevalence, and because the second two lack universal recognition as instincts.

Two Nonuniversally Prevalent Instincts$_2$

All the important complex animal Instincts$_2$ are universally prevalent in all the members of a species. If a behavior pattern appears which is only in a few members of a species, we have to conclude either that it is not an instinct or, possibly, that it is a latent or repressed instinct. Because man is the only animal notable for repressed drives and emotions, it is possible that there are certain instincts that are latent in most men but manifest only in a few anomalous specimens. We will mention the two possibilities which come to mind, one of which is a well-known psychophysical phenomenon, while the other is alleged to be a verifiable religious (mystical) phenomenon.

(1) *Hypnotism.* A subject under the influence of hypnotic suggestion will carry out complex operations without knowing why, as if directed by some unseen force. This behavior obviously is similar in basic phenomenal characteristics to animal Instincts$_2$. However, it differs in one very important respect. The "unseen force" is not "nature" but the commands of the hypnotist. Could a hypnotic subject conceivably abandon himself to some superior force, such as nature, rather than to another human being? If he could, and if he could accept and perform unlearned functions under the control of that higher force, we would seem to have something definitely comparable to complex Instincts$_2$. This consideration leads us to our second possibility, "glossalalia," in which a subject seems to abandon himself to a superior force, in this case God, and carries out certain functions which he never has learned.

(2) *"Glossalalia."* The glossalalia, or the miraculous power of speaking in foreign tongues, is a phenomenon that is said to have been rather common among early Christians; and, according to some accounts, it still takes place in certain religious communities. Insofar as the human subject in such an experience (if we are to believe the claims) would be suddenly overtaken with the power of enunciating real words that he does not understand, the experience would have the characteristics of a complex animal Instinct$_2$. Thus we would have here the possibility of a bona fide complex, albeit usually latent, human Instinct$_2$. Unfortunately, however, there is no evidence so far that this phenomenon actually takes place. Researchers investigating the glossalalia have not been able to identify any foreign language (spoken by an "inspired" subject) that the subject could not have known from previous experiences (including early and subconscious memories).

Two Nonuniversally Recognized Instincts$_2$?

Unlike hypnotism and the glossalalia, the following two possibilities seem to be universally prevalent, but in various ways they fall short of being universally recognized:

(1) *The process of developing hierarchical social rankings.* This process is widely prevalent in the animal world, even among the higher primates; but it is often referred to as a result of the other instincts (the mating

Instinct$_2$, the Instinct$_2$ for fighting for a mate, the Instinct$_2$ for following a leader, etc.), rather than as a complex Instinct$_2$ in its own right. This same process, as prevalent in the human race, is neither characterized as a complex Instinct$_2$ nor ascribed to a convergence or interplay of multiple Instincts$_2$ but, on the contrary, is often rationalized as related to this or that goal or this or that need, justified on the basis of the natural superiority of those at the top of the hierarchy, or vilified on the ground that those who should be at the top are actually at some lower echelon and vice versa. Even the egalitarians, socialists, and communists who refuse to recognize the existence or validity of prevailing hierarchical arrangements always seem to replace them, or want to replace them, with other hierarchical arrangements based on merit, productivity, superior understanding of the masses, etc. Even liberal democracies seem to have their own subtle hierarchies in which "superior strength" becomes equated with "ability to win over a majority" or "the knack of cooperating with greater numbers." Why is it that a process that is so universally prevalent is not universally recognized as Instinctive$_2$, or at least ascribed to a conflux of Instincts$_2$ in the way that humans sometimes ascribe the hierarchical arrangements of mammals to such a conflux?

(2) *The process of developing syntactical structures and language.* Noam Chomsky and his followers have theorized that the production of language itself, with all its immensely complex grammatical interconnections, is an unlearned ability that is innate to the human species, and that is a clear break with even the most advanced communications systems developed by subhuman animals. Since Chomsky is speaking of an unlearned innate ability issuing in a certain type of complex behavior (speech), it would seem to provide us with a solution not only to the question we have raised about the existence of a complex Instinct$_2$ in man, but also possibly an answer to the question posed in Chapter 1 regarding essential differences-in-kind between man and animals, for according to this interpretation language would be a significant and specifically human complex Instinct$_2$, not found at all in other animals.[5] But a subtle obstacle prevents us from designating language formation unequivocally as a complex human Instinct$_2$. For although language (like the hierarchical arrangements just discussed) is an exoteric, universally prevalent phenomenon, and although (unlike hierarchical arrangements) the existence of language among humans is universally recognized, nevertheless the recognition of language as an instinctive phenomenon with similar earmarks, attributes, and structures in *all* human cultures is far from universal.

The vast majority of both laymen and experts would argue strenuously either, (1) that what *we* call "language" has no clear essential characteristics in common with, e.g., logographic languages such as ancient Egyptian, or (2) that even if language is essentially similar in all cultures, it is still not instinctive but is a tribute to the rational ingenuity and inventiveness of men that is passed down from generation to generation by often haphazard and definitely "nonprogrammed" educational and cultural processes.

It would be unthinkable—wouldn't it?—to suggest that human language, which is hardly recognized by anyone as an instinct, is a species-specific complex Instinct$_2$. On the other hand, it *was* suggested earlier in this chapter that if we did encounter something really instinctive (i.e., truly unlearned, not consciously devised or planned), we would find it difficult or impossible to admit that it was "instinctive." Here, perhaps, we come face-to-face with an ultimate truism (which may also be taken as an ultimate paradox), that the more "unconscious" something is, the less conscious of it we can be.

3: The Heredity-Environment Controversy: What Is Behind It and Can It Be Resolved?

No man is voluntarily bad; but the bad become bad by reason of an ill disposition of the body and bad education. . . . And in the case of pain too in like manner the soul suffers much evil from the body. . . . All of us who become bad become bad from two causes [evil constitution of body, and bad environment] which are entirely beyond our control. . . . But . . . we should endeavor as far as we can by education . . . to avoid vice and attain virtue.—Plato, *Timaeus* (86E–87A)

It is . . . [a] capacity for one-sidedness which bids us to observe things from one angle only, and if possible to reduce them to a single principle. In psychology this attitude inevitably leads to explanations in terms of one particular bias. For instance, in a case of marked extroversion the whole of the psyche is traced back to environmental influences, while in introversion it is traced back to the hereditary psychophysical disposition.—Carl Jung, *Flying Saucers: A Modern Myth of Things Seen in the Skies*

Our discussion of the possible influence of instincts—which are presumably inherited through the genes—upon human personality, values, and behavior would be incomplete and one-sided if we made no attempt to set hereditary propensities, including instincts, in the context of their possible limitation and modifiability by environment. Even among animals an instinct may never be expressed if a favorable environment is not found; and the environment may also either enhance or supersede instinctive drives (we have reason to believe that this supersession of instinct takes place even more frequently with men than with animals). For example, Chomsky observes that actual linguistic structures are a product of the interaction of man's inherited linguistic "genetic program" and suitable environmental influences (although, in opposition to what he considers to be the "distortions" of behaviorism, he gives the decisive edge to the hereditary factor).

The questions that are raised about environment and heredity very often take this form: "what are the *relative*, or *proportional*, contributions of heredity and environment to this or that human characteristic, considered as an effect?" Such questions seem to presuppose that environment-plus-heredity constitutes the sum of the factors that condition human ability and behavior, and that it might be possible to divide up this total in terms of a certain percentage of environmental influence plus a certain percentage of heredity-conditioning, adding up, of course, to 100 percent.

Unfortunately, this sort of answer cannot be given, even in terms of approximate percentages, for most of the environment-vs.-heredity problems that occur. Many major conditions or changes that affect human beings are the result of highly variable interactions between heredity and environment. A very slight change in environment, plus a slight difference in heredity, can very often produce a major difference in features, a difference that seems all out of proportion to the environmental and hereditary factors that are considered causative. For instance (we cite here an example utilized by Anastasi), there are two hereditary strains of the Drosophila fruit flies, one of which (Type A) tends to have more eye-facets than the other (Type B).[1] However, the number of eye-facets is also affected by the temperature; flies bred at lower temperatures tended to have more eye facets. But genetic Type A is much more affected by cold temperatures than genetic Type B. And warm temperatures produce much less variation in the relative number of eye-facets possessed by the two genetic strains than do cold temperatures. Therefore, there are some Type A flies in warm temperatures that have fewer eye-facets than some Type B flies in cold temperatures, and innumerable variations are possible. One could not make a meaningful assessment of this particular trait simply in terms of the proportional influences of heredity and environment.

The science of genetics has made immense progress in recent decades; much of the new knowledge has to do with the influence of genetic factors that possibly have an effect on human behavior. Sociology and behavioral psychology have made perhaps equally impressive strides in tracing, isolating, and specifying environmental influences on the human subject. Some evolutionists have developed mathematical formulas for evaluating the relative efficacy of genetic mutations in view of certain environmentally influenced factors, called "selection coefficients." But it does not seem probable that any scientist or metascientist will be able to describe with mathematical precision the complex interactions of heredity and environment as they affect specific human characteristics or aptitudes.

The problem of giving an accurate description emerges even with regard to physical diseases in man. For example, there is strong evidence that diabetes is inherited; however, the disease may be mild or even nonexistent in a genetically predisposed individual if environmental factors (diet, etc.) are favorable to good health and if psychosomatic stresses are minimal. We know that sickle-cell anemia is a hereditary disease in blacks; but we also know that the genes for sickle-cell anemia have thrived precisely because of an environmental advantage (freedom from malaria) that certain forms of the genes (heterozygous forms) have enjoyed in certain times and places (e.g., North America). Likewise, myopia (near-

sightedness) is hereditary; but the extent to which a genetically predisposed individual will be afflicted depends on his home environment,
occupation, and other nonhereditary factors.

When we come to mental or personality traits, it is even more difficult to
distinguish and weigh the hereditary factors in contrast with the environmental ones. There is strong evidence that schizophrenic and manic-
depressive psychoses are in some degree hereditary mental disorders, but
many psychiatrists still think it possible to cure such disorders solely by
changing personal attitudes and/or environmental situations. Some
biochemical researchers, on the other hand, have made a strong case for
considering most cases of schizophrenia as necessarily related to nutritional or metabolic disorders. It is possible that several or all of the above
factors are operative in creating a condition like schizophrenia. Manic-
depressive psychoses, meanwhile, are sometimes being effectively treated
and controlled, if not exactly "cured," by chemotherapy (lithium).

Understandably enough, geneticists tend to emphasize the importance
of hereditary factors, while psychiatrists, biochemists, and other specialists
emphasize factors of which they have greater knowledge and that they are
professionally predisposed to consider most important. Thus "territorial"
disputes emerge.

As a case in point, consider the many-sided controversy about the
"cause" (or causes) of homosexuality. F.J. Kallmann, a geneticist, in his
studies of forty-four homosexual male twins, found that the twin brothers
of each homosexual were also homosexual and seemed to have a similar
degree of homosexuality. Such evidence for a physical, even hereditary
cause of homosexuality has been substantiated by the work of M. Sidney
Margolese, an endocrinologist, who has found that in heterosexual males
the amount of androsterone is always greater than the amount of
etiocholanolane, while the proportions are exactly the opposite in
homosexual males.[2] Such findings are challenged (a) by the Freudians,
who trace male homosexual tendencies to certain Oedipal conflicts of the
young child (and, in turn, trace certain manifestations of schizophrenia to
unacknowledged homosexual tendencies); (b) by Jungians, who see
homosexuality as a result of one's unconscious identification with one's
opposite-sex image (leading to "projection" of the relatively unconscious
same-sex "Persona"); (c) by some followers of Konrad Lorenz, who
theorize (on the basis of experiments with animals) that homosexuality in
human beings is "conditioned" by exclusive exposure to one sex at a
critical period of development; and (d) by theorists who connect
homosexuality with painful experiences with one's opposite-sex pajent, *or*
with influences from one's peer group or cultural trends, *or* with a number
of the above factors in conjunction.

As another case in point, measurable intelligence (IQ) also seems to be a
factor strongly influenced by heredity, as indicated by recent studies of

identical twins. But there is almost equally strong evidence that one's intelligence—as measured by IQ tests, at least—is affected by environmental variables such as one's economic and social class, positive reinforcement by one's parents and peers, the values prevalent in one's culture or subculture, and other nonhereditary factors.

In all these areas there is heated debate, and those on one or the other side of the debate will often tend to downgrade and belittle the importance of the factors emphasized by the other side or sides. Sometimes the debate becomes acrimonious.

At this writing, the heredity-environment debate is probably the most intense with specific regard to three topics: (1) the question of race and intelligence, (2) sociobiology, and (3) the extent of "extended" secondary sex characteristics.

(1) *Race and intelligence.* In 1969, Professor Arthur Jensen, an educational psychologist, published an article in the *Harvard Educational Review* [3] expounding the thesis that the lower average IQ scores of blacks were attributable not to cultural deprivation but to a genetic deficiency. He based these claims on the "fact" that, after a long series of attempts, reliable "culture-fair" tests had been developed for all other major racial or ethnic groups—American Indians, Latinos, Orientals, etc.—but not for blacks. Jensen emphasized that he was not ruling out the possibility that individual blacks might be in the higher IQ ranges, even in the "genius" range, and that his thesis applied only to blacks as a "population," i.e., as a distinct racial group. But, granted this racial genetic handicap, we must, concluded Jensen, resolutely dismantle government programs such as "Head Start," all of which are destined for failure because they invariably presume that it is possible to overcome the IQ gap by strategically improving the cultural environment of the "disadvantaged," especially blacks. [4]

Shortly after this thesis was published, William B. Shockley, a noted physicist and Nobel Prize laureate (as coinventor of the transistor), began travelling around the United States stirring up intense emotional displays by publicizing Jensen's thesis. Shockley also made known his own personal conclusions: (a) that blacks are so generally genetically inferior to whites that they are unwittingly contributing to social "dysgenics," i.e., "retrogressive evolution through the disproportionate reproduction of the disadvantaged"; and (b) that inferior blacks, i.e., most blacks, should be rewarded monetarily for having themselves sterilized.

Opposed to the theses of both Jensen and Shockley is evidence from experienced researchers showing that the gap in IQ between blacks and whites as population groups, which amounted some decades ago to a twenty-point difference, has been steadily narrowing, apparently as a result of environmental, educational, and socioeconomic changes. Some see this phenomenon as proof that intelligence as measured on culture-free tests—if such tests are ever devised—would be found to be the same in whites and blacks, and they contend that Jensen, instead of concluding that there was some inherent deficiency in blacks, should have more reasonably and honestly concluded that there was a deficiency in his testing procedures or presuppositions or both.

The problem is further complicated by: (a) the fact that the precise nature and number of variables constituting "intelligence" is not known; (b) the fact that all IQ tests now in use, including those that are supposedly culture free or nearly so, are obviously not culture free with reference to blacks; and (c) the fact that the large number of environmental and psychological advantages and disadvantages that would have to be taken into account in testing an individual or group, even if we knew what factors constituted intelligence, would be unmanageable.

(2) *Sociobiology.* In 1975, Edward O. Wilson, a professor of zoology at Harvard University, published a book entitled *Sociobiology: The New Synthesis* (Cambridge, Mass.: Belknap/Harvard University Press) that turned out to be as controversial as it was long and scholarly. Wilson's basic idea, which was taken up and propounded by a number of other scientists, was to develop a comprehensive science in which data from genetics, neurobiology, molecular biology, and other sciences would be coordinated with zoological, anthropological, and sociological insights to produce a "total view" of animal and human societies as biologically conditioned and biologically explainable. As applied to animals, sociobiology offers specific explanations and sometimes even mathematically formulated genetic calculations of probability for territoriality struggles, mating habits, social hierarchies, male dominance, etc. Applying the same sort of thinking to human societies, sociobiologists have come up with seemingly plausible explanations of aggressive and altruistic behavior, conformism, homosexuality, machismo, courtship customs, marriage customs dictating that wives should be younger than husbands, the divisions of labor, and even ethical values.

Although sociobiologists have generally been very careful to qualify their emphasis on genetic determinants in the case of man with an insistence on the importance of human adaptability and man's power to change the environment, their theories have met with strong opposition, particularly from sociologists, but also from psychologists and other scientists who see racist, sexist, and/or outmoded hereditarian implications in the sociobiologists' observations and conclusions.

(3) *The extent of "secondary sex characteristics."* Sex is inherited through different combinations of the x and y chromosomes, and some so-called secondary sex characteristics are likewise inherited (e.g., differences in skeletal structure, pitch of voice, cranial hair, and sex preferences that are usually found in males and females, respectively). These facts are beyond dispute. But there are many laymen and some scientists who are wont to extend the range of inherited "secondary sex characteristics" to encom-

pass a host of temperamental or personality traits, especially in females. Thus it is claimed that women are by nature submissive, more interested in art than in mathematics, not as susceptible as men to strong visual sexual stimulation, and inclined to be more emotional, more personal, more altruistic than men.

Feminists seem to be of one mind in rejecting the notion that such traits are natural, inherited, or instinctive in women as distinct from men. Even such things as the "maternal instinct" and male "aggressiveness," which are evident in apes and thus (by evolutionary inference) might seem to be instinctive also in humans, are denied by the feminists and those who support their view of the matter, including a number of widely respected scientists (of both sexes).

Reading the literature on these and kindred questions, one gets the impression that such disputes involve something more than the "evidence" cited for or against the various positions involved. It is true that most and perhaps all of the available evidence is ambiguous and inconclusive. But suppose, for example, that it were discovered that blacks, owing to their physiological and metabolic makeup and their nutritional habits, do not efficiently synthesize or assimilate certain vitamins (e.g., Vitamin B_1, a deficiency of which has been shown to correlate with lower IQ scores). Suppose also that sociobiologists discovered a specific gene responsible for aggressivity. Suppose, moreover, that it were demonstrated that relative proportions of sex hormones correlated positively and perfectly with the "extended" secondary sex characteristics mentioned above. Would many minds be changed? Quite to the contrary, there is good reason to believe that most interested persons would continue to hold to their previous views. The new, "conclusive" facts would be "interpreted"—provided they were not simply ignored. The disagreements we are discussing seem to be very deeply rooted and not subject to change merely because of the discovery of some new "fact."

What are the sources of such seemingly perpetual disagreements? For one thing, the subject matters are extremely complex. The presence or absence of certain vitamins in blacks (to use the example given above) might seem to many to be clearly a physiological problem or an environmental problem or a combination of the two, but many physiologists and physicians are inclined to deny on principle that nutrition affects the intelligence of most slightly subnormal children and would challenge the results of such studies and strive to discredit them; and the fact that blacks as a whole are consistently several points behind in IQ, while apparently attributable to genetic differences, may be attributable wholly or partially to the largely environmental factors that cause the more successful middle- and upper-class blacks, those with generally higher IQs, to tend to propagate fewer children than lower-class blacks, just as middle- and upper-class whites tend to have fewer children than lower-class whites. Again, the discovery of a specific gene for aggression would not even slightly inhibit a dedicated Marxian-Freudian psychologist such as Erich Fromm from continuing to maintain that, with the coming of the post-capitalist communist society, human aggression, violence, and injustice will be completely (or at least nearly) eliminated. Finally, the proportions and constituents of male and female hormones may seem to be clearly traceable to hereditary factors; but the feminist or environmentalist may choose to emphasize the equally evident fact that impulses and tendencies of most females can and will be expressed only in certain acceptable ways, ways dictated by culturally conditioned role expectations.

Let us go a little further. It is quite possible for environmental influences to lead people to have a hereditarian bias. For example, a member of the upper caste in the formerly official (and now unofficial) caste system of India would be influenced by his environment to look upon members of the lower caste as hereditarily inferior. In speaking of the lower caste, he would be using the language of the hereditarian but thinking the thought of the environmentalist. In a different situation, it is possible that a person could be *environmentally* conditioned to consider all questions about "feminine" traits or "racial IQ" in purely *environmental* terms; in that case, it would seem almost literally impossible for such a person even to recognize, let alone accept, a hereditary factor.

At this point, we are ready to put aside specific questions about whether the environmentalists or hereditarians have the edge on controversial questions concerning feminine traits, racial intelligence, etc., in order to explore some deeper and more subtle sources that may be stoking the fires and fanning the flames of such typical heredity-environment controversies.

A number of attempts have been made in the recent past to understand (and perhaps indirectly to moderate or resolve) long-standing disagreements by getting behind the "intellectual" pros and cons to temperamental dispositions or attitudinal presuppositions. One of the most noteworthy of these attempts was made by William James in an effort to understand certain apparently unresolvable philosophical disputes that had persisted over the centuries. Attributing many such disputes to a subrational temperamental bias, James distinguished two major temperamental types: the "tender-minded" individual, who is strongly attracted to "abstract and eternal principles," and the "tough-minded" individual, who is primarily a lover of facts in all their crude variety.[5] A philosopher with the first kind of temperament typically becomes a rationalist; his main concern is to create all-embracing conceptual structures or ideals by means of which to unify experience. A philosopher of the second type will tend to become an empiricist, devoted to facts, wary of any principles or ideals that are not derived from systematic scientific analysis. These two "camps" have characteristically been unable to communicate with one another or to "convert" one another since the earliest days of Western philosophy when Plato was skirmishing with the Sophists, and the conflict has extended to more modern times when empiricists have been at loggerheads with rationalists, positivists with idealists, logical empiricists with phenomenologists, and so forth.

Carl Jung took up the same theme in a chapter on philosophical dichotomies in his book *Psychological Types* (1921). Jung begins with James' theory of tender-minded and tough-minded types, and then proceeds to relate this to his own more extensive and elaborately developed theory on "introversion" and "extroversion."

It is not quite clear whether either James' or Jung's typology would help explain a controversy in philosophical anthropology such as the environment-heredity dispute. James says that a tender-minded individual is characteristically authoritarian, while his opposite has anarchistic tendencies. Are hereditarians more authoritarian than environmentalists? One can think of examples, but the evidence is not conclusive. Jung describes the introvert as one whose attention is primarily focused on inner determinants, while the extrovert is primarily subject to determination from extrinsic, empirical factors. Are hereditarians characteristically more introverted than environmentalists? Again, this particular question has not yet been subjected to thorough investigation.

One researcher, however, has carried out an extensive investigation of basic attitudinal preferences among hereditarians and environmentalists. In *The Nature-Nurture Controversy* (1942) Nicholas Pastore analyzed the biographical details and intellectual positions of twenty-four English and American psychologists, biologists, and sociologists, and arrived at the conclusion that eleven of the twelve environmentalists were "liberals or radicals" in sociopolitical orientation, while eleven of the twelve hereditarians were "conservatives."

Pastore defined the "liberal" as one who was "characterized by a belief in the necessity of change" and by the fact that he was "favorably disposed toward the democratic concept." The "radical" was committed to an even greater degree of change. The "conservative" was "pessimistic with regard to the potentialities of the average person, or . . . critical of attempts to broaden the participation of the citizenry in governmental affairs," and was also characterized by "acceptance of the *status quo*."[6]

If we accepted Pastore's working definitions and accepted the positive correlation between sociopolitical attitudes and environmental or hereditarian bias, we would have a possible handle for dealing with the more intractable of the nature-nurture controversies. We might even conclude from Pastore's research that the only way to mitigate the opposition between hereditarians and environmentalists would be to bring about improved communication and understanding on a sociopolitical level among liberals, radicals, and conservatives.

Might we go still further and find a correlation between sociopolitical orientation and temperament? Such a correlation would be an indirect indication that one's temperament might tend to influence one's position on questions in philosophical anthropology, such as the various nature-nurture disputes. Some students of the subject have already looked in this direction. One psychologist who conducted an exhaustive study of temperament attempted unsuccessfully to find a correlation between conservative-radical tendencies and temperament.[7] Another decided to treat radicalism and conservatism as two independent variables, in conjunction with James' "tender-minded"/"tough-minded" classification of temperament, rather than deriving radical/conservative attitudes *from* temperament.[8] This would seem to indicate that temperament, if it does influence one's views on heredity and environment, may be at best only one of a number of influences.

In a way, however, those who look to temperament for even a partial explanation of the heredity-environment controversy may be starting out from an unduly one-sided and even biased presupposition that foredooms the effort. Temperament, at least in the minds of theorists such as Carl Jung and W.H. Sheldon, is considered a kind of innate, inherited endowment—a simple Instinct$_1$, to use the terminology we introduced earlier. But what environmentalist, knowing this, would accept the proposition that he was an environmentalist—or anything else—"by temperament"? And why should the environmentalist take the hereditarian's position seriously if that position itself is only a matter of temperament and not the result of the careful evaluation of evidence? On balance, reducing the environmentalist-hereditarian controversy to a matter of temperamental differences, far from throwing light on the dichotomy, tends to confuse matters still further and to cause bad feeling among all concerned.

A more productive approach toward an essential understanding of a seemingly irreconcilable dichotomy like nature-nurture is well illustrated by a book that has had an extraordinary influence on psychology since 1950, *The Authoritarian Personality*, by T. W. Adorno et al. In this work, Adorno and a number of other European psychologists, influenced by the Freudian emphasis on instinctive (i.e., hereditary) drives, collaborated with a number of American psychologists interested primarily in the precise measurement of attitudinal traits that were presumed to be mostly environmental in origin. As a result of their research, they came up with scales for "ethnocentrism" (E), "politico-economic conservatism" (PEC), and "prefacist tendencies" (F). They found that high scores on the E-scale (which can be an indication of hereditarianism) tend to correlate significantly with PEC-scales and also tend to be predictive of traditional ideas about sex roles. By concentrating on the analysis of attitudes as such, while temporarily suspending questions about the respective roles of heredity and environment in producing the attitudes, these researchers may have pointed the way toward the sort of approach that is most promising both for detecting a "causal" source of heredity-environment bias and for predicting such bias. They also seem to offer the possibility of a fairly reliable means of testing for the presence of conservatism and its opposites, as defined by Pastore. However, none of their tests were specifically set up to test Pastore's thesis of a correlation between hereditarianism and conservatism, and those who have continued the research begun by Adorno have not addressed themselves to this specific thesis, either. All one can do at present is to suggest that if a representative group of environmentalist and hereditarian psychologists were to test specifically for an attitudinal correlation between hereditarianism and conservatism, and between liberalism and environmentalism, confirmation of Pastore's thesis might be forthcoming.

Whatever the likelihood of a correlation between the "conservative-liberal attitude syndromes" and one's bias on questions of heredity and environment, it seems highly probable that any cultural alliance between conservatism and hereditarianism would be not only complex but self-contradictory and self-defeating. For instance, as was mentioned above, a caste system has been perpetuated in India for thousands of years apparently on the basis of a belief that skilled and unskilled laborers are genetically inferior to warriors and priests. This "hereditarian" position has been bolstered by a conservative-aristocratic sociopolitical structure. Adherence to this sociopolitical system by the upper castes, in turn, was promoted and reinforced by a "hereditarian" view of human behavior. A rather circular, self-perpetuating process thus arose.

Ironically, this system was (and is, to the extent that it still exists in practice) self-defeating. According to Theodosius Dobzhansky,[9] the caste system in India must lead to genetic changes, over generations, that will, genetically speaking, weaken the upper castes and strengthen the lower ones. He cites two main reasons for this. First, higher-caste incompetents cannot be relegated to lower castes or easily demoted and thus tend to remain in the higher castes, diluting the gene pools of these castes. Second, the aristocrats are wont to enjoy temporary illicit sexual unions with lower-caste women and thus are continually passing on their "superior" genes to the lower castes. Paradoxically, Dobzhansky believes, if one seriously wished to ensure eugenic improvement (in India or anywhere else), the best means of doing so would be to promote equality of opportunity in a "liberal" system in which the superior, more talented individuals would be attracted to those with similar abilities and tastes, would marry without respect to social rank, and would produce many genetically superior progeny, leaving any progeny that happened to be inferior to find a level that suited them, even if this meant their "dropping out" from unrealistic role-expectations that placed intolerable pressure on them. In sum, Dobzhansky asserts that a "liberal" solution would be the best means of assuring maximal and optimal hereditarian influence. However, this solution may reflect Dobzhansky's own liberal-environmental bias.

While granting that Dobzhansky's insights may be unwittingly biased towards environmentalism, we should not ignore the very real possibility that this paradoxical insight of his may have a direct bearing on the areas of particularly acute controversy mentioned above, i.e., racial inheritance of intelligence, the genetic programming of social behavior, and the prevalence of "extended" secondary sex characteristics.

In analogy with the Indian caste-system example, one might conjecture that, if one *really* believed in the superiority of IQ in whites, the best way to perpetuate such superiority would be to allow maximum mobility (based on aptitude) and access to the best educational facilities to *other* races (black, yellow, and red), thus assuring that whites with defective intelligence would not monopolize the superior facilities, place obstacles in the way of the education of the more talented whites, and in general dilute or tarnish the total performance of those who are supposed (by reputation) to be in the upper echelons of intelligence. Again, if one *really* held that there was a gene for altruism, the best and perhaps the only way to establish that point would be to provide the optimum social environment for the encouragement of cooperative and unselfish behavior. Likewise, those who *really* believe in male superiority in molding world affairs should, in order to assure and maintain this superiority, allow maximum upward mobility to women, thus weeding from their own ranks the incompetents whose only real claim to their preeminent positions is their male sex, and who by remaining in these positions tarnish or cast doubt on the "superior" male image.

However, to the extent that white students and their parents have been "environmentally" conditioned to a strictly hereditarian interpretation of educability, they could be expected to resist having to prove their supremacy through such an unorthodox and paradoxical liberalization. To the extent that professors of sociobiology have been environmentally conditioned to think of themselves and other law-abiding citizens as more liberally endowed with genes for altruism, they would hesitate to risk wasting resources and energy trying to create for lawbreakers or potential lawbreakers an environment that might be more conducive to altruistic behavior by all. And to the extent that believers in the worldly superiority of males have been environmentally conditioned to accept a strictly hereditarian interpretation of masculine and feminine roles, they would be conditioned against allowing even the basic "liberal" changes that might assure that superiority or even make it more credible.

All of which could mean, if Dobzhansky is right and if our analogies are right, that if currently advantaged groups succeed in denying opportunities to the disadvantaged, the "victory" of the former will be clouded by inevitable uncertainty as to whether their "superiority" was real or artificially engineered. Conversely, if these same advantaged groups are unsuccessful in attaining their objectives, they will assure for future generations the emergence not only of genetically superior people in the disadvantaged group but also the emergence of the worthier members of their own group.

4: Men and Women: What Is the Difference, Really?

It is essential to understand that the concepts of 'masculine' and 'feminine,' whose meaning seems so unambiguous to ordinary people, are among the most confused that occur in science. It is possible to distinguish at least three uses. 'Masculine' and 'feminine' are sometimes used in the sense of activity and passivity, sometimes in the biological, and sometimes, again, in a sociological sense. The first of these three meanings is the essential one and the most serviceable in psycho-analysis. When, for instance, libido was described [in a preceeding passage] as being 'masculine,' the word was being used in this sense, for an instinct is always active even when it has a passive aim in view. The second, or biological, meaning of 'masculine' and feminine' is the one whose applicability can be determined most easily. Here 'masculine' and 'feminine' are characterized by the presence of spermatozoa or ova respectively and by the functions proceeding from them. Activity and its concomitant phenomena (more powerful muscular development, aggressiveness, greater intensity of libido) are as a rule linked with biological masculinity; but they are not necessarily so, for there are animal species in which these qualities are on the contrary assigned to the female. The third, or sociological, meaning receives its connotation from the observation of actually existing masculine and feminine individuals. Such observation shows that in human beings pure masculinity or feminity is not to be found either in a psychological or biological sense. Every individual on the contrary displays a mixture of the character-traits belonging to his own and to the opposite sex; and he shows a combination of the activity and passivity whether or not these last character-traits tally with his biological ones.—Freud, *Three Essays on Sexuality*

In Chapter 3 I have tried to show how difficult it is to isolate "environmentally conditioned" or "hereditarily conditioned" differences, especially when we come to a matter of controversy such as the question of the so-called "masculine" and "feminine" traits that go beyond the scope of the universally accepted "secondary sex characteristics." However, we may still, with some optimism, investigate a slightly different question, which can be phrased thus: "Granting that inherited genetic makeup interacts with environment in very complex ways, has it brought about any fundamental, long-standing (if not eternal) 'existential' differences between men and women?"

In the six-week-old human embryo, both male and female, the sex organs are identical.[1] It is only gradually that these organs, along with the glands, begin to differentiate into what will eventually be a clear-cut physical sex difference. It is only rarely that a "hermaphrodite" is born, a child with both male and female sex organs, and thus an exception to the rule of complete sex differentiation by the time of birth.

In the physically differentiated male or female, the basic structural distinction from the time of conception is so clear-cut that every cell manifests the organism's sex-characteristics, so much so, in fact, that it is possible to identify an individual's sex by microscopic examination of samples of his or her cells. "Behind the scenes," however, there is still some ambiguity, for the male hormone, androgen, and the female hormone, estrogen, are both present in both sexes. It is the predominance of one or the other hormone that contributes to the dynamic and physiological male and female sex differences; and it is the relative proportion of androgen to estrogen that "determines the degree to which the individual develops masculine or feminine characteristics."[2]

The fact that physical (anatomical-structural and physiological-dynamic) differences are relevant to various personality characteristics and behavioral patterns is illustrated dramatically by tests that have been done with various animals. For instance, injections of the male hormone into hens resulted in increased growth of their comb, in a falling off in the rate of egg laying, and in crowing, male courtship rituals, and increased aggressiveness (bringing with it a rise from the lowest ranks to the top position in the flock). Similarly, injections of female hormones into a male toad over a period of two years not only caused a change in the toad's behavior but a complete change of sex. Thus it seems that no rigid separation of physical sex characteristics from personality and behavior is possible.

On the other hand, there are no one-to-one correspondences, either. If one had complete knowledge of the relative hormonal balances in an animal organism and in addition was able by a series of skeletal, muscular, visceral, and cranial measurements to calculate accurately the degree of male-female (M-F) structural predominance (some investigators have tried to do this), it is doubtful whether he would be able to make reliable predictions about personality traits, etc. on this basis.

But the fact that there *are* psychological and behavioral traits distinctive to males and females is recognized by almost everyone, including Mrs. Judith Loftus in Mark Twain's *Huckleberry Finn*. She has just caught Huck Finn in the act of impersonating a female, and after seeing him thread a needle, catch a piece of lead in his lap, and throw it at a rat, she tells it to him "like it is":

> The woman kept looking at me pretty curious, and I didn't feel a bit comfortable. Pretty soon she says:
> "What did you say your name was, honey?"

"M—Mary Williams" . . .

". . . What's your real name, now?"

"George Peters, mum."

"Well, try to remember it, George. Don't forget and tell me it's Elexander before you go, and then get out by saying it's George Elexander when I catch you. And don't go about women in that old calico. You do a girl tolerable poor, but you might fool men, maybe. Bless you, child, when you set out to thread a needle don't hold the thread still and fetch the needle up to it; hold the needle still and poke the thread at it; that's the way a woman most always does, but a man always does t'other way. And when you throw at a rat or anything, hitch yourself up a-tiptoe and fetch your hand up over your head as awkward as you can, and miss your rat about six or seven foot. Throw stiff-armed from the shoulder, like there was a pivot there for it to turn on, like a girl; not from the wrist and elbow, with your arm out to one side, like a boy. And, mind you, when a girl tries to catch anything in her lap she throws her knees apart; she don't clap them together, the way you did when you catched the lump of lead. Why, I spotted you for a boy when you was threading the needle; and I contrived the other things just to make certain. Now trot along to your uncle, Sarah Mary Williams George Elexander Peters."

Scientific investigations, after studies sometimes lasting a decade or more, have come to conclusions that go quite a bit beyond Mark Twain's observations about the differences between men and women. For instance, Lewis M. Terman and Catherine C. Miles, who conducted a well-known M-F investigation, summarized some of their conclusions as follows:

From whatever angle we have examined them the males included in the standardization groups evinced a distinctive interest in exploit and adventure, in outdoor and physically strenuous occupations, in machinery and tools, in science, physical phenomena, in inventions; and from rather occasional evidence, in business and in commerce. On the other hand, the females of our groups evinced a distinctive interest in domestic affairs and in aesthetic objects and occupations; they have distinctively preferred more sedentary and indoor occupations, and occupations more directly ministrative, particularly to the young, the helpless, the distressed. Supporting and supplementing these are the more subjective differences—those in emotional disposition and direction. The males directly or indirectly manifest the greater self-assertion and aggressiveness; they express more hardihood and fearlessness, and more toughness of manners, language, and sentiments. The females express themselves as more compassionate and sympathetic, more timid, more fastidious, and aesthetically sensitive, more emotional in general, . . . severer moralists, yet admit in themselves weaknesses in emotional control and (less noticeably) in physique.[3]

More recent studies confirm some of these findings and also suggest other specific differences: e.g., a more accurate spatial orientation and sense of direction in males (this is one of the few traits concerning which there is relatively universal agreement) as contrasted with greater perception of detail in females; greater speed and coordination in males as contrasted with greater manual dexterity and agility in females; male interest in things as contrasted with female interest in persons; female superiority in memory, vocabulary, and facility of speech; and the fact that males are more easily aroused sexually by visual stimuli than females are.

Yet some writers are not impressed by all these specific behavioral differences. Rather than just factoring out a series of M-F behavioral traits, they would like to go beyond these scattered details, looking for what might be called a basic M-F temperamental orientation, a psychological differentiation that would sum up all the scattered differences and, in a sense, get to their root. Freud had attempted to do this, but commented in *Civilization and its Discontents:*

> Sex is a biological fact which, although it is of extraordinary importance in mental life, is hard to grasp psychologically. We are accustomed to say that every human being displays both male and female instinctual impulses, needs and attributes; but though anatomy, it is true, can point out the characteristic of maleness and femaleness, psychology cannot. For psychology the contrast between the sexes fades away into one between activity and passivity, in which we too readily identify activity with maleness and passivity with femaleness, a view which is by no means universally confirmed in the animal kingdom.[4]

Oswald Schwartz, a neo-Freudian psychologist, abandoned such M-F categories as "activity" and "passivity." Instead, he developed the theory that men and women are psychologically distinguished by a basic perspective or attitude toward the world. The woman feels in continuity with the material world, understands it intuitively, exists *in* her environment rather than with it. The man, on the other hand, feels a sort of estrangement from the world around him and is always trying to capture it and disarm it through concepts. The man thinks up philosophical problems about how things really exist "in themselves"; women consider such problems superfluous and contrived.[5]

The most serious attempts to distinguish fundamental, radical male and female personality orientations have been made not by psychologists but by certain philosophers of the rationalist persuasion.

Immanuel Kant, the eighteenth-century German philosopher who is noted mainly for three somewhat abstruse treatises on various aspects of reason, wrote in his younger years a treatise in which he tried to distinguish the two sexes on the basis of their different aesthetic orientations. Women, according to Kant, are particularly endowed with a sense of the "beautiful," which is characterized by smallness and variegation. Men, on the other hand, are signalized by their feeling for "sublime" objects, i.e., aesthetic objects that are simple and large. Ideally, marriage is a natural union in which those two aesthetic orientations find optimum complementarity.[6]

For those who are not able to follow Kant over the shifting sands of aesthetic orientations, the theory of Søren Kierkegaard, the nineteenth-century Danish existentialist, may offer another option. Kierkegaard distinguished between psychological and metaphysical sexual differentiation. Psychologically, woman is distinguished from man in that in her the psychic is expressed in a corporeal way, leading to an emphasis on beauty, delicate sensitivity, and heightened sensuousness. Man, on the contrary, never feels completely at home with his body; he strives for rational control and dominance in such a way that his body becomes a mere vehicle for his attempts to express physical and psychic strength.[7] For those to whom this sounds too much like a sophisticated paraphrase of certain clichés ("men are stronger than women," etc.), Kierkegaard's "metaphysical" distinction may seem to be an even more abstract expression of role-stereotyping. Following up on some ideas of the German idealist G. W. F. Hegel, Kierkegaard described woman "metaphysically" as being-for-another (finding fulfillment in altruism), while man is characterized as being-for-self (finding fulfillment in reflection).[8] Simone de Beauvoir, a twentieth-century existential phenomenologist in the Sartrean tradition, sees an element of metaphysical chauvinism in this distinction, and in her book *The Second Sex*[9] she is quick to call attention to the fact that the Hegelian "being-for-another" can be quaint metaphysical jargon for servitude. In defense of Hegel, however, it should be pointed out that, in the original Hegelian dialectical-phenomenological context, being-for-another and being-for-self, whether these terms are applied to sexual relationships or to other things, are always merely two different aspects of one and the same thing; it is not possible for one to manifest being-for-another without also existing "for-self," and vice versa.[10]

Whatever the merits of these psychological and philosophical attempts at sex differentiation, we can see the possibility—the danger—that the impetus to classify will go awry. And women, doing a little classifying of their own, might well describe the more audacious of such attempts as manifestations of the "typical" male pastime of compartmentalizing and categorizing things.

At this point it might be best to return to the bisexuality of the human fetus, and take this as a kind of symbol and watchword for our further investigation of M-F differentiation. It is perhaps natural for us to want to classify but, in a very real sense, there are no men and no women per se, except on the merely physical level of M-F sex organs, glands, and chromosomal makeup. When we move to the levels of physique, physiology, temperament, personality, behavior, and "metaphysical" characteristics (if there be any such), there are only M-F *predominances,* which have a way of distributing themselves in infinitely variable and unpredictable ways.

Plato was one of the first philosophers to attempt to recapture and represent this infinite variability. In the *Symposium* he recounts, in a semihumorous way, a myth according to which there were, in the beginning, three sexes—a double-male, a double-female, and a bisexual creature. Each of these creatures was divided in half by Zeus, who was envious of their happiness. Thereafter each half was forever seeking its appropriate counterpart, leading to three types of sexual attraction: male for male, female for female, and male for female. Behind the humorous aspects of the story, there is a serious intent, that of showing that in the real world there is no "eternal feminine" or its masculine counterpart, but only a series of polarities that work themselves out in very complex ways in human nature and human associations. We may conclude, with Plato, that "masculinity" and "femininity" are only ideas or abstractions, which are never found "in pure form" in the real world.[11]

Thus, rather than look for a neat definition of each of the sexes individually, it makes more sense to try to understand how mutual definition and redefinition takes place in this or that culture or historical period. At the present time, as women are entering more and more into roles that were once defined as exclusively male, such redefinition must take place. (Men may be forgiven, however, and perhaps women too, if they occasionally lapse into nostalgic remembrance of the bygone days before "future shock," when men and women had very exact notions of their respective places in society, expectations in congruence with these notions, and—no doubt—in many cases less neurotic frustration and fewer "identity crises.")

The relationship (that is, the congruent and continual mutual definition) of the sexes may have far-reaching ramifications socially and politically. Karl Marx, in his *Economic and Philosophic Manuscripts of 1844,*[12] theorized that the character of man's relationship to woman will not only symbolize but also influence his relationship to nature and society. For example, a man who exploits women will carry over the same exploitative attitude to those other areas of life. There is much to be said for this observation, whatever one may think of Marx's formula for establishing a proper mutuality between the sexes (i.e., communism).[13] On the other hand, the most extreme feminists, those who reject childbearing and all other "preliberation" roles, may end up obliterating their social movement from the face of the earth, because, as some sociobiologists take delight in pointing out, such women, by not reproducing themselves (or reproducing only minimally), would in effect be "passing the torch" to women who have no ideological bias against the wife-and-mother role. In terms of

Darwinian natural selection, the feminists would be "selecting against" themselves.

It is useful to try to visualize a society in which women are copiously or even equally represented in all hitherto "male" professions such as, for example, medicine, philosophy, and politics. We may expect (though feminists may feel uncomfortable with this idea) that these women will bring some particularly feminine traits to their profession, and that, owing to the influx of such great numbers of the other sex, the "role expectations" or images of these professions may gradually change. "Feminine" traits (as currently conceived) may win out, e.g., physicians may become less interested in pathologies than in persons, philosophers more interested in aesthetics and ethics than in logic, politicians more interested in the traditional "housewifely" task of tidying up their own jurisdictions than in extending their control to ever larger ones. Many such changes would doubtless be for the better.

But if we wish to prepare ourselves for eventualities, we should note that: (a) there would be a gradual shift in cultural values, including changes in the prevailing ideas about greatness, competence, even genius, in the spheres of life that previously were associated almost exclusively with a single sex role; and (b) once women were heavily represented in a previously "male" profession or occupation (or vice versa for exclusively "female" professions), the two sexes might begin to differentiate themselves in specific ways within the profession or occupation, in new ways that are not now envisioned. Feminists notwithstanding, the development of a "unisex,"[14] a merging of sex traits into an undifferentiated sameness, is highly doubtful; and the idea that, if only we rigidly control environmental variables, there will be no significant M-F personality differences or role orientations seems an extremely Baconian[15] viewpoint for embodied personalities and embodied minds to take.

Above all, however, we must not allow such sex-trait squabbles to blind us to an all-important message coming to us through the feminist movement, namely, that those who are satisfied with mere sex-identity will never become persons and will never be able to appreciate others as persons. And this would be a calamity, for in evolutionary terms, the development of the concept of personhood is a later and "higher" development than that of sexual differentiation.

5: What Is the Future of Human Evolution?

In the human species, the reflective coiling of the individual upon himself leads to the coiling of the phyla upon each other, which in turn leads to the coiling of the whole system about the closed convexity of the celestial body that carries us.—Teilhard de Chardin, *The Future of Man*

Matter developed its organized forms until it became capable of embodying living organisms; then life rose from the subconscience of the plant into conscious animal formations and through them to the thinking life of man. Mind founded in life developed intellect, developed its type of knowledge and ignorance, truth and error, till it reached the spiritual perception and illumination and now can see as in a glass dimly the possibility of Supermind and a Truth-Conscious existence. In this inevitable ascent the Mind of Light is a gradation, an inevitable stage. As an evolving principle it will mark a stage in the human ascent and evolve a new type of human being; this development must carry in it an ascending gradation of its own powers and types of an ascending humanity that will embody more and more the turn toward spirituality, capacity for Light, a climb toward a divinized manhood and the divine life.—
Sri Aurobindo Ghose, *The Mind of Light*

The evolution of human society has brought with it some profound changes in our perception of sex roles. Perhaps if we could understand more about human evolution as a total phenomenon and something about the laws governing this evolution (if there are such laws), the way might be prepared for a deeper and more balanced understanding not only of sex roles and the values related to those roles but also of many other aspects of contemporary civilization—political, economic, religious, psychological, etc.—and the concomitant values. Thus we "time-out" now to allow ourselves the luxury of a look at human evolution in its totality—although in the context of our main objective of understanding man, it must be a very general inspection indeed, a brief overview intended principally to throw some light on man's current evolutionary situation.

There is disagreement among biologists and anthropologists about the present status of human evolution. The official scientific doctrine in the Soviet Union states that biological evolution in the human race has come to a halt; the only thing going on now is social evolution, the dialectical progress of man through and beyond capitalism to enlightened (Marxian) socialism. Some Western scientists also hold that the organic evolution of the human race has ceased and been superseded by cultural evolution.

Others prefer to think of both evolutionary processes—organic and sociocultural—as still ongoing and in intimate connection.

It is not our task to try to resolve these disagreements. What interests us here is the notable bedrock of agreement that is to be found on all sides of the question. All evolutionists seem to agree that, so far as man can know, the sociocultural evolution of man is now just as important as (if not more important than) his organic evolution. It is especially important for us to realize the relatively greater significance of sociocultural evolution when we come to the problem of the "future" of human evolution. Instead of concentrating speculatively on questions concerning how the organs, genes, blood types, etc. of man are now undergoing evolutionary change (if indeed they are), it behooves us to focus on those other aspects of evolution, that is, the building of social and political systems and the development and transmission of our cultural heritage, if we want to grasp present-day evolution in its most important aspects—the aspects of evolution over which man may just possibly have some small measure of control.

But, granted that the most noteworthy developments in human evolution are taking place in the sociocultural realm, is it permitted, does it make any sense, to ask questions about the "future" of this evolution? Can we know anything about the direction in which human evolution is now moving (if it is moving) and the goals (if any) toward which it is tending? Offhand, the answers to such questions would seem to be beyond our ken. Certain and accurate scientific knowledge is concerned with the present and the past, not the future. However, if we can content ourselves with possibilities (and perhaps even a few probabilities), it should be possible, using available scientific information, to project or "extrapolate" some of what the future may well hold. If a physicist knows the present position and speed and direction of a space vehicle, he can predict its future course with a high degree of probability. And every voter in contemporary America is familiar with the extremely accurate election-day computer technology, which allows commentators to predict results in many elections long before complete returns are in.

Pierre Teilhard de Chardin, in the first of his posthumously published books, *The Phenomenon of Man*,[1] advocates the use of similar predictive methods to "chart the course" of the future evolution of mankind. He cites the example of the engineer or physicist who is able to determine the course and the landing site of an arrow shot in the air—provided he has knowledge of variables such as the angle at which it is shot, its speed, and the wind velocity. So also, Teilhard maintains, if we focus on the past and present of human evolution and cull out the most significant developments without getting lost in tangential or trivial details, we can gain some insight into man's future (and evolution's future also, since the emergence of man is the culmination of all evolutionary processes, and the only thing that gives them their meaning). To do this would require something like a bird's-eye view of the total spatiotemporal expanse of evolution.

Teilhard offers such a view in the early pages of *The Phenomenon of Man*, in which he demonstrates how the process of aggregation and complexification in subhuman evolution seemed to have one goal in sight—the production of a brain, and with it the highest state of consciousness. With the development of the human brain and proper environmental conditions the main goal of consciousness was reached, namely, the point at which consciousness "turned upon itself" in reflective thought. At this point "the circuit was closed" and man's physical (organic) evolution was completed for all practical purposes. But the social and cultural evolution of mankind was just beginning. And it is by examining the stages of sociocultural evolution that we can garner the best index for assessing man's present psychic condition and future goals.

A number of authors, including Teilhard, agree in dividing up the past development of mankind into two major stages: primitive consciousness and modern individualized consciousness. Teilhard, as we shall see, goes beyond most of these authors and speaks of a third and final stage transcending the perfection of "modern" consciousness. But let us begin with the first stage.

The earliest stages of human consciousness, according to most close students of the subject, were characterized by an extraordinary sense of unity with nature and with one's fellow man—a feeling and way of looking at things that modern man can imagine only with difficulty. Teilhard designates this as the stage of "primitive coconsciousness," thus emphasizing the fact that, in many respects, it was not a consciousness of separateness but one of conjunction. Oswald Schwartz, a Freudian, describes this early stage as an original unity in which

> men lived in a perpetual present. Reality and dream were one. Life and death were parts, successive stages in one and the same process: birth was [a] return to life and death [a] continuation of life. . . . Symbol and reality were the same. . . . Cause and effect were not yet separated.[2]

Carl Jung's depiction of the primeval stage agrees in all essential respects with that of Schwartz:

> Primitive man . . . assumes that everything is brought about by invisible, arbitrary powers; in other words, that everything is chance. Only he does not call it chance, but intention. Natural causation is to him a mere semblance. . . . We modern men have learned to distinguish what is subjective and psychic from what is objective and "natural." For primitive man, on the contrary, the psychic and the objective coalesce in the external world.[3]

All in all, we have here the picture of men who were simply not conscious of many of the distinctions that we take for granted—distinctions between our ego and the world, cause and effect, the sign and the thing signified, reality and imagination, etc.

It was in the second stage that the many distinctions that we are so familiar with began to take root and develop "through millennia of painful differentiations."[4] In this second stage, according to Claude Lévi-Strauss,

passage from the state of Nature to the state of Culture is marked by man's ability to view biological relations as a series of contrasts; duality, alternation, opposition, and symmetry, whether under definite or vague forms, constitute not so much phenomena to be explained as fundamental and immediately given data of social reality.[5]

The "oppositions" and "alternations" that Lévi-Strauss speaks of did not, of course, emerge all at once. Historically, they underwent long and slow elaborations among ancient civilizations, through the Middle Ages, and up to our own twentieth century. At present, we are almost a world away from primitive and ancient man, owing to the sharply different orientation of modern consciousness. To gather an idea of how great this difference is, we have only to reflect on one example of an opposition that we now take for granted—the notion of "self" opposed to the world, with its concomitant corollaries of individuality, personality, and freedom. In the primitive and ancient worlds we do not find anything approaching these concepts. The medievals, it is true, used some of the terms ("freedom" etc.), but it was not until the Renaissance that the notion of the self as a "self-contained unit"[6] began to take on the signification of an imperious right to pursue happiness and develop one's personality in one's own individual way, free from intellectual dogmatism, social or economic pressures, and political monoliths.

According to Teilhard de Chardin,[7] however, the indubitable progress in all these "freedoms" that man has achieved in the last three centuries has not been without some devastating side-effects. The intellectual freedom of science has brought with it weighty moral problems concerning the proper use of our power over the elements; the new-found economic patterns have brought on tensions caused by having one's material fortunes tied to the shifting uncertainties of "fluid money"; and the quest for political and social freedom has brought in its wake the problem of the responsibilities connected with freedom, once it has been attained. Couple these problems with the Darwinian insight that life is progressing onward and the Einsteinian perception that all spatial and temporal movements are intimately connected and you have the necessary and sufficient conditions for a crisis in consciousness. For one can no longer concentrate on the provincial and the present without taking into account the global and the future, even the distant future. For example, we can no longer concentrate on wars (for many thousands of years one of mankind's favorite activities) without thinking about the spectre of global atomic war and the end of civilization; we can no longer concentrate on technical progress without considering pollution levels and the other ecological consequences of such "progress." Because of our new awareness of the interconnectedness of our personal situations with developments throughout the world and effects throughout time, Teilhard tells us, we sense that our world is fast approaching a "critical threshold," a state of extreme tension and extremely concentrated energy. According to the Teilhardian theory, such critical thresholds in past stages of evolution have always been the harbingers of "leaps" to new and higher stages of life.[8] We have no reason to believe that the evolutionary laws will change. Thus we may expect—or so the theory tells us—that the present tensions are simply signs that the human race is gathering momentum for another critical "leap" in consciousness—a leap to a stage of consciousness comparable (in its newness and qualitative difference) to the first dawn of self-consciousness that took place in some man (or some group) after the long night of primitive coconsciousness had passed.

It must be observed at this point that not everyone will be able to follow Teilhard's thinking in regard to the "critical threshold." According to existentialists, libertarians, and others who adopt similar individualist philosophies, our present stage of "differentiation" is the pinnacle of evolutionary development and should be maintained at all costs. In their estimation, there is no massive *evolutionary* crisis; there are only individual problems and personal crises. Actually, there is no way for a Teilhardian to argue with these apologists for individualism on a strictly logical level, for the differences of opinion here arise out of basic differences in systems of value and differences in "seeing." If one does not "see" that, in spite of the indisputable benefits of self-consciousness and individual freedom, there is something still higher and more important, then there is very little that can be done to convince him. Thus Teilhard calls this choice between alternatives a "fundamental option," the option either to stop at individualism or else to move beyond it.

There are others, from many ideological persuasions, who prefer to take the second option, i.e., that of expecting and preparing for something beyond individualism. Many of them are "collectivists" who, taking their cues from the darker aspects of individualism (selfishness, loneliness, avarice, etc.), as well as from the intuition that the paradisiacal sense of unity of the "first stage" should not be rejected in toto, have predicted a future stage in which mankind will return, in a greater or lesser degree, to a communal consciousness. Karl Marx, for example, concentrating almost exclusively on the socioeconomic aspects of life and drawing historical-dialectical conclusions from the breakup of feudalism into capitalistic individualism and competitiveness, foresaw a third and higher stage in a "socialist" society to come.

From a very different perspective Charles Reich, concentrating exclusively on the situation in the United States since the eighteenth century, describes the early days of the Republic in terms of what Jung and Schwartz would call the "second stage," i.e., the differentiation process. This process, according to Reich, became complete in the ruthless capitalistic entrepreneurship of the nineteenth century, began to reverse itself with the coming of the "organization man" in the twentieth century, and is now undergoing radical transformation into the new and different "Consciousness III," which Reich portrays as a state of general (nationwide) accentuation of conscious unity and noncompetitiveness.[9] In 1970, when Reich published his analysis, he claimed that Consciousness III had all but arrived, and cited the so-called counterculture, "the Movement," and the existence of thousands of experiments in "communal living" as evidence of the fact. By 1980 most of the communes had gone out of existence, and most leaders and followers in the counterculture and the Movement had joined the Establishment or otherwise chosen, as some of them put it, to "work within the System." The fate and even the existence of Consciousness III was uncertain.

In a somewhat similar and parallel vein, a Canadian visionary, Marshall McLuhan, drawing daring, apothegmatic inferences from the rapid contemporary developments in technology, transportation, and communication, concluded that mankind as a whole is becoming a "global village," returning "willy nilly" to a very complex and immeasurably expanded form of the tribal life of our primitive ancestors.[10]

Teilhard de Chardin viewed such social theories as contemplating and adumbrating a "third stage" of consciousness, which he called the "collective consciousness" (not to be confused with Jung's collective unconscious). Such thinkers have opted for "socialization" in preference to arrested individualism—and are thus pointed in the general direction of progress. In Teilhard's opinion, however, they do not go far enough. They depict for us a communal existence that seems rather retrogressive; it has all the earmarks of a reversion to the primitive unity, without any clear-cut provision for the promotion of individual consciousness and freedom. And this is a mistake, a defect, for life never evolves backward; and consciousness, having attained the inestimably great benefits of individualization and differentiation, must not in any way sacrifice these priceless attainments in its rush to a "higher stage."

In his speculations about the third and highest stage, Teilhard seemed to follow the lead of Henri Bergson (1859–1941), whose philosophy of evolution left a strong impression on him. Bergson advocated a futuristic "open society," which will gradually come to embrace all mankind, while still allowing for maximum diversity and individual fulfillment.[11]

What kind of massive unity in, and superorganization of, mankind would leave room for such values as freedom and individuality, and even enhance and foster such values? The answer, said Teilhard, is to be found in biology, not sociology. Biology offers to us the example of the *organism*, which is always a unity-in-difference. The greater unity and the harmonious coordination of higher organisms always goes hand in hand with a greater diversification and complexification of parts. Why shouldn't this biological law—that higher unity is always coupled with the highest possible diversity—apply to the evolution of mankind? If it is hard to envision a super-*organization* that does not suppress individual differences, it is easier to hypothesize a super-*organism* that possesses these qualities.

Thus, in accord with this line of thought, Teilhard sees modern movements toward collectivization, i.e., communism, socialism, communal living, as merely surface indications of something deeper and much more far-reaching that is now taking place in human evolution and that may take centuries to be completed, namely, a new biological event: the final evolution of all separate human organisms into a "collective consciousness," a superorganism, in which all "convergent"[12] consciousnesses, without losing their sense of individual identity, will join forces to produce a single supreme state of consciousness. He describes this final state as follows:

> The idea I propose is that of the earth not only becoming covered by myriads of grains of thought [individualized consciousnesses], but becoming enclosed in a single thinking envelope [the "collective consciousness"] so as to form, functionally, no more than a single vast grain of thought on a planetary scale—the plurality of individual reflections grouping themselves together and reinforcing one another in the act of a single unanimous reflection.[13]

Just as the cells and organs of the human body, by carrying out their specific functions, contribute through their organic unity to the creation of a single individualized consciousness, so these individual "grains of thought," when the proper time and circumstances arrive, will unite to create a superconsciousness, without ceasing to possess their own characteristics or losing their sense of self-identity.

Since this experience is in the future, we can comprehend it now only by means of analogies. Teilhard mentioned three of them. The first is the occasional experience men have of voluntarily and consciously "losing themselves" in the enthusiasm and goals of some group they are associated with. In the "collective consciousness" this experience will be intensified and made constant. The second analogy is the state of divine ecstasy or union with all of nature that the mystics of various religions refer to. According to Teilhard, such occasional and rare experiences are anomalous precursors of a state that will become habitual in all convergent consciousnesses. The third analogy is our experience of an intensification of consciousness and self-realization through converse with a close friend. Far from distracting us from constructive self-awareness, this converse enhances and contributes to such awareness. We may conjecture that the same experience may be repeated on a macrocosmic scale when an extraordinary increase of "love-energy" (to use Teilhard's expression) occurs with the coming of the "collective consciousness."

How will such a state come about? Not exclusively by "metaphysical" means, such as prayer, contemplation, etc. Although these things are not unimportant, evolutionary advances in life and consciousness have always required and been conditioned by new changes that have been quite material in nature. Such material changes (we are using the term *material* to include the physical, social, and cultural), preparing the way for the collective consciousness, will be: individual and social eugenics (*social eugenics* includes redistribution of natural resources, population control, international economics, and organized research in all areas affecting human welfare); revision and transformation of now-outmoded political forms (communism, facism, *and* democracy); and a synthesis of the power of science and technology with the vision of religion and philosophy.

Such changes will help to accelerate the inevitable unification of mankind, a unification that has already been in preliminary preparation during thousands of years of evolution. We must realize, says Teilhard, that the ultimate unification of men will *not* come about through conformity to dogmas, ideologies, political nostrums, or fads and fashions. A unity that is truly human must be based not on conformity but on voluntary association and, ultimately, on a voluntarily created superorganism.

Admittedly, a vision of the future such as Teilhard's has an aura of science fiction about it. But has not much of the science fiction of past decades become fact in our present "space age"? In *The Phenomenon of Man* and other essays Teilhard de Chardin tries by elaborate scientific and synthetic reasoning to remove the fictional appearances from a hypothesis that we have briefly summarized. Rather than calling it science fiction, he would prefer to present it as a vision of real human possibilities. And this vision has won the respect of a number of knowledgeable scientists. When Teilhard's Jesuit superiors forbade publication of his works, a group of scientists took charge of his writings and arranged for their posthumous publication. The noted British biologist (and agnostic) Julian Huxley, who wrote the introduction to *The Phenomenon of Man* (the first of Teilhard's major works to appear in print), saw Teilhard's religious vision as a necessary corrective for, and complement to, the empirical and somewhat materialistic emphasis of contemporary biology. The geneticist

Theodosius Dobzhansky concludes his book *Evolving Man* with a reference to Teilhard's hypothesis as an example of the kind of thinking that must be done if man is ever to begin to control evolution.

For thousands of years the Hindu sages and mystics have been telling us that all the differentiations among men are *maya,* i.e., pure illusion, and that it is necessary to rise to a higher state of consciousness to perceive the fundamental and absolute unity of all human spirits.[14] Teilhard's "collective consciousness," which in some ways seems to be a reinterpretation of the notion of the "mystical body of Christ" found in St. Paul's epistles, is perhaps the Christian counterpart of the Indian vision. What Teilhard envisages differs, however, in its insistence—in the tradition of Western Christian cultural values—on the continuance and intensification of the autonomy and individual self-consciousness of the human molecules who are to be drawn into the unity of the organic superconsciousness.

6: Is Man a Unity or a Duality?

There is as much difference between us and ourselves as between us and others.—Montaigne, *Essays*

> Is my own person, at a given moment, one or manifold? If I declare it one, inner voices arise and protest—those of the sensations, feelings, ideas, among which my individuality is distributed. But, if I make it distinctly manifold, my consciousness rebels quite as strongly; it affirms that my sensations, my feelings, my thoughts are abstractions which I effect on myself, and that each of my states implies all the others.—
> Henri Bergson, *Creative Evolution*

Thinking, existentially speaking, is a solitary but not lonely business. Solitude is that human situation in which I keep myself company. Loneliness comes about when I am alone without being able to split up into the two-in-one, without being able to keep myself company. Man exists *essentially* in the plural.—Hannah Arendt, *Thinking*

As we consider the whole span of human evolution so far as we know or can imagine it, one of the most striking and impressive developments is the emergence of self-consciousness and, especially, the emergence of the individual consciousness of freedom and personality that is the characteristic feature of the modern world. This accentuation of individual consciousness has not been an unmixed blessing. Aside from the social side-effects mentioned earlier (and all too evident everywhere we look), the emergence of the sense of individuality has also confronted us with a more subjective, Sphinxian riddle, to wit: why is the sense of individual identity accompanied by an equal and opposite awareness of difference—difference between mind and body, will and desire, etc.? Obviously we need to take a closer look at this ambiguous monistic-dualistic experience of individual consciousness.

Is there a difference between the mind and the brain, or are mental processes simply identical with the neural and other physical interactions going on in the brain? Is there such a thing as a human "soul" that is in some way independent of the human body? (If the soul has no such independence, how can we say that it "exists"?) In the sentence "I am thinking about myself" does the *I* that is doing the thinking really differ in any way from the *myself* that is the object of thought? Is there really, as some philosophers and psychologists have theorized, an "unconscious" that is distinct and perhaps in some way cut off from the consciousness-proper? These are just a few of the dimensions or corollaries of the question posed in the title of this chapter, some of which have come to be lumped together under an umbrella-term, the "mind-body problem."

Philosophers have dealt with the mind-body problem in a number of ways. There are monists and dualists and various subspecies of each: materialistic monists and idealistic monists and identity theorists and double-aspect theorists, among the monists; interactionists, occasionalists, psychophysical parallelists, and epiphenomenalists, among the dualists.[1]

There is no need for us to go into all these "ists" and "isms" in a technical way. What follows is only a general introduction to the basic problem of the "unity" or "duality" of man and, coincidentally, to the mind-body problem as well. I shall also try to set the problem in perspective and point out an approach that I think offers possibilities for overcoming some of the ideological disagreements and contradictions that have developed with regard to this problem.

History of the Unity-Duality Problem

In all stages of the history of philosophy "materialists" have shown a tendency to emphasize the material unity of man by reducing supposedly "mental" or "psychic" phenomena to purely physical interactions. One of the earliest materialist positions was expounded by the ancient Greek philosopher Democritus, who theorized that everything, including the human soul, resulted from various combinations of "atoms" and who explained so-called mental phenomena, such as sensation, in terms of a meeting or collision of "soul-atoms" with atoms from external sources. In succeeding ages, as the Democritean atomic theory was superseded by the theory of the four elements (earth, air, fire, water), and later as the theory of the four elements was superseded by the modern atomic theory, different and more up-to-date materialist explanations were given for supposedly "mental" phenomena. In the twentieth century, various attempts have been made by Rudolf Carnap, Gilbert Ryle, Ludwig Wittgenstein, and others to explain apparently "mental" phenomena in terms of contemporary physics or biology.

Nonmaterialists,[2] meanwhile, had all along been resisting the materialists' reductions of mind to matter. Some of them developed their own monistic theories, but most ended up with dualistic accounts of human personality.

The Greek philosopher Plato decided that abstract and "universal" ideas (e.g., "man-in-general") could never be derived from the material world. Thus he hypothesized that our "soul" (which contained such universal ideas) must have descended from an immaterial "heaven" (where it had previously viewed the pure ideas) to the earth, where it was temporarily imprisoned in a body through the process of conception and birth. The individual's consciousness develops as a succession of "remembrances" of things seen earlier in our "previous existence" (i.e., before birth). External sensations are simply stimuli that help to remind us of ideas we already knew. If one completes certain processes of purification, one's soul will be enabled to leave behind all material things and return to the heaven from which it came. Obviously, Plato's theory involves a radical dualism of body and soul, each of which is distinguishable and separable from the other, and one of which (soul) is clearly far superior to the other. Indeed, only the soul is *really* "real"—however real the "world of appearances" might seem to be.

Plato's most gifted pupil, Aristotle, was not satisfied with Plato's utter separation of soul and body. He preferred to look upon soul and body as "form" and "matter," respectively. The body of each living being, including that of a human being, was a kind of content to which the soul gave a distinctive form and character. Thus Aristotle emphasized the interaction between, and the unity of, body and soul. In the case of man, however, Aristotle also claimed that the human form (or soul) had a certain unique substantiality and a kind of independence of matter.[3] Man's soul existed in the body and depended on the body in many ways, but it was independent of the body in certain intellectual operations. Thus we can see that with respect to man, at least, Aristotle ended up with a modified form of Plato's dualism.

In the Middle Ages, various Christian scholastics, strongly influenced by Aristotle's philosophy, used Aristotle's concession of partial subsistence and independence of the soul-form as their philosophical bulwark for "proving" that the human soul "survives" in an "afterlife," thus bolstering certain theological presuppositions that were already widely believed.

Modern philosophy begins in the seventeenth century with René Descartes, who maintained the traditional Christian dualism, but in a somewhat different form. According to Descartes, body is an extended and unthinking substance, while mind is an unextended and thinking substance. He succeeds in distinguishing these two substances *so* well that he has to resort to the hypothesis of the activity of God in order to explain their coordination and unity.

Benedict Spinoza and Gottfried Leibniz, though followers of Descartes, both tried to restore some semblance of intrinsic unity to man. Spinoza accomplished this by means of a pantheistic reduction of all things, including man's body and mind, to God. Leibniz, for his part, reduced all things, including the human body, to certain *immaterial* atoms of consciousness called "monads."

The eighteenth-century British empiricist David Hume had no use for such formulations. He began to raise all sorts of pointed questions about the very existence and substantiality of the mind or soul.[4] A rethinking and reversal of Descartes' notion of an unextended "thinking substance" was thus set in motion. The skeptical thrusts of Hume were bolstered by the thorough-going argumentative talents of the German idealist Immanuel Kant, who supplied formidable systematic demonstrations that the mind or soul should not be considered a substance separate from the body. But even Kant was unable to dissolve completely the body-soul dichotomy; for in his "practical" (moral) philosophy, he still maintained a radical dualism between man's "rational will" and his unruly bodily inclinations.

A new approach to the body-soul problem was offered by Hegel. Making use of some mental groundwork provided by two of his contemporaries, Fichte and Schelling, Hegel depicted both soul and body as two different "moments" (aspects) that result or arise from the development of an essential reality, Spirit, that both produces and resolves (or supersedes) all the dualisms that we find in the world (i.e., subject and object, form and matter, etc.). "Spirit," for Hegel, was essentially a dynamic unity that incessantly polarizes itself into various oppositions before "closing the circuit" and restoring itself to unity.

Further attempts to restore unity to man have been made by the existentialists and the phenomenologists.

The Danish existentialist Søren Kierkegaard, heavily influenced by Hegel, took up a line of thought found in Hegel's *Phenomenology* and described the Self as follows:

> What is the self? The self is a relation which relates itself to its own self. . . . Man is a synthesis of the infinite and finite. . . . A synthesis is a relation between two factors. . . . If . . . the relation relates itself to its own self, the relation is then the positive third term, and this is the self.[5]

Kierkegaard's point was that man's self is essentially the restless oscillation or interrelationship between two opposing aspects, poles, or "moments." What we call the "soul" is simply one of these moments (the moment of the "infinite"), which can be isolated by the mind and considered out of the context of its relationship to the other moment (the "finite," i.e., the body). But the self is *not* the soul. The self is the dialectical unity that (to use Kierkegaard's technical language) "relates itself to the relation" between body and soul.

In our own century phenomenologists such as Edmund Husserl and "existential" phenomenologists such as Martin Heidegger and Jean-Paul Sartre have attempted to dislodge traditional dualistic presuppositions (such as body vs. soul) from Western philosophy, making a new beginning with their own supposedly presuppositionless "phenomenological" analyses of man's experience in the world. Although their respective analyses differed somewhat, it is interesting to note that each of these philosophers still ended up with one or more dualisms of various kinds, e.g., in Husserl, the dualism of "transcendental ego" and "empirical ego"; in Heidegger, the dualism of "authentic self" and "inauthentic self"; and in Sartre, dualisms between the "reflective self-consciousness" and the "prereflective consciousness," and between "the body for-itself" and "the body for-others," among others.

In this extremely brief historical survey (which omits so much!) we have barely scratched the surface. But the survey suffices for our purposes here, showing as it does that only a few philosophers, relatively speaking, have taken what might be called an "extreme" position on the unity-duality question. Plato and Descartes might be called extreme "dualists" and Spinoza an extreme "monist," but in the thought of most of the philosophers mentioned there was and is a certain ambiguity. Kant, as we indicated, rather successfully removed problems about the body-soul dichotomy from the agenda of theoretical philosophy, but in his practical philosophy he perpetuated the traditional dichotomy between reason and sensible inclinations. Kierkegaard tried to unify man through his notion of the self as a "relating," but this relating essentially involved a polarization process, and hence a dualism. Thus, on the basis of what most of these philosophers wrote it seems impossible to say, in a univocal and definitive way, that man is a unity or that he is a duality.

These ambiguities, frustrating though they are to some, may well be very much to the point. Perhaps categories such as "unity" and "duality" are misleading or inapplicable in the strict sense when our subject matter is the human personality. If we can successfully differentiate the proper from the improper usage of such categories, a solution to (or at least a better understanding of) our problem may be facilitated.

Toward a Resolution of the Unity-Duality Problem

The problem we formulated at the outset of this chapter, i.e., that of the "unity" versus "duality" of man, is an exceedingly complex one. It is additionally complicated by our inability to consider it as objectively and dispassionately as we do an experiment in a physics or chemistry laboratory. We are not mere observers; we are actually participants in the problem itself—as well as being the observers, we are the subjects to be observed. If we permit ourselves to become over-anxious in our search for a speedy and clear-cut solution, we may rush into oversimplification. It behooves us to proceed with caution, and a certain modesty.

Two paradigmatic examples of oversimplification deserve mention here. The first involves the philosophical reduction of all physical events, including a man's own bodily processes, to events taking place in the mind. This sort of reduction was defended in the eighteenth century by George Berkeley (Bishop Berkeley), who believed that what we call physical objects and events are merely our own perceptions; i.e., he believed that there is no real external world, independent of our thoughts. A completely opposite type of oversimplification is exemplified by some of our twentieth-century "logical behaviorists," who reduce *all* mental events to merely physical interactions.[6] While many behaviorists maintain that psychological reactions, feelings, and thoughts are effects *caused* by various physiological and neurological happenings in the human body, the logical behaviorists maintain that to talk about a mental event as an "effect" is meaningless. When we refer to an "idea" or a "thought process" we are merely denoting some neural processes taking place in the brain; the idea is not the "effect" of these processes but is identical with them. "Logical behaviorism" is of course a "materialist" position. Those who wish to avoid these two polar extremes of oversimplification generally admit that there is *some* kind of a distinction between the mental and the physical in man; they differ in the ways in which they try to account for the distinction.

So as to avoid not only oversimplification but also ambiguity or equivocation, let us now distinguish three meanings of "unity" and three meanings of "duality." As we make these distinctions, a constructive resolution of the problem may become apparent.

Three Meanings of "Unity"

(1) **Physical unity,** e.g., the unity of a slab of stone, a tree, or a field of grass, can best be characterized as a continuum of extension. Thus it is primarily spatial and implies some multiplicity of parts that are drawn into a physical coherence or unity. (It does not, of course, imply the complete absence of duality or multiplicity; nor do any of the various types of "unity" or "duality" discussed here imply the absence of their opposites. It is simply a matter of emphasis; in a state of unity, the unifying aspects are emphasized over the diversifying aspects—and vice versa in a state of duality or multiplicity.)

(2) **Mental or ideal unity** in its purest form implies the intrinsic coherence of an idea that consists of a certain set of individuating characteristics. For example, my idea of democracy can be analyzed into various essential characteristics—representative government, majority rule, political equality, etc.—and these essential characteristics serve to differentiate this one idea of mine from my other ideas (e.g., my idea of monarchy), and from the ideas of others (e.g., the ideas of my totalitarian enemies about democracy). Another instance of purely mental unity would be the unity of my mind with its ideas. Note that in all these cases no spatial

relationship of parts or elements is implied. The various elements constituting my idea of democracy are not spatially separate from one another; neither are my various ideas spatially separate from my "mind," conceived as the source and/or container of my ideas.

(3) *Physical-mental unity.* The best example of a physical-mental unity is to be found in any conception of man that portrays the body or "objective" aspects as "content" and the soul or mind or ideas of the mind as "form." It is possible to differentiate three species of attitudes toward the unity of man's nature on the basis of the relative emphasis put on the formal and/or the material elements, as follows:

(a) *Emphasis on content over form.* William James recognizes a form-content distinction in the human composite, but tends to emphasize the material aspects. He makes a distinction between the *I* (the self that is doing the thinking) and the *me* (the self that is being thought about), but then discusses the *me* almost exclusively—the physical *me* (body, clothes, etc.), the social *me* (my "image" in the mind of others), and the spiritual *me* (my states of consciousness and the faculties of my mind).[7] After so much has been relegated to the *me,* what is left for the *I*? The most we can say about the *I,* James wrote, is that it is our present thought, i.e., just the thought that we happen to have at any particular moment. However, many of us who also recognize a distinction between the *I* and the *me,* would tend to grant to the *I* a little more territory than James allowed it; we would perhaps grant that the *I* in some way encompasses past thoughts, past acts, feelings, and volitions, as well as an idea that happens to be present at this very moment.

(b) *Emphasis on form over content.* In his theory of human knowledge, Immanuel Kant tends to emphasize the formal aspect to such an extent that (it would seem) there is very little left on the "material" side. After beginning with pure, raw sense-data (a content that seems to have no definite form in itself), he proceeds to supply all kinds of "forms" by which this sensible content becomes defined and perceptible and intelligible to human beings (such "forms" are space, time, and various categories such as "causality" and "existence," which are imposed by the mind on the raw sense-data).[8] From our point of view, we might object that Kant seems to include many things in the category of "form" that we would tend to view as "content," e.g., distance in space, causal relationships.

(c) *"Even-handed" recognition of both form and content.* In other theoretical formulations, form and content are both taken as real, meaningful, and important, and any one-sided emphasis is avoided.

Many contemporary mind-body theories seem to be of this sort. They recognize that the human psyche has a real physical side or content, which is subject to its own biological, physiological, and neurological laws; but also that it has a mental side or form, which follows logical and psychological laws and has a reality of a different sort. Certainly there are many predominantly physical aspects, e.g., my warts and cholesterol and the size of my feet; and predominantly mental aspects, e.g., my moral doubts and my philosophizing about the best possible government. But because of the intermingling of form and content, there is also a great "borderline area" of things that are said by some to be physical and said by others to be mental, e.g., some of the more abstract images or schemata in the imagination, which bear a remote resemblance, on the one hand, to perceptions we have had of actual physical objects, and, on the other hand, to the very general concepts produced by the mind; and also emotions, which seem to be inseparable and indistinguishable from certain physiological and glandular changes but are also "mental."

For example, when an engineer is calculating the stress capacities of a bridge to be constructed, are the very abstract schemata running through his imagination more akin to the aspects and articulations of the bridge-to-be or to the concepts and formulae according to which his specific calculations were made? When I experience the onrush of a powerful emotion such as joy, am I to attribute this to certain minimal physical dispositions without which the experience would be improbable or impossible, or to the proper mental state without which the experience would be defective or go unnoticed? It seems that such experiences cannot be reduced easily to either the physical or the mental, precisely because they are simultaneously both physical and mental.

Because form and content are inseparable unities (the very use of the terms *form* and *content* implies that there is only one thing that happens to have these two aspects), any theory that portrays man as a composite of form and content tends to portray him primarily as a psychophysical unity.

Three Meanings of "Duality"

(1) **Physical duality** implies separation in space.[9] There cannot be two physical things or parts, strictly speaking, except insofar as they are spatially separated. Along with the notion of a purely physical duality, we have the notion of a purely physical cause-effect relationship, e.g., the causal relationship of the cue ball on a billiard table to the carom-effect that it sets in motion upon hitting another ball. Such reactions are known to be subject to definite physical laws, and the nature of the effects can be calculated precisely by the utilization of certain standard physico-mathematical formulas.

(2) **Mental (or ideal) duality.** Two ideas that are different from each other in content constitute a "mental" duality. There is, of course, no physical separation involved in this kind of duality. In conjunction with this notion of mental duality, there is also a kind of mental "causality";

thus, when I go through a process of deductive reasoning and reach a conclusion, the ideas that led me to this conclusion are purely mental "causes" (i.e., premises) that have led me to a purely mental "effect" (i.e., a conclusion). The causal relationships in this case have been codified in "deductive logic"; and by obeying the logical laws of inference we can produce with some regularity the mental effects we desire (i.e., valid conclusions).

(3) *Physical-mental duality.* This is a concept that we seem to presuppose in many of our attitudes, explanations, and practices in everyday life. As in some forms of physical or mental duality, a certain notion of causality is sometimes involved here. Sometimes the emphasis is on the fact that the physical can have an effect on the mental. We say, for example, that certain physical causes, such as menstruation or low blood sugar, can cause mental depression; we hypothesize that certain genetic endowments can cause mental disease; and some psychologists (such as Ernst Kretschmer in Germany and W.H. Sheldon in the United States) have expended considerable effort trying to establish positive correlations between certain body-types and corresponding personality traits. At other times, we emphasize the fact that the mental can have an effect on the physical. We say, for example, that by an act of "will" we can raise and lower our arms; we hypothesize that certain mental attitudes or preconceptions can cause certain "psychosomatic" diseases; and some of us conjecture that belief can sometimes produce direct physical effects, e.g., in "faith healing."

These different possibilities for emphasis are represented in philosophy and psychology. (a) Some positions, e.g., moderate behaviorism, emphasize the fact that physical (environmental) changes affect man's mental outlook and habits. They do not completely deny the existence of "mind," but they attribute mental activities to physical causes. (b) Others emphasize the fact that mental constructs have physical effects. C.G. Jung, for example, hypothesized that certain mental conflicts or neuroses will cause certain definite physical diseases that "symbolize" the neurosis. (c) It is possible, of course, to emphasize the reciprocal causality of mind on body and vice versa, and this approach, corroborated by "common sense," is supported by many.

However we may interpret the interactions of the body and mind, are they really "causal" in the strict sense of the word? Many philosophers have pointed out (correctly) that our ideas of causality are usually related to physical interactions, and that it is not quite correct to speak of the relationship between mind and body as "causal." Certainly the effects of the physical on the mental, or vice versa, cannot be calculated and predicted in any precise way. Likewise, if we consider "mental causality" as a separate species of causality, we must also admit that the relationship between the physical and mental follows no logical laws. Are we thus to conclude that such physical-mental dualisms are not causal relationships at all? Some have concluded this. Or are we to speak of physical-mental interactions as causal in an equivocal or analogous way (i.e., presuming that physical causality is the primary and most important kind of causality, while other types of causality are simply compared to it as to a prime analogate)? Some speak in this fashion also. But yet another option is open to us. We could consider the physical-mental relationship as *the* prime and all-important causal relationship, and then view purely physical causality and purely mental causality as two subtypes bearing certain limited resemblances to, and affinities with, the "prime analogate"—physical-mental causality.[10]

It should be noted that we have been using the expression "mind-body" relationship to connote what is primarily a cause-effect interaction, while the expression "soul-body" relationship has been reserved for a form-content unity.[11] If mind and body are thought of as separate and distinct, then a primary problem is how or "where" two such disparate entitles—if such they are—can become contiguous or even mediately united so that a "causal" interaction can take place. If, on the other hand, soul and body are thought of as harmoniously united and inseparable, then a major problem (at least for a believer in an afterlife) is how, in any sense whatsoever, a bona fide soul could be separated from its body even for an instant.

It has been suggested above that we derive our notion of a soul-body fusion from phenomena characterized by a certain physical-psychical ambiguity, e.g., the emotions and the imagination. If that notion is derived in this manner, then it would seem that "soul-body" and "mind-body" complement each other in an important sense; namely, insofar as it is precisely in the experience of ambiguous, borderline, *soul*-body phenomena (e.g., the emotion of joy, or the imagination of an infinite mathematical series) that we "see" the possibility of the mutual approximation to, and *meeting* of, each other on the part of *mind* and body respectively, related alternately as cause and effect. If this is the case, then it would seem that the reason we interpret certain abnormal states such as autism, catatonia, stroke, and coma as anomalous (i.e., as deficient in, or devoid of, the usual causal mind-body interactions) is that we do not have evidence of the normal "borderline" phenomena (e.g., emotional expressions and/or the power of making imaginative syntheses) that we habitually presuppose to be necessary conditions for healthy mind-body interaction.

To return to the question with which we began this chapter: it appears that man is partly a unity of soul and body, partly a mind-body duality. Those who find disconcerting the idea that man is both a unity and a duality should observe that even in the realm of the material and inorganic: (a) unity is always a unity of X with Y, i.e., the unity of something *with* something; and (b) duality involves a duplication of some *single* entity or type or quality. One should expect this paradox to persist and perhaps be even more pronounced in the realm of the human psyche, where a man can become "one" *with* himself and can also distinguish his *single* self into an *I* and a *me,* a mind and a body.

7: What Is Freedom?

Regarding man as a subject of observation from whatever point of view—theological, historical, ethical or philosophic—we find a general law of necessity to which he (like all that exists) is subject. But regarding him from within ourselves as what we are conscious of, we feel ourselves to be free.

This consciousness is a source of self-cognition quite apart from and independent of [observation-oriented] reason. Through his reason man observes himself, but only through consciousness does he know himself.

Apart from consciousness of self no observation or application of reason is conceivable. . . .

Every man, savage or sage, however incontestably reason and experiment may prove to him that it is impossible to imagine two different courses of action [free choice between two alternatives] in precisely the same conditions, feels that without this irrational conception (which constitutes the essence of freedom) he cannot imagine life. . . . All his impulses to life, are only efforts to increase freedom.—Tolstoy, *War and Peace*

> The most I hope is to induce some of you [Harvard divinity students] to follow my own example in assuming [free will to be] true, and acting as if it were true. . . . In other words, our first act of freedom, if we are free, ought in all inward propriety to be to affirm that we are free.—William James, "The Dilemma of Determinism," in *Pragmatism*

Freedom is not merely a speculative matter. Having or not having it has far-reaching practical consequences. Our moral judgments, for example, which are concerned with "right" and "wrong" actions, seem to imply that we have the power to make free choices. If we did not have this power, then nothing could be right or wrong in the moral sense, but only "fortunate" or "unfortunate." If I become a mass murderer and rapist of children, it is too bad for me that I must risk being rather unpopular, and too bad for those I kill and rape and for their friends and relatives—but nothing I do is really morally "wrong," or could be, since I am not free *not* to do what I do. Certainly all our notions of "punishment" would have to be revised if we presupposed that the "wrongdoer" was not free in his "criminal" or "evil" acts. We would not do away with punishment altogether. The parent might still punish his naughty child in the hope of influencing (i.e., determining) the direction of its future behavior, and society might still restrain the so-called criminal as much as was necessary to protect itself. But, one would think, the expressions of moral censure or disapproval that ordinarily accompany the punishment of criminals would be patently senseless and unjustifiable—even sadistic—and would have to cease.[1]

A thinker who takes a monistic approach to the understanding of individual self-consciousness is bound to show this propensity when he turns to the concept of freedom. Thus the materialistic monist, who denies the existence of anything other than bodies, will, if he admits that freedom has any reality at all, interpret freedom in terms of proprioperceptive feelings of spontaneity, kinesthetic sensations, etc. This approach is best exemplified today in behavioral psychology and in the Anglo-Saxon analytic and scientistic philosophical tradition.

The idealistic monist, who denies any real determination by matter, wonders why others have problems with freedom as *self*-determination ("What other kind of determination is there?" he asks). But in this case all meaningful distinction between freedom and "external" determination disappears.

On the other hand, any dualist who recognizes a causal relationship between mind and body is heir to the "freedom problem" in all its vigor. (a) He creates the problem by designating one area of the individual (i.e., the intellectual soul, or mind, the domain of "freedom" as opposed to materialist "necessity") as separate from, and equal or superior to, the other area, body. (b) Having recognized this real separation or distinction, he is also the only one who recognizes the existence of a real problem (in demonstrating how one separate area can affect the other separate area). (c) If he is an abstract dualist, he may construe freedom as the freedom *from* determination by matter. This implies that he grants some reality to the material world, but looks upon it as a potential menace to his nonmaterial self. (d) If his dualism is less abstract, he may go further and construe his freedom as the ability to "determine" himself and his world. And (e) if he is infected enough by the monistic insight to admit that the sphere of matter can have an effect on the sphere of mind or will, he will also try to develop the idea of freedom as a "reciprocity" between the two spheres.

In the analysis that follows, we will develop stages (c), (d), and (e) as three successive stages in the development of the idea of freedom typified in the development from "free choice" to "free will" to "liberty." First, some definitions: (1) *Free choice* is conceived as a state of indetermination, i.e., of not being determined or necessitated by material or biological or unconscious forces to some specific set line of action, or to the adoption of a particular alternative. (The term *alternative* implies that at least one other option could have been chosen, i.e., that one could have done or chosen otherwise than one actually did.) (2) *Free will* is conceived as the power of self-determination, i.e., the ability to act in certain ways predetermined by oneself. The idea of causality, i.e., being a "cause" of one's own bodily actions or external expressions, is also included in this notion.[2] (3) *Sociopolitical freedom, or "liberty"* implies, negatively, a lack of undue restraints and obstacles in the political and social spheres; and positively, the ability to work for certain goals in one's external environment, despite the fact that one must to some extent be determined by that environment.

We will begin with an investigation of free choice, but, as we shall see, the second and third meanings will also be implicated as we work toward a solution.

Free Choice

The major objection to "free choice" was posed quite explicitly in Plato's *Timaeus,* in which Timaeus, commenting on something similar to what we would call the "environment-heredity" complexus, says,

> No one is voluntarily wicked, but the wicked man becomes wicked by reason of some evil condition of body and unskilled nurture. . . . And when, moreover, no lessons that would cure these evils are anywhere learnt from childhood,—thus it comes to pass that all of us who are wicked become wicked owing to two quite involuntary causes.[3]

Contemporary versions of this objection may be posed in terms of external circumstances ("nurture") or inner determinants ("nature") or both. A good example of a nurture theory is that of B.F. Skinner. In his book *Beyond Freedom and Dignity* we are told flatly that we should forget about freedom and buckle down to the task of controlling human behavior in the only way it can be controlled, through "operant conditioning," i.e., the systematic use of positive and negative "reinforcements" to encourage behavior "we" like and to discourage all other types of behavior. Another approach, with the emphasis on "nature" rather than "nurture," is that of Sigmund Freud, who tends to explain all behavioral abnormalities in terms of repressed impulses from the "unconscious," which date very often from early childhood experiences and are apt to appear or explode in various ways later on in life. Some other psychologists would prefer to say (along the general lines already adumbrated by Timaeus) that human behavior is determined by an interplay of both types of influence—inner impulses or drives and external circumstances. But one thing should be noticed in many hypotheses of this sort about human behavior: no room is left for free choice. It does not even enter into consideration.

It is perhaps to be expected that a variable such as free choice would be ignored. For it must be admitted that, in considering most of our choices, whether externally or internally influenced, we find it almost impossible to *prove* freedom of choice, if we define this freedom as "the ability to have done otherwise." For our actions are never "could do's," but *deeds*. "Could do's" exist only in the mind. Philosophers of freedom have spent many pensive hours considering whether an individual could choose X instead of Y (in a situation where X and Y are thought to be viable but opposed alternatives that could not be simultaneously chosen).

(1) Many of them have concluded that when we say "A person, P, could choose X instead of Y" we are simply referring to logical possibility. Anything that is not self-contradictory is a logical possibility. If P does not try to choose X and Y simultaneously, it is logically possible that he could choose X even after he has actually chosen Y (so long as he is willing to forfeit Y). But some other interpretations are also possible.

(2) If we understand "P could choose X instead of Y" in the sense that P possesses some psychic capacity to choose X instead of Y, then the statement could refer either: (a) to our rational-logical capacities, so that we end up saying, in effect, "P possesses the rational capacity of discovering logical possibilities"; or (b) to a capacity (which we think we have) of withdrawing ourselves physically from our present involvements, so that in this case we end up saying, in effect, "P possesses the capacity to withdraw psychically from his involvement in Y, so that he is now open to choosing X." Examples of 2(b) would be the bachelor who suddenly loses his commitment to bachelorhood, and becomes detached from bachelorhood's delights, so that he is now open to the alternative of marriage; or the rape victim who allows herself to be raped in order to save her life, but withholds internal consent to the rape and by so doing immediately opens up to herself any alternatives that are contrary to the rape, although she may be temporarily prohibited from actually choosing these latter alternatives. In such cases, it is precisely the lack of psychic involvement in some choice, Y, that leaves one open to choosing some alternative, X, opposed to Y; and this indirect openness to other options seems to be essentially what we mean by "free choice." But if we were to insist that, in order to prove that P has free choice, P actually must choose X instead of Y, we would be defeating our purpose; because, as soon as P actually chose X, he would immediately be faced with a new problem (or rather, a new appearance of that old, traditional problem of free choice), namely, whether P could have chosen Y instead of X![4]

And so free choice could be taken to imply, at the most, a rather negative capacity to withdraw psychically from deterministic influences, through a kind of return-to-self; and the feeling that we have the power of withdrawing from all kinds of contingencies to our own inner sanctum seems to be responsible for our conviction that we are not controlled or determined by any of those factors outside ourself—whether these factors fall into the category of "nature" or of "nurture." But in addition to this rather negative "power" of psychic withdrawal, do we have any positive power to control and direct the self? For it is one thing to avoid determination from extrinsic factors, and quite another to *determine ourselves,* in such a way that the "self" enters into the equation of our choices and behavior as a variable, in addition to various involuntary factors, and perhaps even superseding these latter. This brings us to the question of "free will," which we defined above as self-determination.

Free Will

(1) *Free will as effort-expenditure.* Can we ever be certain that we are not just a bundle of desires and reactions driven this way and that by the winds of circumstance or the floods of raw impulse? Do we have any evidence that continually, or very often, or at least at certain points in our life *something* called the "mind" or "self" enters into the picture and by the power of its "will" takes charge of its circumstances, passions, etc., and makes itself "the master of its fate," as Tennyson's poem would have it? William James, who dissuades us from expecting any scientific proof of such "freedom of will," suggests that we nevertheless look to our own experience for some persuasive nonscientific proof of this freedom.[5] He bids us to examine the experience of "effort-expenditure" for the best-available evidence that "free will" is a significant factor in human behavior. Following up on this suggestion, we offer several observations.

(a) In the expenditure of extraordinary physical effort, we sometimes seem to go beyond the limits of the possible as defined by common sense and science alike. A case in point is an incident related to the newspapers some years ago. A child was trapped under the wheels of an automobile. The child's mother, although she weighed only ninety pounds, found the strength to lift the automobile off the child, just enough to make it possible for the child to be saved. The mother was not a trained weight lifter and, in fact, she suffered severe back injuries. We know, of course, that in emergency situations the sudden release of the hormone adrenalin into the system will give us unusual energy, but the laws of physics do not offer us much hope that a ninety-pound individual could lift a car weighing many hundreds and perhaps thousands of pounds without the aid of some kind of external lever. There are of course many such stories in circulation—some of them probably apocryphal, but surely not all of them—from which one might infer that man has a remarkable ability to use what is popularly called "will power" to do things ordinarily thought to be impossible. The belief that a scientific application of the will enables man habitually and systematically to exceed ordinary physical limits has led to the discipline and art of karate.

(b) The expenditure of effort in the moral sphere gives us perhaps another persuasive clue to the presence of freedom. Immanuel Kant tells us that it is precisely when a person performs his duty in spite of great personal hardship and real suffering that he knows that he is acting freely, i.e., from his own sense of duty and from no other motive. For example, if, in spite of all my inclinations to the contrary, I perform an act of benevolence out of humanitarian considerations for someone whom I loathe, I may be fairly sure that it is "human freedom" that makes such behavior possible (since animals—it is said—never go against their inclinations).[6]

(c) If one questions whether such moral acts are evidence of freedom, one may still perhaps be persuaded that acts of supreme self-sacrifice, e.g., laying down one's life to save a stranger from being killed,[7] do seem to give positive proof that there are no ulterior goals or satisfactions motivating one's act (since death obviously prevents the possibility of further pursuit of goals or satisfactions).

(d) It may be necessary, however, to go even further than this in order to gain greater clarification of the freedom of such an act. It is conceivable that an individual in thus sacrificing his life would have the strange but nevertheless real motive of attaining posthumous recognition and fame. For a more convincing proof, therefore, we might have to look to a case in which an individual was willing to sacrifice his life for a stranger even though he believed that no one would ever know about it. It is almost impossible to think of an example meeting these conditions, since we would have to visualize an individual whose whereabouts were unknown to anyone, whose death would result in complete corporeal disintegration, and who did not even harbor the hidden hope that someone might indirectly find clues to his existence and his heroic act. But this hypothetical case, or approximations to it, would no doubt intensify our conviction that the act was indeed "free."

(e) Even if we could locate such an individual, there is still the possibility that he might believe in a heavenly reward or "afterlife," and perform his "selfless" action simply for the apparently avaricious goal of attaining an unusually great recompense in the "next life."[8] Thus it may be necessary, if we wish to be sure that this act is completely self-determined (i.e., not determined by any base motives), to require that our hypothetical individual also be an atheist or agnostic or belong to a religion (e.g., Buddhism) that does not propound any belief in an afterlife.[9]

(2) *Self-determination and knowledge.* Just how important is knowledge for the achievement of full self-determination? Socrates thought that knowledge was the one necessary and sufficient condition for moral freedom (i.e., freedom from passions or vicious habits). He claimed that it would be impossible for a person really to know good and then refuse to will it. Thus he placed the highest importance on education as the single most liberating influence in society. If we were to take Socrates seriously, we might considerably trim down and simplify the prerequisites for freedom that we have listed above. Indeed, we would need only one prerequisite—adequate knowledge—and everything else, self-control, self-determination, social and institutional freedom, etc., would follow.

This view seems to be at variance with the widespread supposition (at least in Western philosophy) that there is a distinction to be made between knowledge and action, between purely theoretical or speculative truth and practical freedom. If we are thinking in terms of this dichotomy, the Socratic formula for freedom makes little sense. However, Socrates himself may have been referring to a different species of "knowledge"—to an intimate practical awareness of that which is good for oneself. We might say that he was concerned with that borderline area in our psyche where knowledge and action converge and become indistinguishable from each other.[10]

Perhaps the closest thing in our Judaeo-Christian tradition to this conception of knowledge is the biblical usage of the term *knowledge*. In the book of Genesis, for example, "the knowledge of good and evil" seems to refer not to theoretical speculation about right and wrong but to the practical experience of both good and evil; and the phrase "Adam knew his wife" refers not merely to Adam's being acquainted with his wife but to intimate sexual experience. In the New Testament, when Jesus says "the truth shall set you free" he is not, of course, speaking of abstract, speculative truth (which has never been reported to set *anyone* free—except from practical concerns). Thus there does seem to be a sense in which knowledge of the good is the only thing necessary for freedom. However, when we use the term *knowledge* in its more usual sense, we must bolster our definition of freedom with a few other accoutrements, in addition to knowledge. Abstract knowledge is at best only the beginning of freedom.

(3) **Determination vs. self-determination.** If knowledge, concrete or abstract, were the necessary and sufficient condition for freedom, would it still be proper to speak of freedom as "*self*-determination"? Wouldn't the "determination" in this case be derived from the knowledge one has, rather than from the self? If we automatically began to perform moral acts in response to the appropriate knowledge, how could we call it freedom? Prima facie, there appears to be a contradiction here: we can't be "determined" by knowledge and still be free. Some have tried to solve this apparent contradiction by saying that, although we are determined by our knowledge, we are free to pursue knowledge and to assent to it and thus "allow" knowledge to "determine" us.

The problem of determination-by-knowledge, however, is just one aspect of a larger problem: Is self-determination compatible with *any* kind of determination, whether by knowledge or by one's own passions or by environmental influences? Does any increase in such forms of determination cause a corresponding diminution or even eradication of the possibility of self-determination? This seems to be a general assumption on the part of many who extol freedom as self-determination.[11] These thinkers, commonly called "libertarians," tend to contrast freedom and determination, and some even consider them irreconcilable opposites.

There are others, commonly called "reconciliationists," who question the validity of the basic assumption that there is an opposition between, or incompatibility of, freedom and necessity, or free choice and determination. Two notable proponents of this position are Kierkegaard and Hegel.

Kierkegaard maintained that the opposite of freedom is not necessity but sin, i.e., according to Kierkegaard, a "lack of faith." In Kierkegaard's view, one who does not have faith has not experienced God's saving grace. The man who lacks this experience, and continues to lack it, is not free. Contrariwise, the individual who has this experience is free, no matter how many determinations he may encounter in his environment, his personal background, or his limited ideas. In fact, we might say that such an individual is free precisely *because* he allows himself to be conditioned by, affected by, and determined by God's grace.

Hegel considered determination to be not only compatible with freedom but necessary for the perfection of freedom. According to Hegel,[12] there are three developmental stages of freedom: (a) the stage of indetermination, which implies the ability to withdraw psychically from external interests and even internal desires; (b) the stage of determination, i.e., self-determination on the basis of our knowledge of our needs and potentialities and of the world; and (c) "absolute" freedom, in which we freely "determine ourselves to be determined" by a moral society and the laws and customs of that society.

Sociopolitical Freedom

The "determination" found in Hegel's third and highest stage is considered the greatest boon to freedom, and indeed, its culmination. In order to understand what Hegel means, we should analyze our conception of the "true friend." Essentially, we might define the true friend as one whom we freely prefer precisely because he would not accept or tolerate the sacrifice of our freedom under any conditions; thus, in a very real sense, he "forces" us to be free. If we could extend this notion to society at large, we can perhaps, without too much fantasizing, visualize a society that in all essential respects is geared to promote and safeguard our freedom. If a free individual finds such a society, it is rational for him to align himself with it. If he does not find such a society, it is equally rational for him to try to create one, in order to complement his freedom with appropriate objective structures and guarantees.

Hegel's notion of freedom sounds similar to that of the seventeenth-century English political philosopher Thomas Hobbes, who defined freedom ("liberty") as an absence of external restrictions on the activity of any being. But this similarity is only apparent. Hegel goes beyond Hobbes' negative requirement of the absence of restraints and adds that the free man must find positive reflections of, and incentives to, freedom in his environment; and, even more importantly, he must have attained to a requisite consciousness of freedom by going through the first two stages (a) and (b) mentioned above.

I think it important that we, like Hegel, go beyond Hobbes in our definition of freedom. If we define it simply as the "absence of external restrictions on our activity" our freedom becomes synonymous with our relative success in gratifying ourselves or in attaining power and is not much different from the uninhibited and unimpeded activity of any animal (as Hobbes himself admits).[13] We go beyond this external view of freedom by requiring: (a) the ability to resist merely raw impulses; (b) the fullest possible knowledge of circumstances; (c) an understanding of our own needs and capabilities; and (d) the ability to put our knowledge into effect. If we then (e) express our freedom externally, and (f) allow ourselves to be "determined" only by the best, most beneficial determinant factors (people, laws, institutions, etc.), we will have attained freedom in a most comprehensive sense.[14] In this sense, freedom is especially to be contrasted with "gut reactions," lack of inhibition, and nonreflective spontaneity, as well as with license, extreme individualism, and antisocial behavior.

8: How Does Consciousness Develop?

Mind . . . reveals its independence of its corporeity in the fact that it can develop itself [prematurely]. Children often have a mental development far in advance of their years. . . . *In general,* however, it must be admitted that intellect does not come before its time. It is almost solely in the case of artistic talents that their premature appearance is an indication of excellence. On the other hand, the premature development of intelligence generally which has been observed in some children has not, as a rule, been followed by great intellectual distinction in manhood.—Hegel, *The Philosophy of Mind*

If we concentrate overmuch on the idea of freedom, we may get the impression that man is the animal who raises himself by his own bootstraps, makes himself free, and perhaps even tries to permeate his environment with the freedom he discovers. But this would be a distortion, at least if we are to believe the developmental psychologists. For they tell us that there are predictable, though not rigidly predictable, sequences or stages in human development—the stages by which man is, in a certain sense, almost "programmed" to develop in consciousness, and even in the consciousness of freedom itself. Many of the developmentalists would agree with the existentialists that "man is determined to be free," but they would of course mean something different by this expression than the existentialists do.

In this chapter we will be concerned not so much with relating or sifting the masses of valuable information that the developmentalists have unearthed as we are with focusing on a few of the better-known facts about early human development—facts that will help us to a better understanding of the emergence of human consciousness, that strange and multifaceted power of an embodied psyche.

The adult human being distinguishes various aspects, states, or powers of consciousness such as sensation, understanding, will, and imagination. If he reflects a little on his experience, however, he finds that these distinctions are artificial. In ordinary conscious life there are for him no pure sensations, i.e., sensations free from any admixture of thoughts or volitions; there is no pure experience of willing, i.e., volition divorced from concomitant thoughts, emotions, and sensations; and so forth. In truth, each of the powers of consciousness just mentioned is thoroughly intertwined with other powers; each continually stimulates and is stimulated by the others. If a power such as sensation or perception seems to have a certain independence from other operations, this is the result of relative *emphasis,* e.g., the experience of thinking about an *idea* so intensely that we seem to forget momentarily about our background perceptions and sensations, or the experience of being so distracted or attracted by *sensations* around us that we seem to put aside all conceptual thought. But in reality, our sensations are inundated with all sorts of ideas—ideas of colors, relative sizes and shapes, specific identifying characteristics, etc.; and, in thought, one who closes his eyes cannot shut out his proprioception of his own body or sense impressions from the imagination. Even so, we must distinguish sensations from thought in order to be able to talk about them and study them; and such "artificial" distinctions must provide the basis for our present study.

In studying the powers of human consciousness, a number of options are open to us.

(a) We can try to isolate various "faculties" in the human personality and/or soul, e.g., the faculties of intellect and will, or the faculties of sight, memory, and imagination. This approach has been adopted by some philosophers and psychologists, who have tried to differentiate these faculties on the basis of the specific objects toward which they are directed and the ways in which the faculties assimilate their objects.

(b) We could attempt to describe various operations and aspects precisely in their dynamic interrelationship in the mature consciousness. Hegel used an approach of this sort in Part I of his *Phenomenology of Spirit,* where he traced the processes by which sensations lead into perceptions, perceptions into understanding, understanding into self-consciousness.[1]

(c) We can contribute something to the understanding of the powers of consciousness by physiologically pinpointing their "causal" nexus in various lobes of the brain or in processes in the brain or other parts of the anatomy. This has already been done by physiological researchers with reference to the five external senses and various aspects of memory, perceptions, conceptual understanding, etc. But much still remains to be done, especially with regard to the more sophisticated mental operations.

(d) One might also throw some light on the powers of consciousness by describing and analyzing their appearance at various "normal" stages of human development. This approach, which is based on developmental psychology, is exemplified in the works of Jean Piaget, Erik Erikson, Arnold Gesell, and other developmental psychologists who utilize their empirical data as a springboard for philosophical speculation about the nature and differentiation of human consciousness. Other approaches are also possible. Thus the developmentally oriented approach, which is being used here, is just one of a number of possible pathways to a better understanding of consciousness.

Preliminary to analysis of the development of consciousness, certain general observations should be made regarding the "normal" stages of human development.

(a) These stages involve references to "average" ages at which certain phenomena begin to appear in children or adolescents. Such averages sum up, in a rather neat way, a wide diversity of cases. We may say, for example, that a child begins to crawl in the ninth month "on the average." However, the inception of crawling that is "averaged up" may actually occur, in individual cases, from the sixth to the twelfth month.

(b) There are wide differences not only among children but apparently among generations, as well. For instance, Dr. Harvey Kravitz of the Northwestern University School of Medicine, who studied the sequences according to which an infant discovers and plays with the various parts of his own body, reports that "hand-to-hand activity occurred about four weeks earlier in our series than the data reported in a study made thirty years ago. Hand-to-foot play occurred about five weeks earlier." He concludes, "this would seem to indicate that today's infants are more advanced."[2]

(c) Most of the studies of developmental stages on which we draw (e.g., the Gesell Institute study by Doctors Ilg and Ames) were conducted on American or European subjects, and thus may be affected by cultural patterns and emphases that prevail in the United States.

(d) When we infer that changes in external infant behavior indicate the existence of certain internal capacities we are no doubt drawing analogies to our own adult external behavior and to the internal states that seem to be associated with that behavior. The infant cannot tell us, of course, whether the analogies we draw are correct. And logically speaking, when we *say*, for instance, that expressions of anticipatory behavior in the infant give evidence that "his memory has developed," what we *mean* is that the type of behavior we observe in the infant is associated in our *adult* experience with memory.

With all these qualifications in mind, we may now consider the apparent genesis of various states of consciousness in the course of normal human development.

(1) *Sensation.* "Sensation" is sometimes confused with "perception." Strictly speaking, *sensation* refers to one's bare awareness of sensory stimuli or a sensory environment. When we associate these sensory stimuli with certain "objects" or clusters of sensation, or if we begin to specify and discern any concrete objects or facets of our environment, we are leaving sensation behind and getting into the sphere of perception.

In our normal adult consciousness, there is no such thing as pure sensation. The closest we get to it is perhaps in subliminal states, e.g., the confused awareness we sometimes have as we are just beginning to rouse ourselves from sleep.

This state, of which we can attain only an approximate idea, is probably the constant state of the "neonate," the newly born infant. William James speculated that during the first few days after birth the infant is in a state of pure sensation, a state in which "the Object which the numerous inpouring currents of the baby bring to his consciousness is one big blooming buzzing Confusion. That Confusion is the baby's Universe."[3] This early state of "pure sensation" seems to be characterized by disorganized, chaotic incoming currents of sense stimuli, i.e., Confusion with a capital C. The newly born infant gives an external sign of his reaction to this "Confusion" by his difficulty in focusing his eyes.[4] Is the infant aware of the presence of objects? How could anything really be "present" to him before he even begins to differentiate himself from objects in his vicinity? Psychologists tell us that the infant in his earliest days is in a state of "coenesthesis," which may be defined as a vague, bodily grasping-together of an organism-field or global mass. There is no subject-object differentiation in this state. The infant has no ego. And he gives signs of his lack of awareness of ego, for example, when he fails to realize that a slight noise or disturbance in his room is just in the background and is not affecting his ego; he cries as if the noise or disturbance were going on within his own body. And if something *is* affecting his body (e.g., a wet diaper), he fails to make allowance for the fact that the wetness is only a passing personal misfortune and cries as if the whole world were wet. For the infant, the whole world *is* wet!

(2) **Perception.** Perception goes beyond sensations by relating sensory input to specific concretions, or "things." Perception is not concerned with raw sensations but with sensations organized and focused into some finite object of attention. The infant probably takes his first step in the direction of perception when he begins to focus his eyes, usually during the first month.

A greater advance occurs at about the sixth month when he begins to let objects go from his hands, instead of clinging to them instinctively. This is significant because it seems to imply a rudimentary dissociation from the external world and its objects (whereas the previous habit of clinging implied the opposite, an immersion of the ego in the external world—which is incompatible with any bona fide perception). A fuller development of perception takes place toward the end of the first year, when the child becomes easily distracted by all sorts of objects and tries to grasp them, play with them, pull them apart.

This general interest in perceptual objects reaches a culmination when, during the second year, the child, just learning to talk, begins to ask the names of things—as if the process of naming and identifying objects were the most important thing in the world. At this stage, we might say that the child has well-developed perceptual powers and is ready to advance to understanding and reasoning.

(3) *Memory.* Perhaps the first major sign that an infant's memory is developing appears during about the second month, when he begins to show signs of anticipation—at the approach of his mother, as he is about to be fed, etc. Feelings of anticipation are always based on some memory of gratification in the past combined with a desire to reexperience the gratification. Later on, during the second year, the vague memories of infancy become more explicit and the child is able to refer to "yesterday" or times past. (It is worth noting in this regard that a child's memory of the past seems to differ considerably from an adult's. Because of the rapid biological processes taking place in the child's body, things in the outside world seem to move rather slowly; yesterday may easily seem like a year ago. Aged persons, on the other hand, whose systems are slowing down, seem to be encountering a world that is going faster and faster, and a year ago may seem like yesterday to them. Thus accurate communication of memories may be a problem when the communicators are extremely far apart in age.)

(4) *Imagination.* There is some dispute about the precise difference between imagination and memory, and sometimes the terms are confused, e.g., when someone talks about "imagining" a scene from the past. Strictly speaking, *memory* applies to past events and *imagination* applies to a mental depiction of objects or events without any necessary reference to a past time. Thus I can imagine my life in the womb *or* my future maturity, but my personal *memories* can pertain only to actual past states or events. Perhaps the first strong indication of the presence of imagination in a child is when the child begins to simulate; e.g., the child reacts to a picture as if it were the thing it represents, plays with dolls as if they were real persons, arranges blocks or other objects into the facsimiles of buildings, etc. Further developments take place as the child learns to play and "make believe" in more complex ways. In later childhood and adolescence, daydreaming and fantasizing indicate a highly developed imagination—something that will be of great importance for many creative and artistic activities of adult life.

(5) *Understanding.* In the forming of concepts of the understanding, we leave behind the various "perceptions" we have experienced now and then, and we try to focus on certain perduring qualities or essential features that remain throughout all these perceptions. Thus, while our perceptions (e.g., the perceptions of trees and colors) are constantly changing, our concepts (e.g., a concept of what a tree is, or what is meant by *blue*) are relatively stable.

The first indication of the advent of conceptualization in the child is often found before the beginning of the third year, when he begins to show awareness of *general* names (e.g., not this or that "kitty," but "cat"; not this doll or that drum, but "toy"). To foster this awareness, he will begin to ask—persistently—about the general names of things, a habit that can become quite annoying to parents, relatives, and friends of the family. His persistence seems to be motivated by a desire to categorize. (Later on, as an adult, he will find out how fallible and misleading some of his categories are; but for the present, categories seem to be a most important thing within his mental horizons.) The categories that he forms supply the basis for logical inferences or ratiocinations that tend in the beginning, of course, to be sketchy or erroneous (e.g., "all cats have tails," thinks the child; "therefore this Manx that I see couldn't be a cat").

A more advanced stage of categorization is exemplified in the tendency of young teenagers or preteens to create collections of various sorts—dolls, parts of cars, rocks, people, sayings, useful principles, etc. Prowess in logical inference from one category to another is illustrated by a positive delight in argumentation for its own sake, an interest that seems to thrive for the first time in the early teens, much to the annoyance of some parents and teachers. More advanced adult stages are the types of inference involved in the study of science, technology, philosophy, and the humanities.

(6) *Will, or volition.* One might be tempted to say that manifestation of will begins early in infancy, e.g., when an infant shows his stubbornness by a temper tantrum, or a seven-month-old baby turns his head vigorously to the left and right to avoid taking the food from the spoon that his mother is holding. However, these examples would be better characterized as "willfulness," for "volition" in the strict sense seems to entail some sort of goal-orientation, or an effort to attain personally selected ideals. The first major manifestation of this tendency seems to take place during the "age of obstinacy" (ages two to five) when the child begins to say "no" and disobeys his parents in order to assert himself and to pursue certain goals that may happen to conflict with the goals his parents are interested in.

Provided an impasse does not result, the child and his parents normally will be able to work out some sort of compromise regarding their respective goals. As the child continues to pursue *his* goals and aspirations, in developing towards adulthood, he will naturally tend to favor the ones that he has been previously successful in attaining. (The ability, however, to choose and successfully accomplish *arduous* goals may be a sign of greater maturity or "freedom" of will, as we have indicated in the previous chapter.) An ultimate stage of volition takes place in adolescence and adulthood, if and when the individual chooses realistic as well as challenging goals, and if he develops the capacity to coordinate his goals with those of others whose goals will sometimes conflict with his own.

(7) *Self-awareness.* Perhaps the first definite sign of self-awareness that we see in the child is at about the ninth month, when he begins to show resentment when objects are taken away from him. From this reaction, we may infer that he has a rudimentary self-concept, since he seems to consider the object his "property," and the notion of property is related to

the notion of the self (that which "appropriates" the object).[5] More advanced stages occur: (a) during the second or third year, when the child learns his own name and begins to respond to it; (b) during pubescence (about eleven to twelve years of age), when the boy or girl, undergoing rapid physical and hormonal development, begins to be acutely (sometimes painfully) aware of his or her own *body* and the bodies of others, as almost independent entities; and finally (c) during middle adolescence (about fifteen to eighteen), when the teenager not only attains an abstract concept of a "self" but proves that he or she has the ability to appreciate and enjoy this self—through the positive and active pursuit of solitude (as distinct from mere avoidance of uncomfortable social encounters), sometimes manifested through keeping a diary, writing poetry, and other "private" pursuits.

(8) *Social extensivity.* An elementary stage of social awareness seems to be reached at about the sixth month of infancy when the baby begins to try to attract company by crying, laughing, making noises, and also in rather "offbeat" ways (e.g., by coughing or banging his head against the crib). During early childhood, his attraction to his peers seems to be related to developments taking place in his "understanding" at this time: he is interested in all types of objects and interested particularly in having some challenging and fascinating human "objects" around him. During puberty, his interest in others seems to be motivated by the same preoccupation that characterizes his interest in himself: a preoccupation with the physical. Thus, there is a tendency among younger teenagers to wear the same clothes and to imitate the hair styles and speech mannerisms of their peers; and the nicknames that they use often refer to physical characteristics (e.g., "Shorty," "Red," "Beanpole").

For the teenager to advance beyond a predominantly physical awareness of others to a more personal awareness, a certain prerequisite seems to be necessary: he must have developed a self-concept in the strict sense. It would seem impossible for an individual to have any deeper or more advanced awareness of others than he has of himself. If we are to accept the "ego," the "self," or the "mind" as in some sense distinct from the body, the distinct awareness of the selfhood of others goes hand-in-hand with a correspondingly distinct and advanced awareness of one's own self. Thus the two orientations—self-awareness and social sensitivity—are intimately connected and foster each other, though they may seem offhand to be opposing tendencies.

(9) *The "aesthetic" sense.* Are young children capable of experiencing and enjoying beauty in nature, music, art, etc., in any significant ways? Children do take evident delight, now and then, in flowers, songs, melodies, and art objects; and there are occasional child prodigies in music to make us reevaluate any prejudices we may have about the aesthetic capabilities of children per se. But for aesthetic sensitivity to

develop in the fullest sense—in most cases—it seems clear that a certain stage of maturity must be reached. Indications that this stage has been reached are to be found chiefly in the late teens, when the young man or woman becomes capable of experiencing what Freud calls "the oceanic feeling" (a sense of intimate relationship with nature and the world as a whole); begins to seek out aesthetic experiences in literature, nature, or the arts, in a spontaneous way (and not just as a school requirement); begins to develop some of the "social graces"; begins to evaluate religion positively or negatively in terms of aesthetic criteria; and becomes susceptible to "romantic love."[6]

Perhaps romantic love itself is the best and most dramatic example of the development of a mature aesthetic sense. In its personal orientation and idealism, it goes far beyond the mere physical infatuations of early adolescence. In its appreciation of fine and delicate feeling and beauty (the sort of thing that younger children will often irreverently refer to as "yucchy"), it drives home to us the lesson that, for aesthetic experience in the fullest possible sense, a certain degree of physical maturity is a prerequisite.

(10) *The ethical sense.* Freud theorized that the Super-Ego (the unconscious source of moral ideals) begins to make its appearance in early childhood, after the sometimes traumatic experiences of the "Oedipus Complex." However, without resorting to any theories of the unconscious, Freudian or otherwise, we find impressive evidence of a definite moral sense developing during the "age of obstinacy." The obstinate behavior and selective disobedience of the young child is not just a manifestation of a strong will and/or diabolical possession; it is a sign of ethical awareness. Until the child begins to evaluate and criticize the goals set down for him by his parents and society, in terms of his own rudimentary goals, he can only be a "conformist" (or "stubborn," if he simply ignores the external goals); but when he begins to weigh his subjective ideals against objective norms, he is just beginning to develop an ethical sense, which involves reflection on, and self-determination of, his own behavior.

This ethical sense often develops slowly and imperceptibly (hence the doubts of people in criminal justice about the age at which young criminals can be held to be responsible and culpable for their acts). Even in puberty, the ethical sense does not seem to be very sophisticated; young teens and preteens have a tendency to judge right and wrong in terms of a necessarily very limited range of experience and knowledge of facts, and their sense of justice (as junior-high school teachers can attest) borders on the strictly mathematical ("an eye for an eye, and a tooth for a tooth"—the "law of Talion," which became the motto of Old Testament Jews). It is only in later adolescence, when black-and-white categories begin to be tempered and countered by an awareness of and responsiveness to a diversity of persons and their idiosyncrasies, that a full and proper ethical sense is evinced. Later on, the young adult, in the spontaneity and positivity of his acceptance of personal, familial, and community responsibilities, will give concrete testimony concerning the extent and degree of the ethical sense that he has attained in adolescence.

There are other "powers" whose time of origin, in terms of normal stages of human development, are difficult to hypothesize. For example, is there a span of time during which the sense of paradox, or that of irony, ordinarily first comes to the fore? Paradox involves an ability to find deep meaning where there is apparent contradiction—something that is never possible at the level of mere "understanding." Irony seems to involve considerable insight into the vagaries and contradictory elements in human nature—something that can be acquired only by experience. Is there a normal time for the appearance of a "religious" sense? Carl Jung showed that religious consciousness can be very important for psychological development in middle age, but he did not prove that middle age is the time in life when the religious dimension of experience normally begins, and the history of mankind seems to indicate otherwise; it is the young men who "see visions," while the old men "dream dreams," the Scriptures tell us (Joel 2:28). So there are some problem areas. What we have done in this chapter is merely to call attention to the appearance of some of the better-known powers of consciousness at certain normal stages of human development.

What are the implications of the theories of the developmental psychologists for philosophical psychology? Various disputes have arisen in the history of philosophy concerning the relative priority of this or that "faculty." Some philosophers have argued, for instance, that the intellect is prior to the will; others that the will is prior to the intellect. Some have claimed that memory precedes imagination; others vice versa. Some have maintained that the understanding precedes self-consciousness; others have claimed to "deduce" understanding from ego-awareness. If we restrict ourselves to the examination of temporal succession and natural genesis (i.e., the viewpoint we have adopted in this chapter), we may conclude tentatively that there are indications that understanding precedes volition, memory precedes imagination, and self-consciousness precedes understanding.

The psychologists' observations on the development of consciousness may have some bearing on the question raised earlier concerning instinct in man. If we believe the claims of some of the developmentalists, the human being seems almost to have been programmed "by nature" to be "obstinate" at about the age of three, to be relatively serene and stable at about the age of five, to be extremely interested in his or her personality at about the age of seventeen, and to be idealistic about freedom and impatient with established ways of doing things at about the age of twenty.

If the developmentalists were unanimous in such observations, and if their studies included a wider range of cultures (especially a good sampling of non-European and "third-world" cultures), one would have to conclude that there must indeed be something "instinctive" about these developmental stages. Although there is something approaching unanimity in regard to some developmental phenomena, the representative sampling of different cultures is only just beginning. It seems likely, however, that such a sampling will show that at least some of the stages of consciousness we have discussed are conditioned not only by "nature" (natural human organic development), but also by "nurture" (social, cultural, environmental, and geographic influences).

9: What Is Maturity?

Human good [happiness] turns out to be activity of soul in accordance with virtue, and if there is more than one virtue, [it is] in accordance with the best and most complete. But we must add "in a complete life." For one swallow does not make a summer, nor does one day. . . . Yet evidently happiness needs the external goods as well. . . . For the man who is very ugly in appearance or ill-born or solitary and childless is not very likely to be happy, and perhaps a man would be still less likely if he had thoroughly bad children or friends or had lost good children or friends by death. . . . Why then should we not say that he is happy who is active in accordance with complete virtue and is sufficiently equipped with external goods, not for some chance period but throughout a complete life?—Aristotle, *Nicomachean Ethics*

If we were studying developmental stages of some plant or animal organism it would be strange indeed if we did not give some attention to the organism's ultimate stage of development, that of "maturity." Such inquiry into the mature state of the organism would seem to be not only the logical culmination of our investigation of the early and intermediate stages but might also be expected to throw some light upon the significance of these stages. If I know the natural goal for which something is headed, I will be better able to appreciate the importance of the steps it takes toward that goal, and also to judge whether this or that development is really a step in the right direction. Similarly, our investigation of the stages of human consciousness would be both incomplete and inconsequential if we did not try to determine something about the ultimate state of consciousness normally attainable in human development.

The question we are posing here is similar to a problem that Aristotle dealt with: "What constitutes human happiness?"—only we might want to substitute "fulfillment" for "happiness."[1] Aristotle's emphasis was on the peaks of happiness (he thought contemplation was the highest form of happiness and therefore that only philosophers could be truly happy); our emphasis will be more democratic. We are interested in what sorts of fulfillment the normal individual can reasonably hope for and should seek out (on the penalty, perhaps, of losing out on it altogether) in the course of his development. We are not concerned so much with personal goals (important as these are in their own right) as we are with the general thrust of consciousness and self-consciousness, as they come to maturation in human existence.

The term *maturity* is defined by different psychologists with varying emphasis on physical, emotional, sexual, mental and/or spiritual development. The kind of definition one hears will depend to a great extent on the school of thought that is behind the definition. A behaviorist may be expected to emphasize different factors than the Freudian; the Freudian will come up with a different emphasis than the Jungian, the personalist, or the existential psychiatrist.

Is it possible to by-pass these "in-house" disagreements about the relative significance of specific factors in maturity and focus simply on the problem of "mature existence" generally? Offhand, one might answer in the negative. The question seems far too broad. After all, *existence* is a term that we apply to rocks, elephants, atoms, human beings—it is apparently one of the most general concepts we have. Actually, however, we do not use the word *existence* very often in ordinary discourse, and if we confine ourselves to a few representative English expressions or colloquialisms in which reference is made directly or indirectly to human existence, we will find that the term has come to have some very specific connotations. Some examples follow:

"(S)he's barely existing." This expression normally connotes a lack of basic material necessities—food, clothing, shelter, health, or whatever is considered to be a material necessity by the speaker. It can also apply to a lack of cultural, social, intellectual, or spiritual enrichment.

"(S)he's existing in another world." During the 1960s this was expressed more colloquially as, "(S)he's out of it." In the 1970s, the expression was, "(S)he's spaced out." And more recently? Perhaps "(S)he's an air-head." However the idea is expressed, the implication is that the person spoken of exhibits a pronounced lack of adaptation to, cognizance of, or interest in his or her natural, social, political, or cultural environment. There is some sort of discordance with one's circumstances.

"So far as (s)he is concerned, I don't exist." This is a plaint sometimes heard from lovers, or those who think they are in love. The emphasis is on interpersonal recognition. If people are indifferent to me or fail to notice me,[2] I do not "exist" in their eyes. A further implication would be that if I do not exist in the eyes of others, and especially those persons whom I value highly, then for all practical purposes I do not exist at all.

"I wasn't myself," or *"that wasn't the real me."* Such statements, taken literally, are paradoxical. The speaker seems to be denying that he existed, at least at a certain time or place about which he has embarrassing memories because of his actions or reactions, which he regrets for some reason. The regret or embarrassment is caused by a disparity between his actions, etc. and his standards, ideals, or aspirations. To the extent that there is such a disparity, to the same extent the speaker considers himself to be deprived in some very real sense of "existence."

Examining these expressions, we see, negatively, that a *"lack* of existence" connotes some sort of deficiency in material accoutrements, social acceptance, cultural enrichment, etc. Putting the matter more positively, we may say that human "existence" implies a three-fold fulfillment: (1)

fulfillment from physical objects, including one's own body; (2) fulfillment from other people (or society or civilization); (3) fulfillment from oneself, and ultimately from one's "better self" or "ideal self"—the ideal ego that we project for ourself, which inwardly censures one or congratulates one for certain types of behavior. (Advocates of religious or mystical fulfillment might want to add a fourth category: fulfillment through "peak" experiences of contemplative union with God [or nature]—a union in which, they tell us, one comes to exist [lives] "really" for the first time.)

There seems to be some relationship between the first three areas of existential fulfillment and the various stages of human development. For example, the stage of infancy is primarily concerned with the acquisition of physical and biological independence—the development of the baby to the point where he (or she) can not only breathe for himself but can assimilate ordinary food, care for himself physically, and deal in a satisfactory manner with the physical objects around him. At the same time, no one expects the infant or the toddler to relate to "society" in an extensive way or to develop a notion of "personality."

The baby's relationship to the physical world might be characterized as an incessant oscillation of attraction and repulsion. He is frustrated by objects and shoves them away or throws them out of his way; but he is also fascinated by them, a fascination that he sometimes manifests by banging them, breaking them, or tearing them apart. He is upset by or dislikes certain foods, but he relishes others. And so forth. This same process of attraction and repulsion seems to carry over to other subsequent relationships that he takes on during the course of childhood, adolescence, and adulthood.[3]

As childhood progresses, personal relationships normally become wider, extending not only to mother, father, and family, but to the so-called peer group in "childhood proper" (about ages six–ten), and finally, in adolescence, to the opposite sex. In all these cases, there is normally the same sort of ambivalence or oscillation as was found in infancy, between attractive and repulsive impulses. Periods of joy with one's parents, siblings, and playmates are normally interspersed with experiences of disillusionment, jealousy, or at least misunderstanding. The adolescent "discovery" of that diametrical opposite, the other sex, is normally preceded by strange mixtures of antipathy and infatuation; and as the encounters become more sophisticated, more sophisticated versions of the same sort of ambivalence appear—to plague humanity and to inspire poets and novelists.

Such ambivalence or oscillation is also prevalent in one's relationship to oneself. The advances in self-knowledge that characterize adolescence are ordinarily preceded by the so-called "negative stage," a stage of depression, inability to "find" oneself, sometimes even (in extreme cases) thoughts of suicide. And subsequent attempts, in late adolescence and adulthood, to attain some sort of congruity or equipoise between one's ideals and one's practical behavior may aptly be compared with the caterpillar's apparently never-ending efforts to make his tail catch up with his head.

In young adulthood, one begins to bring the *form* of all these various ambivalent relationships—to the physical world, society, and oneself—under one's own control, as much as possible—like an acrobat who is about to do a tumbling act but for now is just setting himself up in a strategic position for the performance to follow.

In adulthood and middle age, there are considerable changes in some aspects of all these relationships. Having children of one's own brings about a different kind of social relationship, in which one finds oneself not only encountering others but also, in a sense, creating the others. Gradually coming to own a considerable amount of one's own property is bound to cause some changes, subtle or not so subtle, in one's attitude toward, and relationship to, one's physical environment.

In late middle age and old age, the control that one began to gain over one's life as a young adult must often be relaxed in the face of changing states in general fitness or health, retirement customs, and the extension or alteration of familial relationships. At least in our cultural milieu, that of the West, older people often do not have the opportunity to control the form of their various relationships to the extent that younger people have. Perhaps there is a certain universality about the words of the author of the Gospel of St. John: "Simon, Simon, when you were young, you prepared yourself and proceeded to do whatever you wished; but when you are old, others will take you by the hand and lead you where you had not intended to go." The adaptation of the older person to the new exigencies he faces will no doubt depend on the character of his own self-concept. If he has set up and pursued a type of personal ideal that was not attainable, or if he has failed to develop any positive and viable self-concept, the sudden crisis of identity brought on by difficult external exigencies can be particularly traumatic for the individual who does not have time on his or her side.[4]

We spoke earlier of the admixture of attraction and repulsion in existential relationships. The "and" is important here. One can conjecture situations in which either the attraction or the repulsion becomes overly dominant. If it is the attraction, the result may be a lethargic conformism, a "drifting along" unquestioningly with convention and the tides of the time; mindless abandonment to creature comforts; or perhaps smugness, an acceptance of, and confidence in, oneself, that is completely uncritical. If the repulsion becomes one-sided the result may be neurotic, misanthropic opposition to society; or overriding ambition that makes one incapable of enjoying the simple pleasures of life; or perhaps a chronic and morbid sense of guilt, the inability to accept oneself or to enjoy being alone with oneself. Obviously, a "mature" existence lies somewhere between such polar extremes.[5]

Is it possible for every person to become "existentially" mature? Insofar as there are "objective" criteria for maturity, it may not be possible for everyone to measure up to them. We have such objective criteria for physical maturity in the sense that certain anatomical and physiological limits are roughly attainable by all normal adults over a certain period of time. We define a dwarf as one who does not reach "normal" musculo-skeletal limits of maturity (although we may still speak about the "relative" physical maturity or immaturity of dwarfs). There is also a rare and incurable disease (Cockayne's syndrome) that accelerates metabolic development and causes old age and death at about the age of fifteen—a life situation that clearly falls outside the normal limits.

We also seem to have some fairly objective criteria for psychological and psychosocial maturity. Psychological maturity is sometimes defined as the ability to deal with one's problems, pursue meaningful goals, and adapt to realistic demands in one's environment. Psychosocial maturity is almost always defined in connection with the ability to enter into "normal" love relationships. These norms seem to be valid, but they may be absolutely unattainable by certain individuals, e.g., a person who, having been constantly abused by his parents and subjected to insuperable frustrations in his environment, moves from hopelessly psychotic behavior to complete insanity. Given the very limited capabilities of psychiatrists at present, it would be almost a miracle if such a person ever achieved complete psychological normality—although psychiatric treatment (psychotherapy, psychoactive drugs, etc.) might afford the individual a goodly measure of relief from symptoms.

Granted that we *do* set up "objective" norms for maturity, granted that perhaps we have to set up such norms (at least as standards to be challenged or revised), the fact is that not everyone will be able to measure up to them. Some people seem to bypass or flout those criteria altogether, as, for example, the so-called "invulnerable" children—children raised with extraordinary environmental (and sometimes also hereditary) handicaps who nevertheless end up as models of normality.[6] And we must also take into account, as Hegel indicates in the epigraph to Chapter 8 of this book, the occasional phenomenon of genius—the Aristotles, the Mozarts, the Einsteins, in whom intellect and "spirit" seem to burst through the normal bounds of corporeal existence even from an early age and produce individuals who seem to stand above all our categories of normality and even seem to suggest criteria or "test cases" that should be used in evaluating such categories.

Coming back to what we have called "existential" maturity, it is important to realize that this notion is simply a synthesis of the various ideas we may have of specific types of maturity. Existential maturity includes (a) physical maturity, insofar as a certain physical development and well-being is presupposed before one can engage in higher human functions and make optimal use of one's physical environment. It includes (b) psychosocial maturity, insofar as it involves deference to others and cooperation and constructive association with others. Because of the importance of awareness of and maximum development of one's emotional and intellectual potential, it also includes (c) psychological maturity. Some would want to add that the concept of existential maturity includes religious and/or mystical fulfillment insofar as the development of self-consciousness, self-appreciation, and self-criticism is furthered by religious and mystical experiences (they might want to designate this latter kind of fulfillment as (d) "spiritual maturity"). If one *means* (a), (b), (c), and possibly (d) when one speaks of existential maturity, and if one possesses certain objective criteria for judging the extent of (a), (b), (c), and (d), then, and to the same degree, one seems to possess objective norms for existential maturity.

There is, however, just one important "catch." Existential maturity does not mean having 25 percent of (a), 25 percent of (b), and so forth. It involves proportioning and synthesizing (a), (b), (c), and (d) among themselves. For example, an individual's psychological maturity has to be judged according to whether or not he suffers physical handicaps; psychosocial maturity is obviously dependent on psychological maturity; and the various forms of "spiritual" maturity may be practically unattainable by one who is psychologically unbalanced. Insofar as existential maturity normally involves this interrelationship of (a), (b), (c), and (d), are there any widespread, publicly accepted objective criteria governing the proper *interrelationship* of (a), (b), (c), and (d)?

The closest we have come to such a consensus is in the oft-cited stipulation of psychologists, psychiatrists, and others that the ability to transcend narcissism, sadism, masochism, etc., and enter into one-to-one love relationships that involve a considerable amount of self-giving is an indispensable condition for true maturity. Perhaps we should follow them and say that the ability to love is a key element in maturity, a kind of pivot around which the constellation of other elements has to be organized in varying fashions. If, on the other hand, we were to conclude that the ability to love is at most just one element among others equally important, then we would also have to conclude that judgments about existential maturity are, at least at present, extremely subjective (or "relative"), in spite of the fact that objective norms are indeed available and recognized for the specific components of such maturity.

10: What Is Love?

The theory of Empedocles [Greek philosopher, 490–430 B.C.] which especially deserves our interest is one which approximates so closely to [our] psychoanalytic theory of the instincts that we should be tempted to maintain that the two are identical. . . . The philosopher taught that two principles governed events in the life of the universe and the life of the mind, that those principles were everlastingly at war with each other. He called them *"philia"* and *"neikos"* (love and strife). . . . The two fundamental principles . . . are, both in name and in function, the same as our two primal instincts, Eros and destructiveness [Thanatos] . . . [Eros] endeavors to combine what exists into even greater unities.—Freud, *Analysis Terminable and Interminable*

Universal benevolence toward all men we may compare to that principle of gravitation which perhaps extends to all bodies in the universe. But, like the love of benevolence, [gravitation] increases as the distance is diminished; and is strongest when bodies come to touch each other.—Francis Hutcheson, *An Inquiry into the Original of our Ideas of Beauty and Virtue*

Civilization is a process in the service of Eros [the Life Instinct, cosmic Love], whose purpose is to combine single human individuals, and after that families, then races, peoples and nations, into one great unity, the unity of mankind. Why this has to happen, we do not know; the work of Eros is precisely this. These collections of men are to be libidinally bound to one another.—Freud, *Civilization and its Discontents*

True love is an emotion which discharges itself in an activity that overcomes self-centredness by expending the self on people and on purposes beyond the self. It is an outward-going spiritual movement from the self towards the universe and towards the ultimate spiritual reality behind the universe.—Arnold Toynbee, *Surviving the Future*

As we have seen, the ability to "love" is considered by a great many psychologists, psychiatrists, and others to be an important aspect of human maturity, and perhaps the single most important aspect. There are many disagreements, however, among the same authorities about what love is or should be. For some psychiatrists love is always related to sexuality in some way; for others it can be and often is a purely altruistic orientation wholly independent of sexuality. Obviously, the "agreement" of two authorities (or two hundred) on the importance of love may be superficial, deceptive, and meaningless if the authorities are in total disagreement about what love is. This fact, coupled with (and perhaps attributable to) a certain perennial ambiguity and confusion when it comes to talking about love, gives us a good excuse to turn our attention to what has been called, with only slight exaggeration, "everybody's favorite subject." We do so gladly, undaunted by the fact that our philosophical attempt to clarify the meaning of love, to define the "indefinable," is doomed to failure. But this is just as well; if our effort were to succeed, we would run the risk of dampening the spirits and incurring the eternal enmity of lovers everywhere!

As almost everyone knows, the topic of love comes up frequently in the works of poets, playwrights, songwriters, and novelists. It is less well known that the subject has been neglected by most philosophers down through the centuries. This neglect becomes particularly noticeable if we compare the voluminousness and seriousness of philosophical writings concerning knowledge, or the theory of knowledge, with those concerning love. The attention devoted to the topic of knowledge has been generous and distributed fairly evenly throughout the history of Western philosophy (i.e., from about the sixth century B.C. on), while the attention given to the topic of love has been sparse and spasmodic.

Perhaps the foremost classical treament of love is to be found in Plato's *Symposium,* a dialogue narrating the proceedings at a banquet at which Socrates and other Greek thinkers expound their views on love. Since the time of Plato, one can find discussions of the subject in Aristotle, Augustine, Thomas Aquinas, Benedict Spinoza, G. W. F. Hegel, Arthur Schopenhauer, Jean-Paul Sartre, Miguel de Unamuno, and others. More extensive, but extremely disparate and far from definitive, treatments of love are found in the writings of the contemporary philosophers V. S. Solovyev, Max Scheler, and José Ortega y Gasset. During the last century, more attention has been given to the subject by psychologists than by professional philosophers. Psychologists such as Sigmund Freud, Erich Fromm, Ignace Lepp, and Oswald Schwartz have written at length on love, almost as if to make up for the long neglect by Western philosophers.

Actually, when one comes right down to it, the widespread diffidence of philosophers on this subject is quite understandable. If it is difficult to "know" and to write about knowledge (and it is),[1] it is just as difficult, and probably more so, to "know" and to write about love. That is, love, with its aura of surprise and mystery, seems even more difficult than knowledge to "pin down" or "objectify."

As if that were not enough, there are probably some other reasons for the comparative neglect of the philosophy of love. One of the chief Renaissance insights evolving out of Western culture has been the realization that "knowledge is power." One who takes this insight seriously will perhaps be wary of devoting too much time and energy to researching a topic that is more associated in our mind with weakness than with power, a topic that may (if one is also a little superstitious) seem to threaten an actual loss of power. (Can you be really sure of keeping your theories completely independent from your practice—even your theory of love?) There may also be just a hint of male chauvinism in the deemphasis of love by philosophers. The male, for historical, environmental, and/or other reasons, has typically considered knowledge to be a male preroga-tive and love to be an (inferior) female characteristic. Since most philosophers have been male, and since a true professional must of course strive to maintain the proper professional perspective on values—need one say more?

Granted that *we* are willing and able to put aside our chauvinism, our drive for power, etc., in tracking down elusive Eros, where should we begin to look for an understanding of love? Perhaps we may appropri-ately begin by looking at what love is *not*, i.e., at that from which love is differentiated, and with which it can be contrasted. Various contrasts have been suggested by philosophers and psychologists.

Thomas Aquinas made an interesting comparison/contrast of love with, of all things, knowledge. When we know something, said Aquinas, we assimilate it to ourselves and change it into our own nature; but when we love something, *we are changed into it.*[2] Thus he concluded that it is better to love God than to know God, but (in line with the same principle) better to know sensuous things (food, fleshly comforts, etc.) than to love them.[3] Some writers have expressed much the same idea by metaphorically describing knowledge as "centripetal" (transferring everything into the ego) and love as "centrifugal" (ecstatic, essentially outgoing, and essentially "expansive").

Most contemporary psychologists approach the matter differently. Erich Fromm, in *The Art of Loving*,[4] sees love as both the opposite of and a remedy for human isolation. While human beings can overcome their sense of isolation to a certain extent through drugs, sexual abandon, group conformity, and various types of aesthetic creativity, the only full solution is to be found in love, which brings about the true interpersonal union with others that is *the* fundamental desire of those who suffer from loneliness and isolation.

Oswald Schwartz, in *The Psychology of Sex*,[5] on the other hand, describes love as the exact opposite of anguish, which is defined as an augmentation of fear to such a high level that it seems to annihilate one's very existence. This extreme state of fear can, according to Schwartz, be extinguished only by love, which enables us to forget about and renounce our own nothingness and open ourselves to the fullness of existence in the world through the perception of, and devotion to, the inner uniqueness of others.

Ignace Lepp, in *The Psychology of Loving*,[6] prefers to contrast love with indifference, which, he observes, is the one feeling-state completely in-compatible with love. I can feel resentment or hostility or even hate toward a person and still love him or her, consciously or unconsciously. But it is humanly impossible for me to feel absolutely indifferent and unconcerned about a person and still love him or her in any real way.

Lepp's remarks notwithstanding, there is no doubt that the opposition between love and hate is the best-known contrast made by the public at large down through the centuries, as well as by philosophers and psychologists. Among the philosophers, Empedocles stands out as one who attached the highest importance to the antithetical relationship between love and hate. For Empedocles, love and "strife" were not just personal, human emotions but cosmic realities that governed the affairs of the universe in eternally oscillating cycles. Love was the principle of unification, strife the principle of division and isolation. At one time the former would prevail, at another the latter; and in the interim the world as a whole (as well as the people in it) would be caught up in an intermediary state of equilibrium and tension between the two cosmic forces.

In modern psychology, a surprisingly similar cosmic view of the antithesis between love and its opposite is presented in the later writings of Sigmund Freud. Freud draws the general outline of the antithesis between love and its opposite in *The Ego and the Id,* where he says:

> I have lately developed a view of the instincts which I shall here hold to and take as the basis of my further discussions. According to this view we have to distinguish two classes of instincts, one of which, the sexual instincts or Eros, is by far the more conspicuous and accessible to study. . . . The second class of instincts was not so easy to point to. . . . On the basis of theoretical considerations, supported by biology, we put forward the hypothesis of a death instinct. . . . Life itself would be a conflict and compromise between these two trends. . . . For the opposition between the two classes of instinct in human beings we may put the polarity of love and hate.[7]

Freud's theory is "cosmic" (or, as Freud put it, "cosmological")[8] because it is concerned with a dualism or polarity that is manifest everywhere—in inanimate elements, material particles, and the cells of living substances. As it applies to human relationships, it very often takes the form of the love-hate polarity. In practice, however, it is very difficult for anyone—except, presumably, a trained psychoanalyst—to distinguish manifestations of love from manifestations of hate, since they tend to fuse with each other. For example, love is very often tinged with varying degrees of sadism or masochism, both of which are, for the psychoanalyst, species of hate. Freud also hypothesized various "transformations" that tend to make the identification of human emotional orientations rather complicated; e.g., in homosexuality, the frustrated little boy with a strong female-hormonal endowment, who is instinctively too weak to compete with his father for the affections of his mother, is forced gradually into the only practical channel for his affections—a love for persons of the same sex.

We have concentrated so far on a series of contrasts of love with things opposite to it, i.e., with things that love is *not*. We have also been indicating, by implication, something of what love is. It is time to explicate further some of the latent positive meanings of love emerging from these contrasts.

For Thomas Aquinas, love is an extension or amplification of our existence in one way or another. For Fromm, love is more precisely an "interpersonal" amplification of existence. Schwartz goes on to emphasize that this amplification is added to our own radical "nothingness." Lepp makes the point that the amplification begins to take place through our attitudes of care, concern, and interest in others. Freud—and Empedocles, too—going beyond the mere psychological view of love, characterizes love as the basic unifying force in the world, the process of attraction that is always either at odds with, or intermingled with, the countless forces of repulsion.

Taking our cue from and summarizing these positive observations, we might tentatively define love as any unifying, attractive force that tends to bring about an amplification of existence. If we may be permitted (at least by poetic-philosophic license) to apply this definition to the subhuman sphere, the definition would conceivably apply to such diverse attractive forces as: gravity; the attraction of the planets for the sun; the tendency of hydrogen atoms to unite, e.g., with oxygen or carbon atoms; more complex processes of unification taking place among cells; and the herd instinct and the mating instincts of animals. In man, perhaps our best example and most appropriate application is "romantic love"—not because it is necessarily the highest manifestation of interpersonal human love, but because it alone seems to synthesize and combine in a unique way all of the main attractive forces prevalent in man—the sensual, the personal, and the intellectual or spiritual.[9] Thus romantic love would not be described as just a unifying force but as a higher-level "unification" of several unifying forces.

Some philosophers, however, would not let us get away too easily with describing love as a unifying force. What are some of their main objections?

OBJECTION A: How can you describe love so glibly as a unity? You contrast love with knowledge, and yet knowledge is also a unifying activity. In knowing an object, I am in some way coming into unity with that object. "Unity" seems to be characteristic of both knowledge and love; therefore you shouldn't point to unity as a differentiating characteristic germane to love alone.

RESPONSE TO A: As Fromm emphasizes,[10] the higher states of love are not unities pure and simple, or "symbiotic unions." Truly human love is a "unity-in-distinction", i.e., a species of unity that is not only compatible with whatever fundamental distinctions still remain but even enhances and fosters them. The same observation might be made about the higher states of knowledge, e.g., scientific knowledge of the world. These states are unities-in-distinction insofar as the knowers remain apart from their cognitive objects but are still united with them in some way. However, there is in love a relative emphasis on unity: Love is a *unity*-in-distinction. The main thing about it is the lover's strange sense of being drawn to the "other," i.e., the object of his love, not the sense of still remaining distinct from the other. Knowledge, on the other hand, is a unity-in-*distinction*, insofar as the essential thing about "objective" knowledge is our conviction that the object is independent from us and not just a figment of our mind, even though we are also conscious of being "drawn to" and intellectually united with our object.[11]

OBJECTION B: I'm not completely satisfied with this answer. One sometimes has the experience of being "lost in thought," to the extent of forgetting about one's personal identity. For some individuals, this is a common occurrence. At least in such cases, the sense of unity exceeds and overshadows the sense of distinctness.

RESPONSE TO B: This seems to be a "limiting case," i.e., a case where the two orientations, knowledge and love, converge. It can happen that an individual at a particular moment is "swept away" by the love for knowledge, in which case his love and his knowledge become for the moment indistinguishable. Or, if in a certain individual the love for knowledge predominated over all other loves, we might say that for that particular individual his knowledge and his love are generally or chronically indistinguishable.

OBJECTION C: I'm still not sure that the facts are as you state them. For one thing, it is well-known to wise and ordinary people alike that "opposites attract." In the inanimate world, two particles that both have a positive electrical charge will repel one another, but if one particle has a negative charge the two will be attracted. Human affairs seem to follow a similar pattern; it is the oppositeness, what you call the "distinctness," that is primary in accounting for the experience of love.

RESPONSE TO C: I do not disagree with this account of love, nor with all the sages who have proposed it, although I would point out the obvious fact that interpersonal attractions and repulsions are much more complex than those obtaining among mere physical particles. However, the main thing that should be emphasized here is that you are speaking in terms of the causation or etiology of love; I am interested in an analysis of the experience of love. You may be quite right—I think you are—that the main cause of love is some distinctness or oppositeness or, to use the electricity metaphor, some "difference in potential"; but even if this is what causes the attraction, the attractive process, which is our concern here, is one definitely characterized by an emphasis on unity or unification.

OBJECTION D: You do not seem to be taking into account some simple and quite common facts about love. When we love something, the desire for that thing causes a sense of longing, pain, and/or isolation that continues until we attain the thing we love. Thus the sense of distinctness (not unity) is accentuated, if anything, by the experience of love.

RESPONSE TO D: Here we come to a certain equivocation in the use of the term *love*. Sometimes the term means the actual fruition of the loved object; sometimes it means a state of desire that has not yet attained its object. In our definition, *love* refers to the total process of desire leading to fruition. If one considers this process as a whole, then it becomes obvious that the initial state of the process, i.e., the state of desire, causes an accentuation of the sense of distinctness, just as you indicate; but the latter stages tend to change this experience into just the opposite, the sense of unity.

OBJECTION E: But it is obvious that not every stage of desire results in "fruition." In fact, it is probable that most cases do not have this result. Thus it becomes unrealistic to consider love as a "total process."

RESPONSE TO E: I don't see any problem here. Just as there are preliminary stages of knowledge that never quite reach their goal, there are also incomplete or preliminary stages of love. And when love is incomplete and unfulfilled, then—as you maintain—an accentuation of the sense of distinctness and isolation may result, rather than the opposite.

OBJECTION F: I will agree that love must be viewed as a process emerging from the state of desire that precedes it. But you seem to be lumping all states of desire together in one category. Obviously, there is a big difference between the desire to acquire or receive, and the desire to give. You should at least distinguish two species of desire, and hence of love, on this basis.

RESPONSE TO F: I would agree with this, but I would prefer to make the distinction in terms of needs rather than desires. Our desires manifest two different kinds of needs, passive and active. Some needs are predominantly passive, i.e., receptive; for example, the need for food, for warmth. Some needs are relatively active, i.e., oriented toward giving rather than receiving; for example, the need of a mother to nurse and care for her child, the need of a man to express his thoughts verbally or nonverbally, or the "need" of God (as the deity is anthropomorphically visualized) to create and give without taking anything in return. Obviously, sometimes one of these needs will conflict with others, in a single individual, as well as among various persons. In such cases of conflict, one's own relative emphasis on this need or that determines the hierarchy of one's "love."

OBJECTION G: I will accept your designation in terms of needs rather than desires. But I cannot accept the rather easygoing way in which you tolerate the relativity of needs and of "loves," as if it made no difference which kind of love were foremost. Surely you must admit that certain loves are more important than others. For example, spiritual and intellectual love should take precedence over material or sensuous love.

RESPONSE TO G: It seems impossible to answer a question like this in an objective way; because if one says, "X should take precedence over all other loves," all he really means is, "I have the greatest need for, and love for, X." There is no way he could prove that others should also feel similarly about X and place the love for X at the top of their hierarchies. Sometimes it happens, however, that because of some need that temporarily outweighs all others (e.g., the need for food during a widespread famine), a temporary "objective" consensus concerning the "highest" love will probably come about. Of course, people caught in a famine would probably not say explicitly, "we love food more than anything else"; they would probably put it more euphemistically, e.g., "man's primary need and his most natural love is for self-preservation."

OBJECTION H: Aren't you disturbed by the possibility that a lower love could come into conflict with a higher love—and that it might win out? Aren't you willing to concede at least that the higher love should win out?

RESPONSE TO H: As I have just shown, your use of the terms *higher* and *lower* seems to be very arbitrary, very subjective. However, I think we can both agree that an absence of conflict among legitimate and natural loves would be a desirable thing. If a conflict between various loves does arise in an individual, we could say that that individual then has a need for Love$_2$, i.e., a second-order unification of each tendency-toward-unity (each Love$_1$) that happens to be in conflict with other tendencies-toward-unity.[12] (Earlier we indicated that "romantic love" was an example of such a second-level unification.)

FINAL OBJECTION: This conversation is getting too cerebral for me. I suppose if I brought up the objection that many individuals, after making second-order syntheses of their own intrapsychic desires or needs, might still come into conflict with one another you would no doubt come readily equipped with a (communal) third-order synthesis to patch up the interindividual squabbles resulting from the different individual syntheses they have made.[13] And then—dare I say it?—one can conceive of fourth- and fifth-order syntheses, final attempts to integrate various communal third-order syntheses among themselves, and then fifthly integrate that fourth worldwide synthesis into the cosmic cycles of love and strife in the universe as a whole—and we are back at the point that Anaxagoras began from.

FINAL RESPONSE: Yes, except that if Anaxagoras were using our terminology, he would prefer to take cosmic love as a "first-order" love, and to proceed from there to cycles of worldwide harmony as a second-order love, and so forth. He might end up with what *we* have called "first-order" love as a fifth-order love. But this is understandable, because we are speaking from the point of view of an individual consciousness of freedom, that we, unlike him, explicitly consider to be the paramount value.

The ancients used to say that Eros (Cupid) was the trickiest and most elusive of the Graeco-Roman gods.[14] In our attempt to define love we have experienced the meaning behind this myth! Even so, I think the efforts we have made have at least increased our respect for "golden-winged" Eros.

11: Paranormal Phenomena: Do They Exist, and If So, What Are Their Philosophical Implications?

Why do so few "scientists" even look at the evidence for telepathy [a form of ESP]? . . . Because they think . . . that even if such a thing were true, scientists ought to band together to keep it suppressed and concealed. It would undo the uniformity of Nature and all sorts of other things without which the scientists cannot carry on their pursuits. . . .

The modern mechanico-physical philosophy [positivism] of which we are all so proud, because it includes the nebular cosmology, the conservation of energy, the kinetic theory of heats and gases, etc., etc., begins by saying that the *only* facts are collocations and motions of primordial solids, and the only laws the changes of motion which changes in collocations bring. . . .

But the positivists . . . are deluded. They have simply chosen from among the entire set of propensities at their command those that were certain to construct, out of the materials given, the leanest, lowest, aridest result—namely the bare molecular world—and they have sacrificed all the best. . . .

Our whole physical life may lie soaking in a spiritual atmosphere. . . . We need only suppose the continuity of our consciousness with a mother sea, to allow for exceptional waves occasionally pouring over the dam [as in ESP] . . .—William James, *Essays on Faith and Morals, Principles of Psychology,* and *Human Immortality*

I am not one of those who, from the outset, disapprove of the study of so-called occult psychological phenomena as unscientific, . . . unworthy, or even dangerous. If I were at the beginning of a scientific career, instead of, as now, at its end I would perhaps choose no other field of work, in spite of all difficulties.—Sigmund Freud, letter to Hereward Carrington (Summer 1921)

In the last chapter we considered the faculty or power of loving, a power that carries with it, in the estimation of poets and mystics, "a touch of the divine," and yet one that is generally considered, rightly or wrongly, to be within the grasp of the ordinary normal human being. In this chapter we consider powers that are generally considered, rightly or wrongly, to be beyond the grasp of most mortals—if, indeed, they are within the grasp of any human beings at all. Assuming that these powers do exist, they seem to appear frequently and dependably only in a select few, and only very infrequently and unpredictably, if at all, in the rest of us. Clearly these powers, if they exist, do so on or near the present "outer limits" of consciousness, whose more "normal" manifestations we began studying in Chapter 8.

The scientific study of so-called extrasensory perception (ESP) and related phenomena has been advanced considerably during the past century. A landmark in this progress was the establishment in London, in 1882, of the Society for Psychical Research (SPR), under the presidency of Henry Sidgwick. An American branch was founded a few years later by the philosopher William James, who became its president in 1894. Other distinguished philosophers who have served in leadership capacities in the SPR, which is still flourishing, include Henri Bergson, F.C.S. Schiller, William McDougall, and C.D. Broad. Sigmund Freud was also a member. During our own century, parapsychology, the scientific study of purported psychic phenomena, has been carried out at several American universities, including the universities of Colorado and Virginia, Harvard University, and especially Duke University, and at many institutions in other countries, including the Soviet Union. The "guiding light" at Duke, and the leading American pathfinder in parapsychological research, was J.B. Rhine, who claimed to have devised a number of scientifically valid and statistically acceptable parapsychological experiments, and who published many of the results of his research in numerous books and articles. Rhine developed, among other instruments, a special deck of twenty-five cards, containing five each of five different symbols ("Zener" symbols),[1] for use in experiments in clairvoyance. Some of his subjects showed a remarkable ability to identify these symbols without seeing them in the "normal" way. In 1937 the American Institute of Mathematics officially confirmed the mathematical reliability of the methods used by Rhine and attested that his statistical measurements and calculations of probability were mathematically sound. (This did not mean, of course, that the institute endorsed Rhine's ideas about ESP.)

An associate of Professor Rhine's, J. Gaither Pratt, obtained particularly unusual results working with a "gifted" subject named "Pearce." In tests of clairvoyance, using the Zener cards, Pearce obtained an average of 7.5 hits (successful guesses) per run throughout a series of 1,825 consecutive trials. Because of the large number of trials, the statistical probability that such results would be obtained by chance was less than one-quintillionth.[2] A British researcher, S.G. Soal, impressed by Rhine's results, carried out some of his own variations on these experiments; and with one subject in particular, Mrs. Gloria Stewart, obtained astronomically high scores (a probability of 10^{-70})[3] over a period of four years.

Research with telepathy has also netted statistically significant results in the United States, England, and the Netherlands. As such evidence began to mount and was double-checked by competent scientists, it seemed even the most skeptical scholars could no longer deny that such effects could no longer be explained by chance. Thus, at least in regard to certain types of "Psi,"[4] we seemed to have reached the terminal point alluded to by Sidgwick who, in his presidential address (1882) to the SPR, claimed that the investigations of a psychical phenomenon would be complete when the statistical results were so overwhelming that "the critic [would have] nothing left to allege except that the investigator [was] 'in the trick' [i.e., guilty of fraud]." At the present time, the most knowledgeable critics of parapsychology do not try to show that the methods used in the investigation of Psi are unreliable, or that the results are not statistically significant; they allege fraud. Professor C.E.M. Hansel, for example, in his book, *ESP: A Scientific Evaluation* (1966), concludes with the rather extraordinary hypothesis that, since successful ESP experiments are impossible to explain statistically, some sort of trickery on the part of subjects and/or researchers must be responsible for the scores obtained by "gifted" subjects. However, the results of many experiments have been checked and corroborated by sometimes skeptical investigators; and in lieu of evidence of collusion or fraud, Hansel's allegations must be adjudged to be unproven.

Before examining some of the philosophical implications of Psi, we will describe and try to differentiate some of the more common paranormal phenomena.[5]

Precognition is said to be the reception by means of ESP of information about future events. The information in question seems to originate *from* these future events; that is, the seer seems to be witnessing these future events in much the same way as he witnesses actual present events. Probably the best-known examples of purported precognition are the "prophecies" of the Bible, e.g., the numerous predictions of a savior or "messiah" in the Old Testament.[6] In the Middle Ages, a monk named Malachy predicted, with sometimes unusual acuity, the popes of the Roman Church who would reign until the end of the world. (There are only two left to go!) In the "secular" sphere, the most famous seer in the Western world is the Jewish physician-astrologer Nostradamus (1503–1566) who, according to some interpreters, predicted the American Revolution,[7] World War II,[8] air travel,[9] and the invention of the aerial bomb.[10] In contemporary America, much attention is given to certain highly publicized self-styled "psychics" (Edgar Cayce, Jeanne Dixon, etc.) who specialize in foretelling events of national or international significance (unfortunately, with an admixture of much error). On a more prosaic level, perhaps the most frequent examples of precognition are premonitions (experienced while awake or through dreams) of the imminent (i.e., within a period of twelve hours) deaths of persons. The investigation of this phenomenon was one of the first tasks undertaken by the SPR, which focused only on precognition in the *waking* state, and concluded with statistics showing that the incidence of such cases was much larger than could be expected by chance.

Precognition of death or other events is a rather rare event in the lives of most people. However, there are certain individuals who seem to have precognitive abilities that are fairly stable and dependable. Such individuals have been sought out by psychic researchers experimenting with precognition, and a few gifted subjects seem to have given definite evidence of paranormal powers in this area. A typical laboratory test for precognition involves guessing the future order of the cards in a deck that is just about to be shuffled and rearranged. In another test, the cards from a deck are taken out one by one, and the subject's task is to guess, not the card that is removed, but the card immediately following, or the one after that.

(One parenthetical remark before proceeding to a consideration of other kinds of Psi: It seems unfortunate that almost all scientific experiments with precognition have utilized humdrum items like cards, dice, number series, etc. It is understandable that researchers should try as much as possible to focus on manifestations of precognition that are statistically measurable. But most examples of supposed precognition in real life seem to be concerned with significant events affecting real people. Without sacrificing too much in the way of accuracy, it would seem possible to do statistical analyses of the sorts of real-life predictions that are usually made; e.g., checking ten personal predictions selected each year by noted psychics over a period of years and comparing the accuracy of these predictions with ten similarly selected predictions made by "control" subjects, i.e., a separate group of persons without any known psychic powers.)[11]

Clairvoyance is defined as the ability to identify objects that cannot be perceived directly by any of the five senses. It presupposes a special faculty for receiving impressions from external objects in paranormal ways. In practice, it is very difficult to differentiate clairvoyance from telepathy, or "mind-reading." For example, an incident reported in the Acts of the Apostles, in which Peter condemns Ananias and Saphira for concealing money from the Apostolic community, would seem to be a case of clairvoyance, since the information about the hidden money was not received through any of the normal sense channels. However, it might also be an instance of telepathy, if Peter had obtained such information by "reading the thoughts" of Ananias and Saphira. In our day, the best-known examples of apparent clairvoyance are to be found among stage performers, most of whom no doubt employ trickery, but a few of whom might be genuine clairvoyants. It should be noted that clairvoyance applies not only to inanimate objects, but to human bodies, whether living or dead. Thus some of the more remarkable cases of clairvoyance involve cooperation of a psychic with police or detectives who are searching for a missing person or for a dead body. In the laboratory, one of the commonest ways of testing clairvoyance is to ask a psychic to name the cards in a deck,[12] after which the cards are inspected and his accuracy is evaluated. Statistically significant results were obtained in using these tests with various subjects, by Rhine at Duke University, and by D.R. Martin and F.P. Stribic at the University of Colorado. Pratt's experiment with the subject Pearce (referred to above) is one of the longest high-scoring series of runs reported.

Telepathy is said to be the paranormal ability to receive information directly from the mind of another.[13] There are several "prophecy stories" recorded in the Gospels in which Jesus displays apparently telepathic powers—e.g., the confrontation with the Pharisees, in which he begins to write their secret sins upon the sand; or the meeting with the Samaritan woman, in which he surprises the woman by telling her he knows that she has had seven husbands. (Actually, as in most such cases, it is hard to tell whether it was telepathy or clairvoyance that occurred, assuming it was one or the other; e.g., Jesus' knowledge of the seven husbands might have had its source in clairvoyant knowledge of the seven husbands' existence, or it may have been that physical objects offered clues to the previous marriages.) Saints and mystics of all religions and in all ages have been reputed to have telepathic powers.

On a more secular plane, "psychics" and fortune-tellers often refer to data that are apparently telepathic in origin. Among "ordinary" people, there are occasional claims of their having received messages in dreams or while awake from people (usually loved ones) involved in some crisis or danger. In the laboratory, a researcher will test for telepathy by asking his subject to guess which Zener symbol he is thinking about (no cards are used, of course, since this might cause clairvoyant knowledge to interfere with telepathic knowledge). One of Soal's subjects, Mrs. Stewart, averaged 7.3 hits per run in a series of 40 runs,[14] in an experiment of this sort, in which an elaborate code system was devised to guarantee that the subject would not be able to derive any (clairvoyant or precognitive) knowledge from the notes made by Soal when keeping a record of his thought transmissions.

Psychokinesis (PK) is defined as the exertion of direct influence by the human will on physical objects or processes, without any intermediary physical instruments, adjuncts, catalysts, etc. "Miracles" in religious literature—e.g., Moses causing the sea to part on his command, or Jesus' changing of water into wine—might be interpreted as outstanding psychokinetic phenomena. In India, down through the centuries, masters of Yoga have claimed to have psychokinetic abilities, as well as ESP. In our day a few reputed "psychics" specialize in psychokinetic performances.[15]

In the parapsychological laboratory, one of the most frequent tests for psychokinesis involves the supposed ability to exercise mental control over dice-throwing.

One wonders, at this point, why some subjects with powers of psychokinesis, clairvoyance, and telepathy are not channeled into successful careers in gambling or the stock market—if their Psi is as dependable as it seems to be. Some psychics claim that their power is a "gift of God" that enables them to help others, and that if they tried to profit monetarily from this gift they would lose it. Whatever one may think of this explanation, one may surmise that if a belief like this were widespread among psychics, the *belief* might prevent them from becoming gamblers and speculators. One may well wonder, however, about the statistical probability of such a belief being held by 100 percent of those who have the abilities in question. On the other hand, there is the possibility that some high-Psi persons have engaged (and are engaged) in gambling, stock-market speculation, etc.—without bothering to tell parapsychologists about it. If the phenomena investigated by Rhine et al. exist, is it reasonable to suppose that only persons studied by parapsychologists are involved? Would not most such persons go about their business normally, using their special powers normally (for them), knowingly or unknowingly?

Mediumship purportedly involves the transmission of messages or information supposedly from deceased persons, in a "sitting" or "séance" conducted by a psychic, or "medium." There are various kinds of mediums: (a) *physical mediums,* who produce "materialized" spirits and other physical phenomena such as tapping noises;[16] (b) *trance mediums,* who are supposedly possessed by a "control" [17] from the spirit world, who puts the medium in contact with dead relatives, acquaintances, etc., with whom the "sitter" wishes to communicate; (c) *"direct-voice" mediums,* who seem to be taken over by a spirit and speak with a voice and inflection often quite similar to the voice that the deceased person had; and (d) *"automatic-writing" mediums,* who are supposedly taken over by the spirit of a deceased person who writes out messages in which there is often an amazing similarity to the handwriting, vocabulary, and expressions used by that person when alive. The Hebrew Scriptures firmly prohibited devout Jews from resorting to mediums, but this rule was broken by King Saul, who obtained a séance with the ghost of Samuel from a medium living in Endor (1 Samuel 28). At present, most mediums are women who engage in séances as part of a purportedly religious ritual (usually connected in the United States with the Spiritualist religion). Although some interesting and scientifically unexplainable results have been obtained in experiments with mediums, no definite conclusions about the authenticity of mediumship have been drawn because of some special problems (which we will discuss below) germane to this type of Psi.

GESP. Finally, since very often clairvoyance, telepathy, and precognition seem to operate in combination, the term *GESP* (*General Extrasensory Perception*) was coined to denote such combinations of various types of ESP.

The possibility of paranormal phenomena such as we have been discussing raises some very interesting questions for the philosophy of science, epistemology,[18] and metaphysics,[19] as well as philosophical anthropology. We will now elaborate on some of these questions.

How can we isolate one particular kind of ESP from others? This is a problem that pertains to all the paranormal faculties we have discussed, and has plagued parapsychologists trying to devise accurate and dependable experimental methods. When an individual has "precognitive" knowledge of a death of a relative, how can anyone be sure that this is not simply clairvoyant knowledge of the weakened physiological state of his relative's body? If a subject in an experiment for precognition correctly calls the fall of dice, could he not actually be influencing the dice to fall in a certain way through PK? When a "clairvoyant" obtains a high score in a DT test with cards, might not his knowledge of the cards result from his precognitive telepathic reading of the mind of the researcher who will check on the cards, rather than actual clairvoyance of the cards?[20] We have already indicated some of the difficulties involved in testing for pure telepathy, and the intricate coding system devised by Soal to preclude clairvoyant knowledge of the notes and records of the researcher. But even if a researcher could accomplish this, could he ever preclude the possibility that his "telepathic" subject is not really reading his *mind,* but only receiving clairvoyant impressions of his brain processes, which are translated into appropriate signals? (A researcher may avoid taking notes but he cannot avoid making connections in his neural synapses.)

Of all the manifestations of Psi, mediumship poses the most staggering problems of isolation. How can we ever be sure that the medium is actually deriving his information from the mind or "spirit" of a deceased person? There is always the possibility that the medium is reading the mind of the "sitter" or other persons who were acquainted with the deceased person, or that the medium may possess clairvoyant knowledge of objects or records formerly possessed by the deceased person.

In order to diminish such possibilities, experimenters have devised such circumventions as the "proxy sitting," in which a proxy, who knows nothing about the deceased person, visits a medium on behalf of the person who was acquainted with the deceased and would be able to identify him. In some instances the "spirit" himself has obligingly tried to salve the doubts of skeptical researchers by splitting up his message into several apparently unrelated segments transmitted to mediums in various parts of the world; it was only when the cryptic segments were pieced together that the message began to make sense.[21] However, even such complicated circumventions as this do not absolutely preclude the possibility that ESP (or GESP) was being used by the medium on an assortment of quite earthly minds, objects, and/or records.

Since the time of Plato, philosophy has been pondering the question of immortality. Is there "life after death," and if so, what is its nature? True mediumship, if it exists, would seem to offer us a possible "empirical" approach to these questions. If only we could obtain a reliable contact with a spirit who could prove conclusively that he or she was essentially identical with some deceased person, and who could give us a description of life "on the other side," our doubts about immortality would disappear—or so it would seem. But the obstacles to verification are obviously insuperable in a case like this. How could we ever be sure that the information conveyed by the communicating spirit (about his own personality and life prior to death) was not obtained by "earthly" GESP? And how could we ever check up on the descriptions he gave us of the "afterlife"?[22] The uncomfortable but obvious answer is that we would have to go there ourselves (by the usual one-way route)—a method of verification that few if any experimenters would be willing to utilize no matter how fervent their devotion to science.

Precognition raises especially difficult questions about the nature of time. If I am really, at the present, receiving information from future events or states of mind, how can I still speak of these things as "future"? Time as we know it always terminates at the present. If the future is present to a consciousness right now, it is no longer the future. If it became established that a psychic really could perceive things, say three hours in the future, how could we explain this? Would we say that the psychic, unlike the ordinary person, sees time as a continuum of movement, rather than successive movements? Could we conjecture that, since future effects are attributable to present causes, the psychic just has an uncanny insight into the present seminal causes and the way they develop and interact to produce future effects? Or would some other explanation be more cogent?

Perhaps the most important philosophical implications of Psi are with reference to the dualism-monism controversies. For example, if one conceives of the human personality in terms of materialistic monism (e.g., the position of the logical behaviorists), we would expect that supposedly "mental" Psi phenomena should be explainable in acceptable physicalistic fashion. However, some of the most feasible physical explanations of Psi have already been eliminated. Psi, unlike radio waves and other types of waves, does not have any known physical barriers—psychic subjects are not affected by walls, lead shields, or other obstructions that have been set up in tests. There is also the embarrassing fact that distance seems to have no effect whatever on many psychics,[23] which seems to contradict physical laws. Perhaps the hardest type of Psi to explain physically is PK, in which definite and observable physical reactions occur without any apparent physical cause.[24]

There are also some nonmaterialistic monistic theories that seem particularly suited to the explanation of Psi, e.g., the theory of Bishop Berkeley that there is no physical world and that all perceptions, sensations, and ideas are impressed directly upon our mind by God. It seems rash, however, to sacrifice our belief in the existence of a physical world for the sake of a theory that can conveniently accommodate ESP phenomena whose reality is at least as open to question as the reality of the physical world that we think we perceive.

One can never be certain that strictly physical and causal explanations will be forthcoming to explain the various manifestations of Psi. However, in lieu of such explanations, the evidence at present seems to bolster a dualist interpretation of man, e.g., the Cartesian theory, which holds that the human mind is a substance in some way separate from matter and possesses certain operations all its own. On the basis of such a theory, we might maintain that a person's mind can *directly* receive impressions from, and cause changes in, the external world; just as it already receives impressions from, and causes changes in, his or her own body. This explanation is at least useful and consistent, if unconvincing, if we are focusing our attention on clairvoyance or PK. But what about telepathy? In the context of dualism as it is usually understood—i.e., my isolated, individual mind in rapport with my particular body—telepathy becomes even harder to understand than in the light of materialistic monism; e.g., it seems harder to explain how an independent "mind-substance" would bridge the distance to another mind than to explain how a mind-brain could come into contact with another mind-brain (at least, in the latter case, there is the hope that a physical law will emerge some day to help explain the connection). In order to explain telepathy-in-the-strict-sense according to dualism-in-the-strict-sense it seems necessary to postulate some sort of supermind that connects individual minds and operates "behind the scenes" to bring individual egos into contact (through some purely spiritual "space") with other egos. William James, as we saw in an epigraph to this chapter, supposed that we humans might be denizens of some "mother sea," the proper milieu into which our minds are plunged, although we *seem* to be separate and independent individuals because we build "accidental fences" cutting ourselves off from others in this intellectual area.[25]

In a similar vein, Carl Jung speaks of a "collective unconscious" that is shared by all men and gives rise to certain common archetypal images. And several thinkers in the history of philosophy have actually developed at some length theories concerning a collective mind or collective consciousness, in which each individual mind or ego participates.[26]

But just how, specifically, could such a hypothesis possibly help to explain a phenomenon such as telepathic communications? At the risk of appearing to descend from philosophy to children's stories, I will end this chapter with an analogy that may throw light on the problem. Let us suppose that there is a certain many-flowered bush and that all the flowers are not only in full bloom but conscious. Having no sense of vision, the individual blossoms will perhaps have only vague external impressions of the other flowers in their vicinity, e.g., if some of the flowers got in the way of the sun, causing a temporary eclipse for the others. Each flower would certainly not have sufficiently detailed awareness of the other flowers to become aware of the stems by which those other flowers are connected at the bottom of the bush. Neither would an individual flower notice that it itself is attached by its stem to the bush, since its petals and pistil would always face in the other direction, toward the sun. Thus the flower would consider itself an "individual consciousness" in its own right, enjoying the sun and the air and aware of the fact that other individual flowers are similarly enjoying the sun and the air. However, every once in a while it would receive quite definite impressions about subjective feelings of enjoyment or deprivation in the other flowers. Since it has only vague external impressions of these other flowers, it realizes that these subjective impressions could not have come from the normal "perceptual" processes. However, neither does it suspect that such impressions might have been received directly from the other flowers through the linkup of stems leading from one to the other; for, alas, our flower does not realize that it is attached to any common stem. Thus it calls the subjective impressions it receives "extraordinary perception" and supposes that somehow or other it results from an intensification of the ordinary external impressions that it receives . . . *Stop!*

. . . You will object: "Your 'analogy' limps. Certainly human beings, with all their advanced perceptual and intellectual powers, receive much more than 'vague external impressions' about other human beings. If individuals were 'rooted' in some collective unconscious substratum, they would know it. Even if they did not perceive the true situation in other individuals, they would be able to perceive it in themselves; because men, unlike flowers, have the power of self-reflection—they can 'bend back' upon themselves, so to speak, and take cognizance of their own 'roots.' "

But *can* they? In Chapter 10 we spoke of the uncertainty of man's "knowledge of his own knowledge," or awareness of his own awareness; and like the flower, we perceive externally only one side or aspect of our fellows—the phenomenal aspects, the body, the expressions and activities—and do not fully understand if these phenomenal aspects are rooted in any source "behind the scenes."

I will not try to carry the analogy any further. Psi—*if* it exists at all—is at present very hard to account for in terms of any of our theories, whether monist or dualist. A dualist theory related to a collective mind might facilitate the explanation of the phenomena we have discussed, but there are obviously some other attendant difficulties (especially the apparent contradiction of this explanation to our experience of the isolation and individuality of egos) that would make us reluctant to accept such a theory without a great deal of further analysis and reflection.

12. Is There Survival After Death?

The seed you sow does not germinate unless it dies. . . . There are heavenly bodies and there are earthly bodies. . . . What is sown in the earth is subject to decay, what rises is incorruptible. . . . This corruptible body must be clothed with incorruptibility, this mortal body with immortality.—1 Corinthians 15:36–53

> O son of noble family, when your body and mind separate, the dharmata [essence of reality] will appear, pure and clear and yet hard to discern, luminous and brilliant, with terrifying brightness, shimmering like a mirage or a plain in spring. Do not be afraid of it, do not be bewildered. This is the natural radiance of your own dharmata, therefore recognize it. A great roar of thunder will come from within the light, the natural sound of dharmata, like a thousand thunderclaps simultaneously. This is the natural sound of your own dharmata, so do not be afraid or bewildered. You have [in the next life] what is called a mental body of unconscious tendencies, you have no physical body of flesh and blood, so whatever sounds, colours and rays of light occur, they cannot hurt you and you cannot die . . .
>
> The whole of space will shine with a blue light, and Blessed Vairocana [the all-comprehending Buddha] will appear before you from the central realm, All-pervading Circle. . . . Do not be frightened or bewildered by the luminous, brilliant, very sharp and clear blue light of supreme wisdom. . . . It is Blessed Vairocana coming to invite you in the dangerous pathway of the bordo [transition from death to new life].—*The Tibetan Book of the Dead*

While the man who despairs marches towards nothingness, the one who has placed his faith in the archetype of life after death follows the tracks of life and lives right into his death. Both, to be sure, remain in uncertainty, but the one lives against his instincts, the other with them.—C.G. Jung, *Memories, Dreams, Reflections*

In the preceding chapter we considered the possibility of the existence of "psychic" powers that transcend the ambits of our normal perceptions and controls over the material world. Now we shall proceed one step further to the question of whether it is possible that there is a state of existence, attainable by man, beyond the limits of our present mortal lifespans. The major religions have given expression to visions of immortality, ranging from the personal immortality of Christianity to the rather impersonal immersion in Nirvana of Buddhism. Many philosophers—Socrates, Plato,

Aristotle, Aquinas, Descartes, Locke, Spinoza, Kant, Hegel, et al.—have defended (or have been interpreted as defending) one concept of immortality or the other, either the individualistic type or what seems (from the Christian point of view) to be an impersonal type. Some of these philosophers have attempted to prove the survival after death of the individual "soul" or some "spirit" transcending individuals and individual lives. Our purpose in this chapter is to reconsider the Christian belief in personal immortality, to determine just what might be meant by this belief; whether there is anything self-contradictory or impossible about the belief; and, if not, in what way it might possibly be implemented.

It is very difficult even to conceive of an empirical proof of "life after death." Some savants have sought such proofs in the parapsychological sphere, i.e., via mediumship. But as we have seen, there is absolutely no evidence whatever that any communications supposedly coming to us from deceased persons through mediums really are, or ever have been, what they purport to be. Unless we can find a way to verify both (a) the existence of communicating "spirits" and (b) the reality of the "other world" that these "spirits" speak to us about, empirical proof of ultimate survival seems to be out of the question, if by empirical proof we mean publicly observable evidence that is accepted as truly conclusive by all rational persons.

In lieu of an empirical proof in this sense, is any other proof of the existence of departed "souls" in the "other world" possible? This is one of the questions we will consider below. Before we get to it, however, some definitions must be given and some semantic problems discussed.

(A) Definitions

The religious notion of the "soul" has undergone a long and laborious evolution since it was introduced in ancient philosophies. We will not concentrate here on its etymological career, but will simply try to differentiate this notion from others that seem synonymous with, or similar to, it, e.g., "mind," "ego," "self," etc. (Note, please, that the following definitions do not presuppose that the soul, mind, etc. actually *exist;* their purpose is limited to summing up what these ideas frequently are taken to mean and the ways in which the terms are frequently utilized. In elaborating on these various definitions, we will refer to *Webster's New Collegiate Dictionary, The Oxford English Dictionary,* and James Drever's *Dictionary of Psychology* [Baltimore: Penguin, 1952].)

(1) **Ego.** The *Oxford* defines *ego* negatively as that which is opposed to a nonego or object. The *Dictionary of Psychology,* in a more positive vein,

states that the ego is "the dynamic unity which is the individual." In line with both these conceptions, we will define the ego as the focal point of self-identity, the *I* that is responsible for unifying all our thoughts and activities (in this regard, see the definition of *I* in *Webster's*), and as a subjective *I* that can be contrasted with objects and with the various objective externalizations of its own self-identity, namely, the *me*.[1] (The ego, insofar as it is thought of as "giving rise" to these expressions—activities, thoughts, and feelings—may be called the "soul.")

(2) *Mind.* The *Dictionary of Psychology* indicates that there is a kind of confusion between the psychological and philosophical definitions of mind, and states that mind in the philosophical sense is the "entity" or substratum underlying (psychic) structures and processes. *Webster's* apparently concentrates on such "philosophical" aspects in defining mind as ". . . memory . . . [and] the element or complex of elements in an individual that feels, perceives, thinks, wills, and especially reasons." The *Oxford* emphasizes the fact that the mind often denotes "cognitive or intellectual powers as distinguished from will and emotions." The emphasis on reason and reasoning seems to be the most important aspect of mind; the mind is taken to be the source of rational thinking (as well as of decisions and volitions), and a kind of receptacle or "substratum" in which many of our thoughts or ideas inhere and perdure. (The "soul" is supposed to give rise to ideas, decisions, and volitions, but also to feelings and sensations.)

(3) *Consciousness* is precisely the sum-total of the things we know, perceive, sense, or intuit.[2] (The soul seems to be the source of the "unconscious" as well as consciousness.)

(4) *The unconscious* usually means (a) that which is "below" consciousness (UC_1): e.g., the Freudian "Id," which is a natural, bodily, quasi-instinctive source of emotions and thoughts. But it can also mean (b) that which is "above" consciousness (UC_2): e.g., the Freudian "Super-ego," which gives "other-worldly" moral directives to the ego; or the Jungian archetypes, supernal symbols and images that come to us from the "collective unconscious" (see Chapter 2). (The soul is supposed to generate the totality of UC_1 and UC_2, and consciousness as well.)

(5) *The self* is sometimes synonymous with "ego," "consciousness," or "personality" (the *Dictionary of Psychology* emphasizes the synonymity of these terms), but sometimes especially connotes a certain totality or comprehensiveness; and it is thus that *Webster's* defines the self as "the entire person of an individual," while the *Oxford* says the self is "an assemblage of characteristics and dispositions which may be conceived as constituting one of various conflicting personalities within a human being." Among psychologists, Carl Jung stands out as one who emphasized this comprehensivity in his use of the term *self.* The Jungian "Self" is a synthetic "union-of-opposites" that encompasses both consciousness and the uncon-

scious, in a totality of present and past acts, motives, or states. (If we conceived the Self in this Jungian sense, the "soul" would stand in contrast as the source or "ground" that makes the Self possible.)

(6) **Personality.** *Webster's* says rather incontrovertibly (and tautologically) that personality is the "state of being a person (human being)." The *Dictionary of Psychology* says, with a little more commitment, that personality is "the integrated and dynamic organization of the physical, mental, moral and social qualities of the individual." Perhaps the main thing to note here is that physical aspects seem to be essential to the notion of personality. When we speak of personality, we are speaking of "temperament," mannerisms, emotions, appearance to other people—all of which emphasize physical as well as mental aspects. (Soul is thought to be the inner subjective source that in conjunction with the body contributes to the formation of personality.)

(7) **The Soul:** UC_1 and UC_2 might appropriately be called the limits or "horizons" of consciousness. Psychologists who deny that there is an "unconscious" (and many do deny it) will deny that there is anything beyond these limits. Those who speak in a positive way about a "soul" sometimes presuppose that there is a hidden source "below" UC_1, an animal soul ($Soul_1$), which gives rise to sensations and emotions; and sometimes that there is an invisible spiritual element "above" UC_2, a higher, quasidivine, possibly immortal soul ($Soul_2$), which is particularly responsible for our thoughts, conscious moral aspirations, and/or higher intuitions.[3] The *Oxford* seems to touch on both these concepts in defining soul first as a "principle of life in man or animals," and then more specifically as the "principle of thought and action in man, commonly regarded as an entity distinct from the body."[4] Sometimes both of these notions of soul are combined into a composite notion of an animal-rational soul that is the source of, and supplies the grounding for, everything (intellectual and sensory) that goes on in the self. Those who speak about "personal immortality" generally speak in terms of $Soul_2$, i.e., a supernal source of intellectual or rational activity, existing somewhere beyond the horizons of our ideas, ideals, and inspirations. (It should be noted, before we go any further, that those who deny $Soul_2$ look upon what we have called the "horizons" as simply limits created by consciousness,[5] while those who accept it look upon these same horizons as both encompassing consciousness and making consciousness possible.[6] We will analyze this difference further, below.) The difference among all the various terms we have discussed so far might be illustrated by the diagram on page 117.

We have concentrated above on certain terms in psychological and philosophical literature that should help to illustrate the meaning of *soul* by comparison and contrast. It should be reemphasized, however, that we are making no judgment about whether any of these entities, all of which go beyond the notion of "body," actually exist.

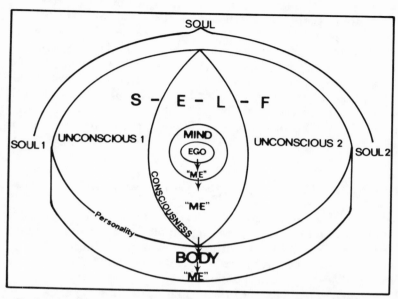

Explanation of the diagram: The ego, or "I," is conceived as the unifying core of persons. The Mind, as the intellectual control center, is thought to be especially near that core. "Consciousness" is a wider term, and includes feelings and sensations. Feelings, sensations, actions and reactions, as well as ideas, all contribute to the *expression* of the ego, i.e., the "me." Consciousness is thought to be bordered by two aspects of the "unconscious," as explained above. Consciousness *plus* these borders or horizons is the Self. The composite animal-rational soul is then portrayed as that which gives rise to, makes possible, or even "causes" the whole Self. (However, the rational component of this soul, Soul$_2$, is sometimes thought to be superior, and to have a special kind of independence.) The conjunction of soul *and* body contributes to human personality.

Before proceeding to the discussion of the main problem, a definition of *spirit* may also be in order. (Questions about immortality are usually framed in terms of "soul" rather than "spirit"; as we shall see later, however, it might be more profitable to focus on spirit rather than soul.) *Spirit* in its various usages seems to connote some kind of a union of the (subjective) self and an (objective) phenomenal expression. In Christian literature, the "Holy Spirit" is taken to be the union or "relation" between the divine mind (the Father) and its expression (the Son). In folklore and occultism, a spirit or "ghost" is supposed to be a union of a deceased human mind (or traces of that mind) and an ethereal or aerial "body" (i.e., some kind of a physical form that looks like the former corporeal body). As applied to living human beings, "spirit" seems to imply a union of, and relation between, one's inner nature and the power to reflect on and express that nature objectively and even *physically;* and in line with this concept of spirit the *Oxford* defines spirit as "an animating or vital principle in man . . . which gives life to the physical organism."[7]

With these definitions in mind, we may now proceed to the semantic problems.

(B) Problems of Formulating the Question about Survival

Consider the following sentence, which is one common way of phrasing the question about immortality: "After a man dies, does his soul continue to exist in another world, i.e., in an afterlife?" This is an innocent-enough question, and seems meaningful. However, the question as put entails a number of troublesome presuppositions. It presupposes, for example:

(1) That a man experiences death, i.e., that death is an experience like any other experience in life. But death, the very moment it "begins," precludes the possibility of experience in the usual sense. In other words, no one can ever have experienced death. In speaking about death, therefore, we are referring to something completely outside our scientific knowledge. All we really know about death is that living people sometimes witness a cessation of activity in dying people; and these living people draw their own tentative conclusions about what may or must be taking place within these dying people.

(2) That if anything remains after death, it must be the soul, i.e., Soul$_2$, the subjective aspect of man that gives rise to the *mind*. It is natural to presuppose this because Soul$_2$ is not visible in life or death; unlike Soul$_1$, it seems to be one step removed from our bodily organism, and it is but one short step from noticing that it is not visible, to calling it an "invisible" entity that still remains. But how could a "subjective" aspect of man remain after death without some objective expression, without some mental activity or memory?[8] It would seem more logical to pose the question of immortality in regard to the "spirit," which is not just a subjective pole but connotes self-conscious reflection and some power of self-expression or self-manifestation.[9]

(3) That the soul "exists." Certainly Soul$_2$ does not exist in the same way that trees, mountains, or atoms, which we can observe and/or measure, exist. In what sense, then, does it exist?

(4) That there is some other world outside our own. By definition,

however, *world,* when used in the sense of "universe," includes all reality. If there is something "outside" this world, it would not, strictly speaking, be a "world"; nor would it be a "reality" in the usual sense of *that* word.

(5) That there can be some kind of continuation-in-time after the end of time. Time "ends" for us in two senses: (a) insofar as time measures one's own bodily motions and processes, an individual's lifetime ends at death; (b) insofar as time measures human history, it ends (or will end, supposedly) with the death of the last human being. If we suppose continuation or perdurance after an individual's death, we contradict the former notion of time. If we suppose a continuance of minds after the "end of the world," we contradict both notions of time.

Thus, we may surmise at the outset that the difficulty of the problem of survival is partly a difficulty of formulating the "question about immortality" meaningfully. Our first task, then, is to reformulate the question in a more meaningful way. Before doing this, however, we must first consider the most basic question of all: "Does the soul exist and, if so, in what sense does it exist?" (If the soul does not exist, we cannot ask the usual questions about "how" it exists, "how long" it exists, etc.)

(C) The Question of the "Existence" of the Human Soul

Some years ago, a gentleman in one of our western states died and left a last will and testament in which a large sum of money was offered to anyone who proved that the soul survived after death. So far as we know, no one came up with a satisfactory proof, and it is possible that the money has still not been paid out. If anyone were to offer such a proof, however, it would seem necessary for him first to prove the "existence" of Soul$_2$ (i.e., the soul that is thought to be independent and perhaps separable from the body) *during life.* This might be more difficult than it seems. The term *existence* seems to be used primarily in two senses: (1) to point out physical objects or physical qualities that have been, or could be, experienced, e.g., rocks, the color and texture of a watermelon, atoms, stars; and (2) to designate purely mental qualities, or mental combinations, such as the number two, goodness, or Oliver Twist, all of which are recognized (by most people) to exist in some sense, although they have never been tangible, measurable, or observable physical qualities or objects.[10] A few esoteric philosophers have claimed that Soul$_2$ is an ethereal (i.e., semiphysical) substance, but most people do not think of it as such. Also, since Soul$_2$ is supposed to "give rise to" the mind and make possible *all* the mind's ideas, we could not say that Soul$_2$ is itself one of these ideas. In short, Soul$_2$ does not seem to exist in either the physical or the mental sense.

To be precise, Soul$_2$ might best be depicted not as existing in itself but as a "ground for existence." Soul$_2$ is considered the ultimate inner source or ground for the thoughts and volitions of the self, just as some ultimate cause might be considered to be the ground for the existence of the physical world.[11] An example may help to show how the notion of Soul$_2$ emerges. Let us suppose that a conscious individual lives in a room, has never been outside that room, has never seen anyone or anything enter that room, and indeed has no evidence that anything exists outside that room. For such an individual, his room is the universe. His ultimate perceptual horizons are the walls of his room. He may suspect that there is something beyond these walls, especially if he hears faint noises or rumblings that don't seem to come from within the room. If he does suppose

that there *is* something in this "beyond," he may also conclude not only that this "something" is causing the noises or rumblings but also that it is a source of his universe (room) or somehow makes that universe (room) possible. The case with one's intellectual universe (mind) is somewhat similar, and somewhat different. A man experiences his own world of ideas, which always has certain boundaries. He has good reason to suspect that there is something outside these boundaries, however, because he experiences his ideas multiplying, i.e., his mental world "growing." If his mental world formerly terminated at the boundary A, and later, after an increase in knowledge, terminated at B, he has positive proof that his former horizons (A) were inaccurate (since they were superseded by the horizons (B)), and he has good reason to suspect that there may be even further horizons (C) beyond his present boundaries. Because he can never control these boundaries completely but can only "discover" them, he may

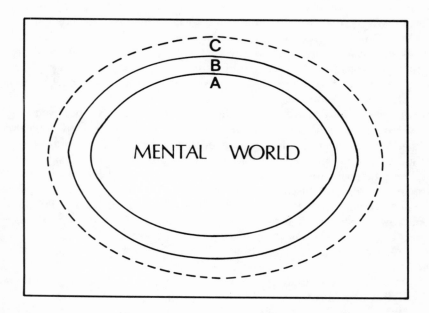

also suppose that they are independent and/or that they supply the grounds for the very possibility of his mental world.[12] If he makes the latter suppositions, he has made the leap to a notion of an independent and subsistent $Soul_2$, which is the "ground" of, or the source for, the existence of his world of ideas.

If $Soul_2$ is conceived as a "ground" for existence, does it itself "exist" in any sense? We have already indicated that the term *existence*, in the two senses in which that term is usually employed, would not strictly apply to $Soul_2$. We might refer to physical existence as $Existence_1$ and mental existence as $Existence_2$; then $Soul_2$, considered to be a real ground for mental existence, might be designated $Existence_3$. I will not be using this terminology in what follows, but I want to emphasize here that, when any references are made to the "existence" of $Soul_2$, this will always be a reference to $Existence_3$, i.e., to that which is thought to exist only in the limited sense that it is thought to provide a real ground for mental existence, and whose "existence" might best be depicted as a "possibility" [13]—the possibility of ultimate horizons supplying the foundation for our present psychic horizons . . .

(D) Cross-examination and Conclusion

READER: Wait a minute! Please. This is getting too complicated. Soul as "possibility" . . . OK, I'll accept that, if you like. Let us agree that the soul could be described as a "mere possibility." Where does that leave us? Certainly we cannot *know* anything for sure about a remote possibility.

AUTHOR: You're right. There could not be any *direct* knowledge of such a possibility, at any rate. I think it would be best to describe our cognitive attitude here as "belief." We can only have a definite knowledge of that which exists and can be experienced in some way or observed; short of this, we have opinions or beliefs.

READER: Then all you are really saying seems to be this: you believe in the possibility of certain mental boundaries that are not created "by" the individual ego but that supply the ground "for" the ego's mental life.

AUTHOR: At this particular point in our discussion, I could say that I harbor a belief in the possibility of a certain ground, beyond the mind, which is a source of mental operations.

READER: I can see how the soul is a possibility, and that this possibility may somehow remain even after what we call death. But this sounds like nothing more than "logical possibility," which you referred to some time ago in your analysis of "free choice." [14] How can you jump from this to *belief-in*?

AUTHOR: I would say that the soul is more than a logical possibility; it is an ontological possibility.

READER: Oh, no! I was hoping we wouldn't have to get any deeper into cosmic abstractions.

AUTHOR: I'll try to spare you. But, since you raised the question, a logical possibility (Possibility$_L$) is just something that is not self-contradictory. As you have already intimated, there are an almost infinite number of things that are logical possibilities. An ontological possibility (Possibility$_O$), on the other hand, is a potentiality, i.e., that which makes something possible. *Some* logical possibilities are also potentialities. If Soul$_2$ is a logical possibility, it may also be the sort of potentiality I have just described, insofar as it would really give rise to mind, and mind is what makes thinking and volition possible.

READER: You say, "*if* Soul$_2$ is a logical possibility . . ." You seem to see no problem in this supposition. But I find it quite problematic. I think you described the soul earlier as a "form," or as something analogous to form. Surely it would be logically impossible for a form to exist without some content.

AUTHOR: This would certainly be the case if Soul$_1$ were our only entitlement to being besouled, but the Thomists and others say that such is not the case with Soul$_2$. They argue that with Soul$_2$ (what we referred to above as the ultimate ground for the existence of mental operations), the "form-content" analogy, which ordinarily requires concomitance of some material content along with the form that actuates or defines it, starts to limp, or at least to wobble. The reason for this, they say, is that Soul$_2$ has certain operations that are independent of matter. Since these operations are independent of matter even now, in this present life, there should be no great difficulty in allowing the possibility that these same operations—and Soul$_2$, which makes them possible—might continue in their independence even after the physical body has disintegrated.

READER: What would happen to Soul$_1$? You seem to have given it up for lost or dead.

AUTHOR: With Soul$_1$ the form-content analogy applies in all its vigor and strictness. Soul$_1$ could not function as a form without something, some content, to in-form, i.e., some body to actuate. But in man, Soul$_1$ and Soul$_2$ are simply distinguishable aspects; they are not really separable from each other. And so, if Soul$_2$ continues to flourish, Soul$_1$ is still there implicitly, and would resume its normal operations if and when it were reunited with a suitable body.

READER: The whole Thomistic argument seems to hinge on the possibility of "independent" mental operations. What would be an example of such operations?

AUTHOR: I think the clearest examples of intellectual operations of Soul$_2$ that are independent of the body can be provided by an examination of some of our notions of time. Can you form a concept of eternity?

READER: I think so, but when I think of eternity I also get sensory images of successions in the world and of history.

AUTHOR: No matter. Your concept of eternity consists precisely in going *beyond* all these temporal successions. What you are doing when you form the concept is to take a look at the totality of time as you know it, and to deny that this "totality" contains everything.

READER: I do the same thing when I form the concept of "infinity." I carry something (e.g., a series of numbers) to its limit, and then I deny these limits. But—if you'll excuse my obtuseness—so what? Eternity and infinity are both negative concepts. They are formed by negating certain finite concepts. But you have to *have* these finite concepts in order to negate them. You have to *imagine* time or a numerical series in order to form the negative idea of "infinite time" or infinity. And I presume one would need a body in order to have a functioning imagination.

AUTHOR: Soul$_2$ would need the body in order to receive objects of knowledge, of course; but that does not necessarily mean it would need the body in order to exist.

READER: Are you trying to suggest that Soul$_2$ would be able to exist in some sort of a "limbo"-state without knowledge? What kind of "existence" would that be?

AUTHOR: Well, definitely an unconscious state, *if* we equate consciousness with the powers of imagining, calculating, reasoning, etc. But if you allow the possibility of a direct infusion of ideas by God—as some Christian philosophers have speculated—it would be possible to characterize this state as a conscious or even supraconscious state.

READER: But if we didn't want to make our argument dependent on (a) the existence of a Christian-type god and (b) the possibility of direct, intuitive, passively received knowledge—I suppose we would simply have to conclude that $Soul_2$, being in a kind of eternal state of "coma" when separated from the body, would for all practical purposes be nonexistent, if existence implies active cognition.

AUTHOR: No doubt. But, I hasten to add, it would be unwarranted to conclude that that state of "coma" would have to be perpetual. I mentioned earlier that the soul as the ground for thinking and volition is conceived as a $Possibility_0$, as a potentiality. The potentiality might remain in a temporarily latent state, and then, finally, when the proper material conditions are restored, the potentiality might begin to exert its congruent effects once more.

READER: To my mind, such a potentiality would be a *remote* $Possibility_0$, indeed. Why not just presume, with probability on your side, that it simply no longer exists in any manner, not even as "unconscious"?

AUTHOR: Because this is a special, relatively anomalous case. In ordinary cases of causal relationships, when both cause and effect are observable, if the effect subsides we can search out the cause and arrive at a judicious conclusion as to whether the cause still exists or not. But if the cause is for some reason. unobservable, we find ourselves in a situation where, although we see a certain effect taking place, and we know it must have a cause, *we don't know what that cause is.* In such cases, we can say that *some* cause, X, makes the effect, Y, possible; but X is a "remote" possibility because we don't know the precise nature of X. The case of $Soul_2$ is like this. We experience thoughts and volitions which seem to go beyond their material conditions, and so we hypothesize a potentiality, i.e., $Soul_2$, giving rise to them.[15] But because we have such a vague intimation of the existence and nature of this potentiality, and no way to directly observe it, we admit that it is a remote possibility. It is not remote because it is farfetched, but because it is largely hidden from view.

READER: I don't understand. We don't have the slightest idea of what the cause is, and yet we conclude that there is some cause back there behind the scenes, and we designate it a "remote $Possibility_0$"?

AUTHOR: An example might help. Let us suppose that there is an oasis in the desert, and a small stream of water is flowing outward to the edge of the oasis. Because of natural barriers (rocks, etc.), we are unable to determine the source of the water. We *believe* that the source must be a spring. However, all we actually see is the water trickling to the edge of the oasis. We are not actually certain that there is a spring, i.e., some receptacle somewhere down below the surface of the oasis, which contains the water under pressure and is the source of the water, or that which makes the flow of water possible.

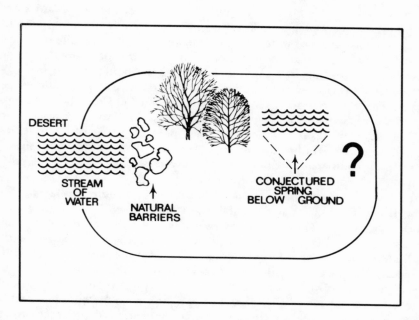

READER: In the case of the spring, I would disagree that the "receptacle" is that which makes the flow of water possible. It seems to me that it would be more correct to say that it is the water under pressure below that makes it possible.

AUTHOR: That would be another way of looking at it.

READER: I think this would have some implications for your theory. In one place you indicated that $Soul_2$ might be an ultimate "receptacle" for thought.

AUTHOR: I think that is the way it is commonly conceived. But I admit that it may also be conceived in a more active fashion, as that which provides illumination, ideals, inspiration. Perhaps it would be best to say that both aspects are involved in $Soul_2$'s "possibility."

READER: Well then, let's follow up on your analogy of the spring. A man dies; the water stops flowing. What happens to all the "$Possibility_O$" of your spring?

AUTHOR: There is a $Possibility_L$ that the water may trickle out again sometime from some $Possibility_O$ (such as a spring), which may just be temporarily impeded from causing its usual effects.

READER: Earlier you distinguished between $Possibility_L$ and probability. I presume that by "probability" you mean exact calculations about possibility. It would be theoretically feasible to make statistical measurements of the probability that water would come again. If we could gather together many examples of such cases in history and determine how many cases with a water phenomenon such as you mention went through a period of temporary stoppage of water flow, we might have some definite statistical evidence that there was not just a $Possibility_L$ but a probability that some $Possibility_O$ would again furnish water. I doubt whether this sort of research would win a Nobel prize, but it could be done. But how could we do this sort of research on cases of the spontaneous and unexpected reappearance of $Soul_2$? Even if you believe in the biblical accounts of the revivification of Jesus and Lazarus, and perhaps some of the tales of revivification in Hindu and Muslim literature, you would have only a handful of confirmatory cases, and thus a very slim probability indeed—something approximating zero probability.

AUTHOR: Such cases, if accepted, would attest to a slight probability for *resurrection*, but not for the $Possibility_O$ of $Soul_2$. Even if the resurrected person began speaking and behaving rationally, this would still be only circumstantial evidence for the $Possibility_O$ of $Soul_2$. For, as I have already indicated, the only bona fide evidence we have for the $Possibility_O$ of $Soul_2$ is our own experience of thought and volition. And so, if you wanted to calculate the probability of the resurgence of *this* $Possibility_O$, you would have to turn to your own subjective experience. And the only reasonably exoteric situation in which there is a cessation of the activities ascribed to $Soul_2$, followed by the reappearance of these activities, is your experience of the cycles of sleeping and waking. Even in sleep, of course, there is some intermittent activity in dreaming that can be ascribed to $Soul_2$, but the comparatively dreamless intervals are the closest empirical approximation we have to a complete cessation of these activities. However, if we used *these* experiences as our basis for calculation, we would not come up with anything like "zero" probability, but rather with the strongest possible positive statistical probability because, as a matter of fact, we always do wake up after sleep; otherwise we wouldn't be talking about it. And if you add to this the consideration that sleep is a state in which the activity of the body increases and predominates, I think it becomes clear why the Platonists believed that the complete release of the soul from bodily influence and impediments through death would make possible the maximum cognitive and volitional activity, just as the release of the fetus from the mother's womb makes possible the full operation of the infant as an autonomous organism. But, of course, we don't want to go to the Platonistic extreme. I think we are both agreed that the soul, even an immortal $Soul_2$, would require a body for complete activity.

READER: I would make that last statement even stronger, and add, "and even for existence." After all, sleep is not death. In order for you to apply your "spring" analogy to $Soul_2$, you have to consider the case where a man not only sleeps but dies. In that case, although Jesus and Lazarus and a few others may have had personal experience of the return of the activities of $Soul_2$ after they had clearly and indubitably died, the rest of us *don't*. (We are not talking here about cases in which a person's heart stops and he is resuscitated by artificial respiration, a pacemaker, etc. Those are not clear, unambiguous cases of death.) If we insist on a clear case of death, and we are honest about it, we would have to say the probability of such revivification is *zero*.

AUTHOR: Not zero—because you personally don't have *any* experience of cases like *this* at all. To come up with "zero" probability, you'd have to have at least one case of personal experience of death followed by no resuscitation. Of course, this is impossible. Actually, what you have here is simply the absence of probability, not zero probability. Probability doesn't apply here. This is the exact point where the "spring" analogy—and all such analogies—end—and not just because we don't have experience of cases. It's rather because we *cannot* have such experience. Death is not something that is subject to experience in any way. As I explained at the outset of this chapter, one requires a living body for "experience" in the strict sense. The body could not *be* dead and *experience* death at the same time. Even Jesus and Lazarus, if we are to suppose that they died and rose again with all their mental activities, would have experienced only the sufferings or distintegration preliminary to death, not death itself. If they experienced death they would still be living at the time of the experience; and so either the experience or the death would contradict itself—unless you wanted to presuppose some sort of nonbodily, second-order experience—a presupposition that would "solve" the problem in a Platonic way by simply assuming that there really is no death and that man is only a soul who is accidentally and temporarily bound up with a body. If you want to avoid that "solution" and its many inconvenient consequences and ramifications, but still conclude that the experience of bodily death is not only inaccessible but self-contradictory and impossible—then you might be led naturally to hold that the very lack of possibility of experiencing bodily death in a bodily way supports the $Possibility_0$ of $Soul_2$ as something above and beyond these experiences.

READER: Maybe we don't have any direct experience of death, but we know for a fact that the dead individual to whom you would like to ascribe the $Possibility_0$ of $Soul_2$ is no longer with us. As far as we can tell, his "spring" has dried up; thought and volition have ceased. And you admitted a few moments ago that there is not for us even a statistical probability that his "spring" will trickle forth again. In view of all this, how can *we* seriously maintain the $Possibility_L$ of a $Possibility_0$ after death. $Possibility_0$ (I'll quote you) is "that which makes something possible." Now I ask you, what in the world could a disembodied $Soul-Possibility_0$ "make possible" after death? One can't imagine a more completely truncated entity.

AUTHOR: It simply comes down to this: $Soul_2$ as a $Possibility_0$ could (for the dead individual, aside from *our* experience) remain ready to make thought and volition possible once again, if and when it was rejoined to its congruent body.

READER: For a Christian, I suppose this would be at the end of the world and after the Last Judgment—events that I, for one, hope will not take place in the near future. And if the human race helps matters by not blowing itself up, poor $Soul_2$ might be lingering in its unconscious state for perhaps eons, unless we are to presuppose some direct infusion of knowledge by a benevolent and solicitous God.

AUTHOR: True, that unconscious state would definitely be a long sleep; but time passes quickly in sleep. Think of Rip van Winkle.

READER: Small comfort to the more active among us who don't look forward to such a dormant afterlife!

AUTHOR: There *is* a way we could avoid this standoff. If it could be shown that certain elements of thought and volition do not depend in any way on physical images as stimuli or objects for cognition *in this present life,* then it would seem possible and even probable that at least that area of thought and volition might continue to function independently of any corporeal apparatus, when the body was no more.

READER: But who can doubt that, in real thought and volitional activity, all sorts of sensory impressions and images are involved. It's impossible to conceive of intellective activity going on without some input and support from the body. Even in very abstract thought, people utilize *some* kind of sensory images or schemata (which, we must presume, are derived from the body).

AUTHOR: I don't think the issue is as clear-cut as you seem to think it is. For one thing, I would observe that one of the distinguishing marks of mystical or paranormal experiences, is that they bring with them the ineluctable conviction that they are taking place independently of ordinary bodily functions and capacities. Unless we are to presume somewhat arbitrarily that all such experiences are delusional, or that the experiencers are really dependent on the body, although "they don't realize it"—we would have to conclude that these experiences offer fairly good subjective grounds for more optimism than you can muster. Specifically, such experiences would strongly urge the belief that $Soul_2$ would not necessarily be unconscious and comatose without the body, but might engage in at least some area of intellectual or supraintellectual (UC_2) activity without requiring concomitance of special bodily conditions. And the greater the intensity of the mystic's or psychic's experience of $Soul_2$'s independence of the body, the more formidable would be his subjective grounds for believing that $Soul_2$ is not just a remote $Possibility_0$ behind the scenes, but a proximate $Possibility_0$ of whose autonomous workings he has direct and indubitable experience.

READER: Perhaps. But how many of us are mystics or psychics? You're touching on a range of experience that is too esoteric to have much bearing on the issue at hand.

AUTHOR: The experience of Soul$_2$'s independence may be more exoteric than you suspect, if some researchers are correct. For example, toward the beginning of this century psychologists of the "Würzburg" school came up with impressive evidence for the existence of "naked" thought, i.e., thought as pure experience sans symbols or vocalizations.[16]

READER: Perhaps the most we could conclude from this is that individuals differ widely among themselves in the extent to which they rely on the imagination, emotions, etc. in their conceptual processes; or that they *think* they differ widely. I personally seem to experience a constant concomitance of sensory images while I am thinking. I rather suspect that all *my* thoughts are fully and decently "clothed." I hope you're not disappointed, but I simply do not seem to have had experiences of the sort that the Würzburg psychologists speak about. And if I do not have any such experience of being completely independent of my body in my most abstract conceptualizations, it seems to me I must react in one of two ways: either I abandon the idea of Soul$_2$ subsisting independent of the body after death, or I insist that Soul$_2$ be instantaneously supplied with a proper body after death, if it is to be considered a decent rational being.

AUTHOR: I can see where you're coming from. Insofar as one is not a mystic and never seems to have had clear and indubitable experiences of Soul$_2$ operating independently from his body, one would have to insist that any *immortal* Soul$_2$ be essentially embodied. And I suppose that the sort of reasoning you exemplify is the source for the various "astral-body" theories that have emerged in various religions and philosophies, and even among some of the early Christian writers. The caterpillar throws off its erstwhile body at a particular stage in its development and takes on a new physical expression, that of the butterfly, which has already emerged within the old. The case with man is thought to be analogous: Man throws off his well-known shape at what we call "death" but preserves some subtle "body" that was latent within the old. This "new" body, hitherto invisible and intangible, will be sufficiently "physical" in the afterlife to at least supply some of the more subtle images and impressions that lay the groundwork for conceptual thought. The essential nucleus of their theory is that there is some very subtle "body" that remains and that can continue to undergo changes or an "evolution" of some sort.

READER: I take it that this "subtle" body would not be something added to Soul$_2$, after some period of time in which Soul$_2$ was denuded of any body whatsoever . . .

AUTHOR: No—because this would involve the idea of an actively operating Soul$_2$ existing independently from its necessary corporeal concomitants—an idea that you, along with many proponents of astral-body theories, find it impossible to conceptualize.

READER: Exactly, and so now, in order to avoid that impossible conception, we have to insist on a stringent criterion: If there is an afterlife, it could not even involve some transition from one body into another—if this required even a few moments of complete separation of a soul from its body.

AUTHOR: The astral-body hypothesis I've just alluded to would, indeed, seem to meet this criterion. The astral body as spoken of, e.g., in Hindu Yoga remains with a person all through his life and after death as well.[17] The astral body as an etherial, quasimaterial body would be possessed by every person along with his ordinary visible and observable physical body. At the time of death, the astral body simply remains and the other is left behind, like a shell or integument that is thrown off. (Some astral-body theories are associated with a doctrine of reincarnation, but this is not an essential feature of such theories, and so it will not be necessary for us to give specific attention here to the question of reincarnation.)

READER: Is the astral body to be conceived as distinct or distinguishable from some "soul"?

AUTHOR: In its essential concept, the astral body seems to be an embodied soul or an ensouled body. Insofar as it is a union of subjective power and objective expression, it approximates to the idea of "spirit" that was delineated at the beginning of this chapter. The astral body, in other words, envisages such a fusion of the physical and the psychic that these two aspects are, for all practical purposes, indistinguishable and absolutely inseparable. If we wanted to be strict about using the traditional philosophical terminology of Christian Western culture, we would have to refer to the immortal "spirit-beings" of other religions as inseparable "soul/astral-body" unities or combinations.

READER: And so—if I may be allowed to sum this up in my own way—while the theme song of the disembodied Aristotelian-Thomistic Soul$_2$ is "I ain't got no body," the theme song of the soul/astral-body combination would be "We're made for each other," or "We'll never part."

AUTHOR: Yes, but I'm surprised you admit that a disembodied Soul$_2$ might even have a theme song.

READER: That was a slip. I have not changed in the least regarding my constitutional incapacity to accept the "Soul$_2$" formulation. But the soul/astral-body-combination theory does seem to offer some possibilities—less "remote" possibilities than we were discussing above . . . How would a Christian relate to a theory like this? It seems that one would have to turn his back on Christian theology, if he espoused a theory like this.

AUTHOR: I don't know why it should be incompatible with Christian theology. The Apostle Paul speaks in the New Testament of Christians arising from the dead with a "spiritual" body, different from the former body, and in the biblical account of Jesus' resurrection, we are told that he was able to walk through doors and walls with his body—which seems to imply that the "immortal" body will not be like the other old body.

READER: However, I also seem to recall some other biblical references in which Jesus, after his resurrection, eats food and asks the Apostle Thomas to place his fingers into the wounds in his hands and on his side. Unless the rules for Jesus are radically different from the rules for you and me, this indicates that there are at least remnants of the old kind of body. In fact, if my memory serves me well, I think Jesus even chides his disciples for thinking that he is a "spirit."

AUTHOR: To me, all this seems to reflect a certain ambivalence or conflict in the Christian theology of the resurrection. On the one hand, there is the belief that a resurrected person would have to be freed from the limitations of the body; on the other hand, there is the realization that a body, a *real* body, would have to have *some* material limitations. The theologians have never been able to reconcile these two disparate ideas.

READER: You referred earlier to "spirit" as the concept of a human mind that also had some power to objectify and express itself. There is also a tradition in occultism[18] that some spirits are able to materialize themselves to a greater or lesser degree. A spirit with unusual powers might be able to materialize himself to the point of developing surface resistance (which might explain the two incidents mentioned just above). But a completely materialized spirit would still be spirit.

AUTHOR: It is fortunate that it is not our task to keep Christian theology self-consistent. Ideas like this do at present seem to contradict the traditional Christian belief that the soul at the Last Judgment will assume the same body that it used to have.

READER: The usual Christian notion of death would also be impugned. If we hypothesize an astral body, death is of course not a separation of soul from body, but a departure of the inseparable soul/astral-body *combination* (i.e., "spirit"),[19] a combination that may later return and materialize itself to various degrees.

AUTHOR: Incidentally, this would seem to solve some of the problems we mentioned earlier concerning "time" after death. If we presuppose an astral body with some basic (although different) physical processes and movements, we have a new kind of inner clock for the measurement of time.

READER: I'm still bothered, however, by the problem concerning *place*. What would be the locus of an expired "soul/astral-body" combination? If it is not anywhere traceable in this world, don't we have to presume it is in some "other world"?

AUTHOR: Not necessarily. We could presume that the objective expression (astral body) is some ethereal substance or force field that is not yet detectable by the instruments we have available, but that could be measured or discerned after suitable instruments are perfected.

READER: It seems to me that you would have to have "ethereal" instruments to detect an ethereal body.

AUTHOR: That may be so. I don't know. Maybe there are some microparticles or waves that are sufficiently ethereal when utilized and directed properly to establish the presence of astral bodies. Something like the Russian development of Kirlian photography, which shows and differentiates "auras" in living beings, also might be serviceable in detecting such ethereal effects.

READER: Unless we relegate these "spirits" to somewhere "outside" our universe, we seem to be ending up with a "ghost" theory in which billions of restless spooks are floating around the universe, unable to ascend to their happy hunting grounds.

AUTHOR: Yes. Unless we presume that the happy hunting grounds are somewhere within our universe. But wherever they might be, it is important to remember that the essential kernel of the notion of a "heaven" in most of the world's great religions is a belief in the attainability of a state of complete inner self-realization, intellective actualization, and control over matter. (For example, Jesus says quite specifically, "the kingdom of heaven is within you.") It is a tradition in many of the world's religions that some sort of process of purification has to be undergone by the soul before it can attain to this state of inner bliss; and thus we are told that the deceased but still unpurified spirit will hover about the material things or places that it used to hanker after inordinately, without being able to tear itself away to attain its higher destiny (perhaps the Christian notion of hell is related to this sort of predicament).

READER: Let us suppose that a spirit *has* been duly purified. Where would it go? I mean, would it be proper to raise the question of place? Are we to conceive of heaven (or the happy hunting ground) as a definite physical place somewhere in the universe? Or will any place do, so long as one has attained inner bliss and perfection?

AUTHOR: The normal physical body takes in necessary energy largely through food, water, oxygen, and heat. If there were some astral body that did not require food, etc., it might be able to imbibe energy directly from light or some other energy source; and I presume it might gravitate upward into the stratosphere where these resources are more abundant.

READER: I hope it has a good sense of direction . . . Actually, I think you are drawing a rather bleak and dreary picture—all those lonely, forlorn spirits soaring around the galaxies, maybe meeting a kindred spirit every million years or so . . . I think that many people, contemplating this conception of immortality, would say, "Well, maybe death's not so bad after all," or even, "Stop the immortality, I want to get off!"

AUTHOR: The bleakness of the picture is not entirely my fault. The tradition in Western philosophy (as well as in Christianity) has been to consider immortality as an individual matter, each "soul" enjoying some sort of private bliss, with possibly some concomitant awareness of the state of other spirits. But we need not conceive immortality in this individualistic way. We could just as easily conceive individual spirits as participating in some collective mind[20] and/or contributing to some Teilhardian collective consciousness.[21]

READER: I still have some social instincts and would not be totally against this hypothesis (although I consider it improbable). But what happens to your supreme collective spirit-consciousness when the world ends? Science tells us that because of entropic processes we are heading towards the inexorable death of the universe, i.e., when energy in usable forms will have been completely depleted. This scientific viewpoint coincides to some extent, of course, with the Christian expectation that there will be some sort of final cataclysmic destruction of the universe. Even energy in the form of light and heat will have been completely used up. What will then be the fate of our hypothesized spirit-community?

AUTHOR: If it so happened that all energy were to be completely used up, I suppose that would be the end of our friends the spirits. But perhaps—I don't want to build up your hopes too high—perhaps these spirits, properly purified, would have gained possession of and control over some supreme inner energy source, making them independent of ordinary physical energy. It may be that with the gradual diminution of physical energy there are inversely proportional increases of the energy of consciousness (what Teilhard calls "radial energy")[22] in the universe. Such a concentration of inner energy may gradually attain a certain independence of its own, subsist in its own way, and perhaps at the end of solar and stellar time (provided the spirits' control over matter is complete) be able to materialize a universe to the spirits' own liking out of the "dead" matter left over from the previous universe, producing matter out of energy, perhaps using some adaptation of Einstein's $E = mc^2$. Thus we would pass from the present situation in which the inner is at the mercy of the outer, to an exactly converse situation in which the outer is under the absolute control of the inner. I guess this must sound like science fiction to you.

READER: Not science fiction. It sounds curiously similar to the old-fashioned idea of God.

AUTHOR: Perhaps you are right. The idea of a supreme inner source of energization at least bears a resemblance to the Holy Spirit in the Christian tradition or the divine Aum in the Hindu tradition, or even to the Aristotelian definition of God as "thought-energy."[23] (But I certainly don't see the need for hypostatizing this idea into a personal, transcendent God.) All I really wanted was to suggest that there may be some formidable spirit, in man and among men, that could *eventually* develop an independent and absolute power of its own.

READER: You realize of course that, at our present state of knowledge, this is a purely gratuitous speculation. Why on earth would one want to believe such an hypothesis? Why unnecessarily make life more difficult or more complex than it already is by projecting future states of perfection aeons away from "spaceship earth"?

AUTHOR: A belief in the possibility of something is a prerequisite for its attainment. For example, if I do not believe I can run a mile in four minutes, I will most likely never do it; in fact I will probably never try. If I believe I might be able to do it, however, I open up the possibility that I may do it. If I *really* believe I cannot understand X, I will probably not make a sincere effort to do so, and I will end up with the very lack of understanding that I predicted. But if I believe I might be able to understand X, I may end up understanding it. Likewise, there may be some latent reserves of energy in the human psyche that are capable of being actualized only by those who believe that these reserves are there and are willing to engage in a patient and diligent search for them.[24]

READER: But even the "leap of faith" should not be taken on the basis of purely arbitrary conjectures about extremely distant goals. The wise man looks intently where he is going, *before* he leaps. If you don't mind, I will stand back and forebear a little longer.

AUTHOR: I am not going to push you over, but one should be careful not to fall into an abyss by failing to leap to the other side in time.

Epilogue: A Return to the Beginning—What Is Man?

At the outset of this book, we began by looking for a clear-cut definition of man, a definition that would effectively distinguish man from all other animal species. We found only approximations of what we sought—unless we want to call the very general, unobservable, and hardly clear-cut "power of reflection on self" a "distinction," and thus stretch language to its limits. As a result, we began to have intimations that there may be some existential reasons why man, who can come up with workable definitions for so many things in the universe, may not be able to perform the same service for himself. Perhaps man may even be described—dare we say "defined"?—as a being in the process of defining and redefining himself.

The subsequent chapters in this book may be taken as further steps toward this definition (or redefinition). Man is the animal who is resigned to death, but also can conceive the possibility of transcending death; who is limited to the five senses, but also can go beyond them; who is a product of organic evolution, but at the same time has the audacity to want to control evolution; who is conscious of a duality, even a plurality, in his nature, but is nevertheless able to attain an experience of unity completely beyond the reach of other animals; who is controlled by every conceivable kind of external and internal necessity, but by his understanding of, and adaptation to, or countercontrol of these necessities is able to attain a high degree of individual and social freedom.

If these statements seem paradoxical, it may be because man himself is a paradox, and a paradox (as contrasted with a straightforward, univocal, scientifically respectable definition) is a statement that in its very formulation shows dissatisfaction with itself and attempts to say more than can be said.

Notes

CHAPTER 1

1. H. Munroe Fox, *The Personality of Animals* (London: Penguin, 1952), p. 108.
2. Ibid., pp. 25–27.
3. Mortimer Alder, *The Difference of Man and the Difference it Makes* (Cleveland: Meridian, 1967). Adler defines a "difference in kind" as a complete dissimilarity in behavior or characteristics, e.g., the different skeletal structures of vertebrates and invertebrates, the different modes of reproduction of mammals as compared with birds. A "difference in degree," on the other hand, is characterized by manifest similarity amid differences, e.g., the difference in speed of two quadrupeds, the difference in length of two reptiles. It should be noted that a "difference in kind" of a specific type of behavior or a specific characteristic implies that *no* instance of that behavior or characteristic be found in one animal, while another animal with which he is being compared *does* manifest that behavior or that characteristic.
4. Duane Rumbaugh and Timothy V. Gill, "Language and the Acquisition of Language-Type Skills by a Chimpanzee," *The Annals of the New York Academy of Sciences* 270 (Apr. 28, 1976): 90–123.
5. A "designator" is a word that is used to refer to a real object, e.g., the word *banana* referring to a real banana.
6. See Mortimer Adler, et al., "A Symposium on Language and Communication," in *The Great Ideas Today* (the 1975 yearbook for subscribers to *The Great Books of the Western World,* published by the Encyclopedia Britannica, Inc., Chicago), p. 83.
7. Ibid., p. 85 n.
8. In the absence of such a clear-cut distinction, one would have to suspect that the main "distinction" between man and other animals is just the fact that man is so extraordinarily conceited that he considers himself different from, i.e., superior to, the "brute" animals. In this case, the feeling of conceit would be a distinguishing characteristic, but it would constitute at most a difference in degree, since animals may be presumed to have sentiments corresponding to conceit or pride also.
9. As a case in point, I noticed a short time ago, through my peripheral vision, that my cat had been staring intently at me for quite a long period of time. When I turned to look at her directly, she immediately looked the other way and began scratching ("grooming"), *as if* to hide a feeling of self-conscious embarrassment.
10. Supposing, of course, that man is still evolving. Some anthropologists deny that he is.

CHAPTER 2

1. In *The Personality of Animals* (London: Penguin, 1952), H. Munroe Fox describes the first twenty days of the life of the worker bee:

As soon as a worker bee has come out of her pupal skin she dries and cleans herself.

After that, she cleans out the wax cell in the comb in which she spent her youth as grub and pupa. ... At the end of three days the worker begins a different job, that of feeding grubs in their cells. ... Next she sucks up nectar from the mouths of older workers who have flown out from the hive, collected the sweet liquid from flowers, and brought it home. ... The worker also takes pollen, which has been brought home by older workers attached to their legs, and packs it into other storage cells. ... After a day or two at this job, the worker acts for a short time as a dustman; she carries dirt outside the hive. After that again, the worker produces wax. ... After this job is finished, the worker may still have one more duty to do in the hive. This is to be guardian at the door. ... Lastly, on her twentieth day out of the pupa, the worker starts flying out of the hive to collect nectar and pollen from flowers and bring this food back to the hive. (pp. 132 ff.)

2. H. Munroe Fox, ibid., p. 140.

3. Natural selection may be defined nontechnically as the favored development of the species or members of species that are best fitted to meet the challenges of the environment in which they find themselves.

4. Cp., Maria Montessori, *The Absorbent Mind* (New York: Dell, 1967), "Only after repeated experiments did we conclude with certainty that all children are endowed with this capacity to 'absorb' culture. ... We discovered that education is not something the teacher does, but that it is a natural process which develops spontaneously in the human being." (pp. 7–8) "The same instinct that makes children defend their spiritual privacy—the obedience they give to the mysterious guiding voice that each seems to hear within himself—this same instinct leads them to submit their work to an external authority, so as to be sure they are following in the right path." (Ibid., p. 274)

5. For fairly readable expositions of these theories, see Noam Chomsky's *Language and Mind* (New York: Harcourt Brace Jovanovich, 1972) and *Reflections on Language* (New York: Pantheon, 1976). In *Rules and Representations* (New York: Columbia University Press, 1980), Chomsky offers further defenses for his basic hypothesis that language is attributable to an innate mechanism, as well as other aspects of his theory.

CHAPTER 3

1. Cf. Anne Anastasi, *Differential Psychology* (New York: Macmillan, 1958), pp. 68–69.

2. Androsterone and etiocholanolone are two chemicals produced in the urine of males when the male hormone, testosterone, is broken down by the body. For Sidney Margolese's studies of homosexuals, see "Androsterone/Etiocholanolone Ratios in Male Homosexuals," *Hormones and Behavior* 1:151 (1970):207–210, and "Homosexuality: A New Endocrine Correlate," *Medical Journal* 3:207 (1973): 151–155. For Kallmann's genetic studies, see F. J. Kallmann, "Twins and Susceptibility to Overt Male Homosexuality" in the *American Journal of Human Genetics* 4 (1952): 136–46.

3. See Jensen's "How Much Can We Boost I.Q. and Scholastic Achievement?" in the *Harvard Educational Review* (Winter, 1969).

4. Jensen admits that environmental deprivation has had some cumulative effects on performance on IQ tests, at least in certain areas of the United States; see

"Heredity and Environment, but Not Race, Found to Influence Intelligence," *The Chronicle of Higher Education* (Sept. 12, 1977): 5. However, a later book by Jensen, *Bias in Mental Testing* (New York: Free Press, 1980) reiterates his earlier contention that the IQ gap of blacks is genetically caused. This book also marshalls a massive array of data in defense of culture-reduced (i.e., culture-fair) IQ tests as the "great equalizers" in contemporary education. According to Jensen, the use of culture-reduced tests has been the key to raising the general level of education and opportunity for all disadvantaged minorities except blacks, and has also been instrumental in identifying individual gifted blacks who otherwise would have been lost in the shuffle because of their low achievement as a result of environmental handicaps. Jensen also argues that IQ scores are useful in the study of juvenile delinquency, since an IQ of 70–90 is positively correlated with male delinquency regardless of race.

5. William James, *Pragmatism: A New Name for Some Old Ways of Thinking* (New York: Longmans, Green & Co., 1907), p. 9.

6. It should be emphasized that Pastore's definitions of *liberalism*, etc. are from the viewpoint of a Western democratic system of government, and more specifically from the viewpoint of a hypothetical "middle-of-the-roader" within that system. Many who pride themselves on being "conservatives" or "libertarians" within the United States system claim that it is conservatism that is carrying on the "true liberal" tradition of minimizing government control. It would be a complex semantic enterprise indeed to translate such terms as *conservative* and *liberal* as they might be used by persons outside the system (e.g., communists) in speaking of their own system or ours.

7. See William Sheldon, *The Varieties of Temperament* (New York: Harper & Row, 1942) p. 29.

8. See H.J. Eysenck, *The Structure of Human Personality* (London: Methuen, 1953).

9. Theodosius Dobzhansky, *Man Evolving* (New Haven: Yale University Press, 1962).

CHAPTER 4

1. In other words, at this stage both male and female embryos contain: (a) identical external genital tubercles that will develop either into a penis plus scrotum or into a clitoris plus labia; and (b) both male and female reproductive ducts, one of which will degenerate and give precedence to the other. Although this interpretation of the early embryonic stages as "physically bisexual" is the majority opinion, this view has been challenged by Mary Sherfey, M.D., in *The Nature and Evolution of Female Sexuality* (New York: Vintage Press, 1973). Sherfey offers evidence that the fetus in the early stages is always female, but may become male by the infusion of androgen at a certain critical stage of development. Since some psychoanalytic theories (e.g., Freud's) are based on the presupposition of initial bisexuality, it is interesting to conjecture the psychological implications of Sherfey's theory, if it is substantiated.

2. Anne Anastasi, *Differential Psychology* (New York: Macmillan, 1958). If, however, a male is less masculine or a female less feminine because of hormonal variations, we cannot immediately conclude that the individual is homosexual. The

relationship of homosexuality to hormonal variations is still a matter of dispute. Some claim there is no relationship whatsoever.

3. L. M. Terman and C. C. Miles, *Sex and Personality: Studies in Masculinity and Femininity* (New York: McGraw-Hill, 1936). Note that no conclusions are drawn here as to whether these differences are innate or environmentally conditioned.

4. Sigmund Freud, *Civilization and Its Discontents,* tr. James Strachey (New York: Norton, 1962), p. 52 n.

5. Oswald Schwartz, see *The Psychology of Sex* (Baltimore: Penguin, 1949), Ch. 8.

6. Immanuel Kant, *Observations on the Feeling of the Beautiful and the Sublime,* tr. John T. Goldthwait (Berkeley: University of California Press, 1957), pp. 57, 58, 62.

7. Søren Kierkegaard, *The Concept of Dread,* tr. Walter Lowrie, (Princeton: Princeton University Press, 1957), pp. 57, 58, 62.

8. See Søren Kierkegaard, *Either/Or,* tr. Walter Lowrie (Princeton: Princeton University Press, 1971), pp. 424, 425. Also H.P. Kainz, "The Relationship of Dread to Spirit in Man and Woman, according to Kierkegaard," in *Women in Modern Philosophy,* edited by Martha L. Osborne (New York, 1979)

9. Simone de Beauvoir, *The Second Sex* (New York: Bantam, 1961), pp. xvii, 59, 410. See also H. Kainz, "A Non-Marxian Application of the Hegelian Master-Slave Dialectic to Some Modern Politico-Social Developments," in *Idealistic Studies* 3:3 (September 1973): 295, 296.

10. For a technical discussion of this, see H.P. Kainz, *Hegel's Phenomenology* [of Spirit], *Part I: Analysis and Commentary* (University, Ala.: The University of Alabama Press, 1976), pp. 30, 69, 141.

11. In the position he takes in the *Symposium* Plato stands in sharp contrast both to Aristotle, whose views concerning the innate inferiority of women prevailed in Western psychology until modern times (see Christine Garside, "Can a Woman be Good in the Same Way as a Man?" in *Dialogue* 10:3 [September 1971]: 534, 544), and to the long-standing Christian (Pauline) tradition that interprets the creation story in Genesis as implying that while men are made "in the image of God," women are made in "the image of man" (see Mary Daly, *The Church and the Second Sex* [New York: Harper & Row, 1953]). In the *Republic* Plato also proposed a revolutionary (for his times) concept of social and political equality in an ideal state. However, Plato was no pioneer "feminist" in our sense of the word; we can also find references to women in his writings that clearly reflect the decisive male dominance in ancient Greek culture.

12. Karl Marx, *Economic and Philosophic Manuscripts of 1844,* edited by D.J. Struik (New York: International Publishers, 1964), p. 134.

13. For a further and speculative discussion of the possible sociopolitical ramifications of changes in the relationship between the sexes, see H.P. Kainz, *The Unbinding of Prometheus: Towards a Philosophy of Revolution* (Roslyn Heights, N.Y.: Libra, 1976), Chapter III(b).

14. Currently, the term *androgyny* is sometimes used to connote this rather negative movement toward "unisex," but so long as the term has not yet been appropriated or copyrighted and still has some plasticity, I would like to suggest that it be taken to refer to a positive ideal that all should aim at, perhaps even as a gauge of personal maturity. *Androgyny* in this sense means simply the ability to

manifest "opposite-sex" characteristics comfortably and naturally and without sacrificing or detracting from the characteristics associated with one's own sex. The end result, of course, would be the avoidance of stereotypes—the rough-hewn male who winces at any display of emotionality and prides himself on his ignorance of art; the fearful female who can only face the world when shielded by "her man," who feels completely unprepared to converse about anything nondomestic; etc. Some psychologists say that androgyny in this sense is a characteristic of those in the higher IQ brackets, but this does not necessarily mean that it requires a higher IQ. It may only mean that those with higher IQs may acquire androgyny more easily (just as they may acquire many other goods and blessings in life more easily). It is noteworthy that Sigmund Freud always stressed the importance in humans of hormonal bisexuality as a biological fact that must be taken into account in personality formation; and that his most famous disciple, Carl Jung, though eventually renouncing many points of Freudian theory, retained this emphasis on bisexuality and even hypothesized that the perfection and individuation of the personality *required* a state of syzygy—the unification of the male and female sexual polarities (which he called animus and anima) within the psyche. An American psychologist who tried to isolate and measure what we have called androgyny is William Sheldon, who in his *The Varieties of Temperament* (New York: Harper & Row, 1942) reports that he and his fellow researchers took "gynandrophenia" (which he describes, on page 286, as "the strength of the 'sissy' element in the male, and of masculinity in the female") as one "positive" temperamental trait, among others. We may be even more positive than Sheldon and note, with Jung et al., that it is the mark of a mature person to be able to combine traits that may *seem* to predominate in this or that sex—rationality *and* feeling, initiative *and* altruism, etc.

15. "Baconian" insofar as it is in line with Francis Bacon's influential recommendation to modern science to seize nature by the throat and "force it to give up its secrets." With a similar if not equal logic, this orientation could conceivably be extended to genetic as well as to environmental variables, but feminists have concentrated on the manipulation of environmental conditions. There are at least two possible reasons for this. First, genetic variables are thought to be less subject to control than environmental variables—an opinion, be it noted, that is becoming less defensible with each new advance in modern genetics. Second, because past traditions that feminists are now opposing were bolstered by biological and genetic arguments for male superiority, feminists are inclined to be distrustful of such arguments in general, even when the genetic evidence appears to support feminist positions on the issues in dispute. Unfortunately, in thus emphasizing (and perhaps overemphasizing) environmental determination of personality, while deemphasizing (and perhaps underemphasizing) the physical (biological, genetic, etc. determinants), feminists may seem to put themselves in a class with those who think "that any soul could be clothed upon with any body—an absurd view. . . . as absurd as to say that the art of carpentry could embody itself in flutes" (Aristotle, *De Anima*, 1, 3).

It should be noted that not all feminists display this strong affinity for environmentalism to the virtual exclusion of all else. And there is even a small minority of "feminists" who champion so-called traditional womanhood and tend to emphasize woman's "uniquely feminine" traits amidst numerous cultural and environmental changes. An apologetic for this latter type of feminism can be found in

A. Stassinopoulos' *The Female Woman* (New York: Random House, 1973). But Germaine Greer's *The Female Eunuch* (New York: McGraw-Hill, 1971) was the apologetic and inspiration for the more widespread feminist movements of the 1970s.

CHAPTER 5

1. Pierre Teilhard de Chardin, *The Phenomenon of Man* (New York: Harper Torchbooks, 1959).

2. Oswald Schwartz, *The Psychology of Sex* (Middlesex: Penguin, 1949).

3. Carl Jung, *Modern Man in Search of Soul* (New York: Vintage, 1966), pp. 132, 140. Jung is here summarizing some of the theories of Lucien Lévy-Bruhl.

4. Teilhard de Chardin, *The Future of Man* (New York: Harper & Row, 1964), p. 249.

5. *Les Structures elementaires de la parente*. Quoted by Simone de Beauvoir, in *The Second Sex* (New York: Bantam, 1961), p. xvii.

6. See Schwartz, op. cit., p. 160.

7. Teilhard de Chardin, *The Phenomenon of Man*, III, 3.

8. For example, Teilhard theorizes that it was a state of extreme tension and compression among "megamolecules" in a milieu of water that brought about the production of the first cell or cells; and that it was at a critical juncture, i.e., when nomadic anthropoids could no longer sustain themselves by hunting, that a more settled and organized form of life became necessary for primitive man (*Homo agricola*).

9. See Charles Reich, *The Greening of America* (New York: Random House, 1970).

10. See Marshall McLuhan, *Understanding Media* (New York: Signet, 1964).

11. See Henri Bergson, *The Two Sources of Morality and Religion* (London: Macmillan & Co., 1935).

12. Because human consciousnesses are free, they may choose *not* to enter into this "collective consciousness" and thus may become divergent rather than convergent.

13. Teilhard de Chardin, *The Phenomenon of Man*, p. 251. Compare the following speculative passage from Lewis Thomas' *The Lives of a Cell* (New York: Viking Press, 1974), pp. 167–168:

> Maybe the thoughts we generate today and flick around from mind to mind, like the jokes that turn up simultaneously at dinner parties in Hong Kong and Boston, or the sudden changes in the way we wear our hair, or all the popular love songs, are primitive precursors of more complicated, polymerized structures that will come later, analogous to the prokaryotic cells that drifted through shallow pools in the early days of biological evolution. Later, when the time is right, there may be fusion and symbiosis among the bits, and then we will see eukaryotic thought, metazoans of thought, huge interliving coral shoals of thought.

14. For a contemporary Indian version of the idea of a transcendent unity of mankind, with particular reference to evolution and consciousness, see part three of *The Essential Aurobindo* (New York: Schocken, 1973), by Sri Aurobindo (Aurobindo Ghose, 1872–1950).

CHAPTER 6

1. A monist denies the dualism of mind (or soul) and body by reducing mind to matter (materialistic monism); or by reducing body to mind (idealistic monism); or by reducing mind-body problems to problems about mentalistic vs. physicalistic language about mind and body as two aspects of the same thing (double-aspect theory). A dualist has the problem of explaining how mind and body are related. He does this by looking upon consciousness as perhaps an epiphenomenon connected with and dependent on physical events; or perhaps as requiring synchronization by God (occasionalism); or perhaps as inherently synchronized without any need for divine interference (parallelism); or perhaps as involved in continual reciprocal interaction.

2. The term *nonmaterialist* embraces all idealists, some empiricists, and some rationalists. For a technical discussion of these categories, see Carl Jung, *Psychological Types* (Princeton: Princeton University Press, 1976), Chapter 8.

3. See Aristotle's *On the Soul,* II, 1, 2; III, 5.

4. It should be noted that I am using the terms *mind* and *soul* in accord with the usages of the authors we are considering and without drawing any sharp distinction of my own between the two terms. As I will point out toward the end of the chapter, however, there *is* an important distinction to be made between the two terms—a distinction to which none of the authors mentioned in this historical survey gave explicit recognition.

5. Søren Kierkegaard, *Sickness unto Death,* tr. Walter Lowrie (New York: Doubleday Anchor, 1954).

6. The fact that this is an extreme oversimplification becomes especially apparent if our logical behaviorist seriously tries to *think about* all the neural processes in the brain that he supposes are identical with his act of thinking. To state that the act-of-thinking-about-one's-neural-processes is identical with those neural processes themselves would either be meaningless, or would imply that the neural processes think about themselves!

7. See William James' *Psychology: A Briefer Course* (New York: Fawcett, 1963), Chapter 12.

8. See Immanuel Kant's *Critique of Pure Reason,* "Transcendental Aesthetic" and "Transcendental Analytic."

9. We are speaking here about "space" on the level of ordinary experience, and in those areas of science that are still conceived in Newtonian fashion. On the level of relativity physics and quantum theory as applied, e.g., to subatomic particles, special problems—which have not yet been solved—emerge because of reactions that seem to go against ordinary laws of momentum, position in space, causality, etc., and because physicists on this level seem to be dealing more with equations and probabilities than with ordinary "first-order" phenomena.

10. The choice of mind-body causality as the prime analogate or paradigmatic example of causality seems to be dictated if and only if we (a) consider the mind-body relationship as a bona fide duality and (b) look upon this duality as *bridgeable,* i.e., such that one pole can come into contact with the other and modify it in some way. An extreme materialist would have to take ordinary causal relations between physical objects as his prime analogate and judge anything that seemed to represent an effect of mind on body or vice versa only insofar as it could be

interpreted in terms of these ordinary relationships. The extreme idealist would have to take the causal relationships of the mind (e.g., syllogistic reasoning) as his prime analogate and consider everything else that appears to be a cause-effect sequence only insofar as it conformed to, or was reducible to, the causal sequence of ideal constructs or ideal entities.

11. A similar distinction between *mind* and *soul* is employed by Hannah Arendt in her book *Thinking* (New York: Harcourt Brace Jovanovich, 1977), pp. 33, 34, 73.

CHAPTER 7

1. One might also argue, however, that if society wished to heap senseless moral recrimination on people who had no freedom, society, which *also* had no freedom, could not really be blamed for so doing.

2. The assertion that a mental operation, such as willing, can be the cause of physical actions raises some further problems. See Chapter 6.

3. Plato, *Timaeus,* 86E, 87B.

4. The distinction to be made here is between "could have chosen" as a logical possibility, etc., and "could have chosen" as an actual, demonstrable power of an individual. It is the latter that causes most problems.

5. See William James' *Psychology: A Briefer Course* (New York: Fawcett, 1963), Chapter 26.

6. Perhaps, taking note of the findings of modern psychology, we should add the proviso that the person performing such "benevolent" acts must be neither a masochist nor what Erich Fromm calls the neurotically "selfless" type of person. For a discussion of the moral ramifications of this problem, see H. Kainz, *Ethica Dialectica* (Nijhoff: The Hague, 1979), p. 25 f.

7. If the person saved were a relation or a friend, the maternal, paternal, filial instincts, the herd instinct, or the sense of kinship might influence one's sacrifice of one's life.

8. For a discussion of this problem, see *Ethica Dialectica,* p. 26.

9. Immanuel Kant, in his *Preface to a Metaphysics of Morals* and his *Critique of Practical Reason,* conjectures that religious motives (e.g., the imitation of Christ, obedience to God's will, the hope for eternal happiness) may be a detriment to morality and hence an obstacle to freedom. He grants that we may believe in these things, but he objects to our taking them as motives for moral actions. (He doesn't tell us much about how we can accomplish the difficult task of keeping our beliefs and our motives apart.) Christian theologians such as Thomas Aquinas would admit that we can be determined by the idea of a supreme reward, but would deny that such determination would be incompatible with our own self-determination. If, says Aquinas, we are determined by our idea of the supreme good, or happiness, this still does not contradict our freedom, since all our attempts at freedom (and not *just* the idea of eternal reward) stem naturally from our idea of ultimate happiness.

10. It is necessary to distinguish here between the Socrates who went around trying to inculcate a definitional knowledge of virtue (this is the Socrates chiefly portrayed by Plato in his dialogues), and the Socrates who, in his personal life, claimed to have an instinctive ability to differentiate good from evil, and who found it very hard to believe that other men did not also have and follow a similar

"voice." Plato, reinterpreting Socrates, emphasizes a theoretical knowledge of "the Good," which is supposed to liberate the intellectual and those with whom the intellectual shares this theoretical knowledge. But Socrates, by his example, emphasized a concrete, experiential knowledge, as an intuitive basis that might be further explicated into theoretical knowledge.

11. An example of this position is to be found in contemporary Sartrean existentialism, in which we are exhorted to avoid the temptation of considering ourselves a thing at the prey of external or internal natural forces, and to rise to the awareness that we ourselves are the absolute origin of our acts (Sartre calls this latter state "good faith," the former state "bad faith").

12. See H. Kainz, *Hegel's Philosophy of Right, with Marx's Commentary* (The Hague: Nijhoff, 1974), p. 15; and H. Kainz, *The Unbinding of Prometheus: Towards a Philosophy of Revolution* (Roslyn Heights, N.Y.: Libra, 1976), Chapter II(d).

13. Our theory of freedom may possibly determine the degree of freedom that we attain in practice. For example, if we believe (like Hobbes) that our freedom consists at best in unimpeded activity, we may be prevented by our own dim view of human potentialities from attaining a higher degree of freedom that would actually be within the scope of our possibilities. Conversely, our definition of freedom may be conditioned by the breadth and intensity of the experience of freedom that we happen to have had in practical life.

14. The compatibility of freedom and "determination by the best" may be illustrated by an example from the sphere of romantic love. A person pondering the respective merits of a number of possible spouses will, unless unduly influenced by extrinsic considerations, almost invariably choose to "be determined" by the one who seems to be most likely to respect and foster his own individuality.

CHAPTER 8

1. See H. Kainz, *Hegel's Phenomenology, Part I: Analysis and Commentary* (University: The University of Alabama Press, 1976), pp. 62 ff.

2. A report by Kravitz, Goldenberg, and Neyhus on their studies of tactile exploration in one hundred normal infants was presented at a meeting of the American Academy of Pediatrics (Section on Child Development) in 1972.

3. William James, *Psychology: A Briefer Course* (New York: Fawcett, 1963), p. 28. This classic textbook, first published in 1892, is still one of the best ever written.

4. Conversely, we might also say that the inability to focus is a "cause" contributing to the confused awareness.

5. Two other considerations tend to corroborate this same conclusion. First, some researchers have determined that the child begins to show some initial special reactions to his own image in the mirror at just about the age of nine months (see *Social Cognition and the Acquisition of Self,* by Michael Lewis and Jeanne Brooks-Gunn [New York: Plenum, 1981]). Second, Jean Piaget, in *The Psychology of Intelligence* (London: Routledge & Paul, 1950), shows that it is only at about the eighth or ninth month that an infant begins to have a concept of objects existing permanently and independently of his own awareness. Prior to that time, infants will not actively search out unseen objects or give any indication that they know objects remain when they (the infants) are not present. This gives us indirect evidence that a self-concept must also be emerging at the same time, inasmuch as

the idea of the permanence of objects requires as a corollary an idea of the independence and permanence of the self from which the objects are distinguished and to which the objects are related as a "constant."

6. It is not possible in this chapter to go into a detailed analysis of romantic love. For our purposes here, it can be defined as a sexual love that is neither merely physical nor purely spiritual (i.e., Platonic) but combines aspects of both. See Chapter 10.

CHAPTER 9

1. Some translation of terminology is necessary here. In English, *happiness* can mean either subjective satisfaction or an objective state of perfection (*felicity*); and while both these meanings are implied by Aristotle, his emphasis is on the objective state, which is close to the connotation of *maturity*. Since in ordinary language we tend to construe *happiness* in the more subjective of its meanings, a more objective-sounding word, such as *fulfillment*, might be substituted for *happiness* in this instance.

2. *Hostility* is not a problem here. One who is hostile is definitely taking notice of me.

3. Sometimes the attraction for one object (or person) is related to a corresponding repulsion for another object (or person); at other times the attraction will be for one aspect of the object while the repulsion will be for another aspect of the same object—a more complex psychological experience. The important thing for our analysis here is that it is the existence of strong attraction or repulsion that shows that a relationship has been set up; if there is only indifference or unawareness, on the other hand, the relevant existential relationship has not yet been established.

4. On this subject, see Carl Jung, *Modern Man in Search of a Soul* (New York: Vintage, 1966), Chapter 5.

5. *Maturity* as construed in this way is analogous to the Aristotelian concept of *virtue*. In his *Nicomachean Ethics* Aristotle characterizes virtue as a mean between the extremes, e.g., the virtue of temperance is a mean between the extremes of overindulgence and "insensibility" (underindulgence), and the virtue of courage is a mean between foolhardiness and cowardice. In the terminology we have developed in this chapter, Aristotle's "man of courage" would be tempering his attraction for noble challenges with a repugnance for unnecessary risk-taking, and so forth.

6. See Maya Pines' article, "Superkids," in *Psychology Today* (January, 1979).

CHAPTER 10

1. There are formidable difficulties in the way of our knowing knowledge—let alone love!—and the following analogy may help to illustrate this. Ludwig Wittgenstein, in his *Tractatus Logico-philosophicus* (1921), gives the example of a person who sets up an elaborate series of mirrors in order to try to catch his own eye in the act of seeing. However, even if some arrangement of mirrors and microscopes enabled us to catch a glimpse of the movements in our eyes, the movements that we saw would not be the same as the act of seeing that saw those

movements. Likewise, it may be impossible for us, in self-reflection, ever to "know" clearly our actual acts of knowledge. We would only really know, for example, certain bodily processes that preceded and led up to, or effects that followed from, the act of knowledge. Both in the case of knowledge-of-knowledge and knowledge-of-love, our subsequent attempts at conceptual clarification will necessarily be conditioned by that inevitable initial lack of concreteness and stability in our "object."

2. Some contemporary philosophers (e.g., Sartre) object to what they call the "eating analogy," i.e., descriptions of knowledge in terms of "assimilation." They would like to emphasize that in all acts of knowing we go out to, we extend ourselves toward, the object to be known. But one could argue that this movement-toward-the-object (called "intentionality") is reducible to the initial attraction for the object, i.e., a function of love (in this case, the love-of-knowledge—an ambiguous example of knowledge, and also of love).

3. It is a presupposition with Thomas Aquinas that knowledge and love are to a great extent independent operations. Thus, I can have an impressive knowledge of something and yet not love it; on the other hand, a person could have an extraordinary love for something while knowing almost nothing about it.

4. Erich Fromm, *The Art of Loving* (New York: Bantam, 1963), Chapter 2.

5. Oswald Schwartz, *The Psychology of Sex* (Baltimore: Penguin, 1949), Chapter 7.

6. Ignace Lepp, *The Psychology of Loving* (New York: Mentor, 1965).

7. Sigmund Freud, *The Ego and the Id,* tr. Jacques Riviere (New York: Norton, 1962), pp. 30–33.

8. Ibid., p. 31.

9. I am speaking about romantic love in its more positive and idealistic sense. As Shirley Letwin points out in "Romantic Love and Christianity" (*Philosophy,* April 1977), another more negative connotation of romantic love has evolved right along with the idealistic one, ever since the concept of romantic love originated in the Western Christian world.

10. Op. cit., Chapter 2.

11. A further development of this basic idea regarding love and knowledge would involve corollaries concerning hate and ignorance. Hate would be characterized as a *distinction*-in-unity (the sort of division that becomes fiercest between those who are similar in their interests, goals, or attributes); and ignorance would be characterized as a distinction-in-*unity* (the illusion of embracing or comprehending an object that really is beyond one's conscious grasp).

12. The presupposition here is that there is a multiplicity of "loves" in an individual, e.g., the love of God, the love of friends, the love of parents for children and vice versa, the love of the opposite sex, the love of knowledge, the love of various pleasure-giving objects (painting, food, music, etc.)—all of which "loves," though manifesting the same "unifying" characteristics, gravitate in different directions and provide potential fodder for intrapsychic conflict, *unless* they are themselves organized and unified on the basis of some naturally more fundamental "second-order" love that is concerned precisely with bringing about intrapsychic harmony or unity. It is possible that some individuals might effect this unity in a hierarchical fashion on the basis of a judgment that certain loves are more important ("higher") than others. But it is also possible that an individual

may consider all legitimate loves, those based on real needs, to be equally important in their own rights and in their appropriate contexts.

13. It is quite conceivable that, even if multiple individuals had successfully made the second-order unification spoken of above, the diversities of emphasis could lead to disorder unless there were some special third-order love (not identifiable with the various first-order loves, e.g., friendship) concerned with obviating such potential disorders. The major manifestation of this love that we are familiar with would be those attempts at sociopolitical structuring that would be oriented toward producing the greatest possible harmony among very diverse human elements. This social structuring would differ from a "love for community" insofar as, while the latter is just one among numerous "first-order" loves, the former would be at least two steps removed from the immediate interests of the monadic individual; in other words, it would be more comprehensive.

14. Cupid, the Roman version of the Greek god Eros, was supposed to be invisible even to his wife, Psyche. Was this the ancients' way of saying that no wife understands her husband or, contrariwise, that every wife can see right through her husband? Probably not, in both cases, but in times like ours one can hardly help wondering.

CHAPTER 11

1. A star, a square, a circle, a cross, and some wavy lines.

2. A probability of "1/1" or the Mean Chance Expectation (MCE) is a score of five hits per run. Normal persons, making several runs through the Zener deck, should be able to average five correct guesses (e.g., if a person went through the deck guessing the "star" symbol each time, this would come up exactly five times). Anything over five hits per run becomes less and less probable, especially if one's record of a high number of hits is sustained over a long period of time. The low probability is particularly significant (according to statistical research in this field) when it is less than 1/5000. For example, a probability of one millionth or below, extended throughout a long series of tests, seems definitely to indicate that the subject whose scores are so improbable has some special ESP ability—provided that there has been no fraud and that other possible explanations have been eliminated.

3. $10^{-70} = 1/10^{70} =$ approximately one-vigintillion.

4. *Psi* is a general term referring to all apparent manifestations of paranormal powers.

5. For those who may wish to delve further into this subject than is possible in this chapter, a good place to begin is Robert H. Ashby's *Guide Book for the Study of Psychical Research* (New York: Weiser, 1972), which lists many of the important books published on Psi during the twentieth century, and provides extensive descriptions of the contents of many of these books. A good introduction is also provided by the various publications of J.B. Rhine, beginning with *Extra-sensory Perception* (London, 1934). Finally, one should be aware of the scholarly journals published in this field, including *The Journal of Parapsychology* (Duke University), the *Journal of the Society for Psychic Research* (SPR) (London), the *Journal of the American SPR* (New York), and the *International Journal of Parapsychology* (New York). To challenge and debunk unwarranted claims of parapsychologists and

psychics, an "antijournal," *The Zetetic* (Buffalo) has been inaugurated by the Committee for the Scientific Investigation of Claims of the Paranormal, headed by philosopher Paul Kurtz.

6. I will refer in this chapter to a number of miracles and prophecies recorded in the Bible simply as apparent examples of ESP or PK, and without necessarily presuming their historical authenticity. However, one should realize a theological risk that one runs in taking this *comparison* seriously. *If* it should turn out that the various forms of Psi are bona fide human powers, and *if* some of the miracles or prophecies of the Bible are bona fide examples of Psi, then these particular miracles or prophecies are no longer "supernatural" in the traditional theological sense. The theologian who became convinced about Psi might have to revise his concept of the "supernatural" as a result (and the philosopher who specializes in astute criticism of the possibility of the supernatural might have to shift his field of specialization accordingly).

7. "The Occident, free from British Isles, Not satisfied, sad rebellion."

8. "The Isles bloodstained for having neglected to arm. Because of the Germans, they and their neighbors around them . . . in wars for control of the clouds."

9. "People will travel safely through the sky."

10. "Live fire will be put in globes . . . will reduce cities to rubble."

11. The relevance or nonrelevance to life of the predictions required of a psychic may even determine his success or lack of it. In independent tests, J.B. Rhine and L.A. Dale showed that the success of a psychic seems to rise and fall in correspondence with his interest and boredom, respectively.

12. This is called the "Down Through" (DT) method. Sometimes the deck of cards is placed behind screens, enclosed in opaque envelopes, or removed to another building.

13. Or the "brain" if, like some behaviorists, you wish to identify the mind with the brain. Presumably, Soviet researchers currently studying telepathy would prefer this definition even though, as we shall see, it presents problems.

14. The probability of maintaining this average for forty successive tries is 10^{-11}, i.e., almost one-trillionth.

15. The most controversial "psychic" in the 1970s was Uri Geller, who claimed to be able to bend spoons by an act of will, to impress photo images on camera film by thought, etc. In 1974 an article was published in the distinguished scientific journal *Nature* reporting favorable results from experiments conducted on Geller under the supervision of physicists at Stanford University. Shortly after publication of this article, however, a British journal, *New Scientist,* published a rebuttal contending that the Stanford experiments were badly planned and therefore inconclusive. One of the most obvious deficiencies in demonstrations and experiments intended to test the authenticity of purported psychics like Geller is the conspicuous absence of professional magicians, who would be able to look for the trickery that is the more-or-less common stock-in-trade of magicians but is almost always undetectable by the layman—including Nobel Prize-winning scientists.

16. All scientific investigations of physical mediums have produced evidence of fraud.

17. The "controlling" spirit often claims to be an Afro-American, Oriental, or Red Indian—on the supposition that "colored" people have more highly developed psychic abilities than white people do.

18. The study of knowledge and truth.

19. The study of the ultimate nature of reality, whether there is anything beyond material reality, etc.

20. G.N.M. Tyrell devised one of the most noteworthy experiments for "pure clairvoyance." He set up a system of boxes with lamps that would light up if the subject opened the lid of the correct box (determined by a switch operated by an assistant who, because of automatic scrambling devices, did not know which lamp he was controlling at any given time). In spite of his success with his subject, Miss G.M. Johnson (26 percent success in 855 trials, $p = 10^{-6}$), we might observe that some human mind devised the "scrambling" mechanism, and that some human mind had to decide which switch to open. Thus Miss Johnson could have arrived at her knowledge by means of double telepathy—an unlikely possibility, but a possibility nevertheless.

21. This is called the "cross-correspondence method."

22. Descriptions of the "afterlife" obtained through the purported mediation of spirits may be found in Bishop James Pike's *The Other Side* (New York: Dell, 1969), in the Afterward; in Jane Roberts' *Seth Speaks*, (Englewood Cliffs, N.J.: Prentice Hall, 1972); and in Yogananda's *Autobiography of a Yoga* (Wehman: Hackensack, N.J., 1971), Chapter 43. The best-known description (obtained through an "angel") is, of course, in the Book of Revelation (Apocalypse) in the New Testament.

23. In tests on PK, it was determined that the effect of distance on the psychic's effectiveness varied directly with the psychic's own belief in the effect of distance.

24. In 1974 an experiment was conducted on "psychic healing," a form of PK in which the psychic by concentration brings about physiological changes (healing) in another person's body. The experiment was conducted by Robert Miller of the Georgia Institute of Technology and Philip Reinhart of Agnes Scott College of Atlanta, Ga. Their subject, a "healer" named Olga Worrall, placed her hands around a cloud chamber and produced wave patterns in the chamber by concentration. She also accomplished the same feat by concentration at a distance of six hundred miles. Since a cloud chamber is supposedly never affected by the proximity of human hands, it would be difficult to devise a scientific explanation for the reaction that took place. See "Research Report," in *Science of Mind* (July 1974): 12 f.

25. James developed no self-consistent theory of this sort; he offered his supposition as a "stab in the dark" to explain things like telepathy.

26. The Arab philosopher Averroes, for example, maintained that there was a collective intellect in which all men unknowingly participated. Teilhard de Chardin's concept of a "collective consciousness" envisions the fully conscious and voluntary participation of individuals in some higher consciousness that is already emerging in mankind (see Chapter 5). Some Oriental philosophies (especially Taoism and Hinduism) also suppose that what we call individual consciousness has broken off from some basic or original unity, and that man's task in life is to recapture, or return to, this unity.

CHAPTER 12

1. In Freud's theory, however, the Ego is a synonym for "consciousness."

2. The *Oxford* emphasizes the fact that *consciousness* involves internal knowledge or conviction, as opposed to uncertainty or mere belief.

3. Soul in its conscious aspects converges with mind. As was mentioned at the

end of Chapter 6, *mind* when used in contradistinction to *soul* connotes causal interaction with the body, while *soul* connotes union. But there can never be a hard and fast distinction between mind and soul, since they are two complementary aspects of the same personality. Thus we should not be surprised that the above distinction is dissolved if and when we consider: (1) that Soul$_1$ in its union with bodily instincts or impulses is thought to share in the causal efficacy of the body on the mind, after the manner of the Freudian Id; and (2) that if Soul$_2$ is thought to be united to some greater entity or force (e.g., God, or a Jungian "collective unconscious," or a Freudian Ego-Ideal as a genetic residue in the human species passed on and further defined and redefined by each generation) it would be thought to share in whatever causal efficacy that greater entity or force might have upon the mind itself. For a further discussion of the relation of Soul$_2$ to a transpersonal Being, see H. Kainz, "The Origin of the Concept of God: A Phenomenological Analysis," *Idealistic Studies* 9:3 (September 1979): 222–28.

4. James Drever's *Dictionary of Psychology* (Baltimore: Penguin, 1952), in congruence, perhaps, with the behavioral orientation of modern psychology, does not include any definition of *soul,* whether animal or human.

5. In the same fashion that a powerful telescope, peering into the stratosphere, would extend man's limits of visibility to a certain horizon.

6. Using the above example, we might presuppose that, somewhere beyond the horizons revealed by our telescope, there were some absolute boundaries containing all other parts of the universe—an absolute receptacle, or an absolute origin.

7. Drever's *Dictionary of Psychology*—perhaps significantly—does not define the word *spirit.*

8. This question caused some difficulties for the medieval thinker Thomas Aquinas. He came to the conclusion that for a human being's mental functions to continue in the absence of a body or a brain it would require an extraordinary but not "supernatural" direct illumination by God.

9. It is necessary, however, to formulate the question here in terms of "soul" rather than "spirit," since the starting point for the discussion of this question in Western philosophy has been a widespread belief in the existence of an independent, separable "soul." Towards the end of this chapter, after an examination and evaluation of this starting point, we will indirectly arrive at a consideration of some of the assets and liabilities of spirit as a starting point.

10. For a more detailed discussion of the kinds of existence, see H. Kainz, *Hegel's Phenomenology, Part I: Analysis and Commentary* (University: The University of Alabama Press, 1976), Conclusion, III.

11. In the ancient (Aristotelian) world, this ultimate cause would be an "unmoved mover" just beyond the outermost periphery of the world. In contemporary cosmogony, the ultimate cause of matter might be considered the hydrogen atom or some smaller particle, and the ultimate source and criterion of motion might be considered light or some aspect of energy. (Obviously, however, there are some big questions remaining about how atoms or light or any material substances could have *created* the universe. Our ideas about a *really* "ultimate" cause are still fuzzy.)

12. He may also be influenced by "mystical" experiences or inspirations, which do not seem to have natural or ordinary causes. These experiences would be

analogous to the "faint noises or rumblings" that we spoke about in commenting on the example of the house.

13. Note that the term *possibility* is not synonymous with *probability*. Note also that there are at least three degrees of possibility: (1) fulfilled or actualized possibilities, e.g., a plan that is implemented; (2) proximate possibilities, e.g., the possibility that if I persevere in thinking I may broaden the sphere of my knowledge; and (3) "mere" possibilities, i.e., remote possibilities, e.g., the possibility that beyond the horizons of my knowledge there may be found an ultimate receptacle (mind or Soul₂), not created by me, which is capable of containing all my ideas ad infinitum. This "mere" possibility, unlike the ideas that I formulate, does not exist in either of the two primary senses adumbrated in the preceding paragraph, but it is nevertheless a "real" possibility because it is natural to suppose that mental phenomena have some mental source. The fact that many people consider it to be more than just a possibility is perhaps due to the subjective experience of illumination or inspiration, which in some people at some times may be so forceful as to suggest some "higher" source for thoughts that do not seem to be attributable to our own activity or to external stimuli.

14. See Chapter 7.

15. If, as was indicated in Chapter 6, the mind is a "cause" of bodily activity in only an analogous sense, a fortiori one would have to say that Soul₂ is a "cause" of mental activity in only some analogous sense. But it is possible to extend the analogy in this way, and de facto we seem to labor under a subjective necessity to think in terms of some sort of causality, analogous or otherwise.

16. See Gerald Myers, *Self: An Introduction to Philosophical Psychology* (New York: Pegasus, 1969), pp. 59–70.

17. The astral-body hypothesis would not only help to explain the continuity between the states before and after bodily death, but would also, along with personal memories, be the key to answering the question about identity ("is this person identical with the person who underwent death?"). In lieu of such a hypothesis, one has the formidable, if not impossible, task of explaining how, at least in cases of complete bodily disintegration (e.g., cremation), a "resurrected" body could be the same as the body that died. Since in this latter case hardly one atom would remain the same, the logical conclusion would seem to be that there is at best a reincarnation here, not a resurrection of the same body.

18. See Chapter 11.

19. As was indicated earlier, *soul* signifies a pole distinct from bodily expression, while *spirit* includes the expression. If the expression of soul is "bodily" in the usual sense of this word, the result is a *person;* if the expression is "bodily" only in some qualified sense, the word *spirit* may be the best way to convey the resulting entity.

At this point, as we begin to explore the "astral-body" hypothesis of survival, it is interesting to note that a number of recent reports on "out-of-body" experiences purportedly undergone by persons who were apparently dead but were later "resuscitated" seem to follow the general pattern that is purely a matter of speculation in our text. The published reports, however, go into much greater detail, and give us some idea of the various "stages" that might be involved if this speculation were correct. According to Raymond A. Moody, M.D., in *Life After Life* (New York: Bantam, 1976), the main "stages" reported are as follows: After "dying," a person begins to hear various noises, e.g., buzzing or ringing sounds, which are usually described as irritating or discomforting. Then he or she feels himself moving through a long enclosure such as a tunnel, cylinder, or "valley." He notices that he can see his own traumatized physical body from a distance, and notices also that he still has a kind of ethereal "body" with the general outlines of head and extremities, but without specific physical features such as hair, fingernails, wrinkles, etc. Then he is met by friends and relatives who have died, and ultimately by a kindly "being of light" who conveys a few probing thoughts inviting the person to reflect on his life. Then a long series of very vivid "flashbacks" begins, starting with significant childhood experiences and leading up to more recent events; and with the help of the "being of light" the individual makes evaluations of, and draws conclusions from, these flashbacks. Finally, some sort of "limit" or boundary line is reached (e.g., a fence, a shore, a line, a bank of fog) that apparently divides this life from something else (perhaps another life). By this time, the person is usually filled with a sense of peace and contentment and is reluctant to return to his former life; but for some reason he either decides or is persuaded to return, or he simply finds himself back in his former body.

These reports are *not* proof of survival after death! Because each person actually "returns" to life there must always be some doubt whether or in what sense he or she actually "died." On the other hand, such reports do *seem* to be the closest thing we have to empirical, if circumstantial, "evidence" of the possibility of survival, and they give us a clear "model" to test for inconsistencies and to examine for suggestive hypotheses.

20. See Chapter 11, end.

21. See Chapter 5, end.

22. See *The Phenomenon of Man*, Book One, II, 3.

23. In the original: *hē nou enérgeia.* See *Metaphysics*, 1072b, 26.

24. The differing possibilities that belief can open up to a person are well illustrated by a story by Rabbi Y.M. Tuckachinsky, which was passed on by Rabbi Samuel K. Joseph in the letters column of *Psychology Today* (July 1977):

> Imagine twins growing peacefully in the warmth of the womb. Their lives are serene. The whole world, to these brothers, is the interior of the womb. Who could conceive of anything larger, better, more comfortable? They begin to wonder: "We are getting lower and lower. Surely if it continues, we will exit one day. What will happen then?"
>
> Now the first infant is a believer, heir to a religious tradition which tells him there will be a "new life" after this warm and wet experience of the womb. A strange belief, seemingly without foundation, but one to which he holds fast. The second infant is a throroughgoing skeptic. Mere stories do not deceive him. What is not within one's experience can have no basis in one's imagination.
>
> Says the faithful brother: "After our 'death' here, there will be a new, great world. We will eat through the mouth! We will see great distances, and we will hear through the ears on the sides of our heads."
>
> Replies the skeptic: "Nonsense. You are looking for something to calm your fear of death. There is only this world. There is no world to come! Our world will collapse and we will sink into oblivion. This may not be a comforting thought, but it is a logical one."
>
> Suddenly the water inside the womb bursts. The womb convulses. Everything lets loose. Then a mysterious pounding—a crushing, staccato pounding. The believing brother exits. Tearing himself from the womb, he falls outward. The second one

shrieks, startled by the accident befallen his brother. He bewails and bemoans the tragedy. As he thus laments, he hears a head-splitting cry, and a great tumult from the black abyss, and he trembles: "Oh my! What a horrible end. As I predicted."

Meanwhile, as the skeptic brother mourns, his "dead" brother has been born into the new world. The cry is a sign of health and vigor, and the tumult is a chorus of mazel tovs sounded by the waiting family, for the birth of a healthy son.

Indeed, man comes from the darkness of the "not yet" and proceeds to the darkness of the "no more." While it is difficult to imagine the "not yet," it is more difficult to imagine the "no more."

Glossaries

GLOSSARY OF NAMES

The following glossary is intended to provide students with a convenient source of reference about some of the persons mentioned or discussed in the text. The entries are not intended to be comprehensive or encyclopedic in scope.

ADLER, ALFRED, 1870–1937, Austrian psychologist, founder of the school of "individual psychology." Adler was a disciple of FREUD, but departed from orthodox Freudianism because of his disagreement with Freud regarding the value of dream interpretation, and because he preferred to interpret psychic pathology in terms of a frustrated desire for power (leading to the "inferiority complex") rather than in terms of sexual libido. Adler saw early sibling relationships as an important barometer to the dynamics of power and inferiority.

ADLER, MORTIMER JEROME, 1902– , American philosopher and educator, director of the Institute for Philosophical Research (in Chicago, Ill.), an Aristotelian systematizer long in the forefront of the "Great Books" movement and the renascence of the Aristotelian-Thomistic concept of man.

ADORNO, THEODOR W., 1903–69, German psychologist who developed scales of social attitudes and personality types.

AMES, LOUISE BATES, 1908– , American child psychologist long associated with Dr. ARNOLD GESELL, first at the Yale Clinic of Child Development (from 1933) and later as cofounder (in 1950) of the Gesell Institute of Child Development.

ANASTASI, ANNE, 1908– , professor of psychology at Fordham University.

ANAXAGORAS, ca. 500–428 B.C., Greek philosopher and cosmologist who held that reality is fundamentally permanent and unchangeable and that "*nous*" (mind or world-ordering spirit) is the first principle of the natural world and the cause of all motion.

ANAXIMANDER, ca. 610–546 B.C., Greek philosopher, a pupil of "the first philosopher," Thales, and cofounder of the Milesian school of Greek philosophy. In holding that the boundless or infinite is the primal substance and first principle of the natural world, he was the first thinker to step outside of the realm of experience for an explanation of nature.

ANAXIMINES, ca. 588–526 B.C., pupil of ANAXIMANDER and member of the Milesian school of Greek philosophy who held that air or vapor is the primal substance and first principle of the natural world.

AQUINAS, THOMAS, 1225–74, Italian-born scholastic philosopher and theologian, of Norman heritage, who utilized the theories of Aristotle as the foundation for a massive system of Christian philosophy that has prevailed intermittently in Roman Catholic philosophical and theological circles since his death. In 1879 Aquinas' "synthesis" was pronounced as "official" for the Roman Catholic Church, but this pronouncement was not (and is not) binding on Roman Catholic philosophers. Aquinas has long been the favorite philosopher of the Dominican Order (which he joined in ca. 1243), much as Augustine of Hippo has been the favorite of the Franciscans.

ARENDT, HANNAH, 1906–75, German-American political scientist and social philosopher noted for her critical evaluation of major modern developments.

ARISTOTLE, 384–322 B.C., Greek philosopher, a pupil of PLATO who downplayed Plato's "dialectical" methodology in favor of a more "scientific" (logically and empirically based) analysis of man and the world. Aristotle also rejected Plato's theory of a completely independent eternal soul, temporarily imprisoned in a body, in favor of a theory that makes the intellectual soul partly dependent on, and partly independent of, the body.

AUGUSTINE, AURELIUS, 353–430, bishop of Hippo and founder of Western Christian philosophy, who treated virtually all of the basic philosophical problems in his attempt to understand the nature of man within a Christian framework. He held that all existence, since it is created by God, is good; thus evil is "good" insofar as it is necessary for goodness. According to St. Augustine, the City of God is constituted by the union of souls in love with the same good; and love, through which we are united with God, is the supreme virtue and the source of all other virtues.

AVERROES (MOHAMMED IBN-ROSHD), 1126–98, Arab philosopher, known principally as a commentator on the works of Aristotle. Some of Averroes' interpretations were subjected to sharp attacks from some Christian Scholastic philosophers, most notably THOMAS AQUINAS. One of the chief areas of contention was Averroes' claim that the Aristotelian "material intellect" is a single, collective intellect shared by all men, a doctrine to which believers in personal immortality and in individual cognition took strong exception.

BACON, FRANCIS, 1561–1626, English philosopher of science who advocated systematic experimentation, observation, and classification in science and contrasted his "inductive" approach with the Aristotelian-scholastic "deductive" approach.

BERGSON, HENRI, 1859–1941, French philosopher noted for (a) his attempt to apply suprascientific metaphysical intuition to the analysis of evolution, resulting in a teleological challenge to Darwinistic emphasis on chance, and (b) his epistemological emphasis on intuition itself.

BERKELEY, GEORGE (BISHOP BERKELEY), 1685–1753, Irish philosopher who is usually classified as a "British empiricist" but is also designated a "subjective idealist." Berkeley emphasized something quite empirical, namely, immediate perceptions, but he believed that these subjective perceptions and the ideas resulting from them are the sole reality—an extremely "idealistic" position, since it calls into question the real existence of any external, physical world.

BONHOEFFER, DIETRICH, 1906–45, German Protestant theologian whose anti-Nazi activities led eventually to his death in a concentration camp. He advocated a "theology of the Cross" that accents the religious importance of acts and events in history.

BROAD, CHARLIE DUNBAR, 1887–1971, British realist philosopher, who adopted the scientific method in his attempt to go beyond science to a total view of the world by considering the facts and principles of aesthetic, religious, ethical, and political experience. He stressed the importance of psychical research and parapsychological theories to fundamental philosophical questions such as causation and the mind-body problem.

BUBER, MARTIN, 1878–1965, Austrian Jewish theologian and religious existentialist, who was active in the Zionist movement. He is best known for his elaboration of the "I-Thou" philosophy.

CARNAP, RUDOLF, 1891–1970, German-born educator, author, and philosopher who brought neopositivism to America. A veteran of the Vienna Circle and thus a representative of scientific empiricism, Carnap believed that metaphysics arose from the failure to distinguish talk about the world from talk about language.

CASSIRER, ERNST, 1874–1945, German neo-Kantian "philosopher of culture," who looked to man's symbolizing activities as the key to the interpretation of culture.

CHUANG-TZU, ca. 369–295 B.C., Chinese Taoist philosopher who preached a doctrine of the equality of all things.

CHOMSKY, NOAM, 1928–   , American linguist noted for emphasizing the innate, genetic sources of language in opposition to those who view language as environmentally or culturally or historically determined.

DARWIN, CHARLES ROBERT, 1809–82, English naturalist who developed the evolutionary theory of the origin of species by means of natural selection. His doctrine of the survival of the fittest holds, among other things, that the existence of a species depends upon its ability to adapt to environmental conditions.

DE BEAUVOIR, SIMONE, 1908–   , French novelist, journalist, existentialist philosopher, and associate of JEAN-PAUL SARTRE for some fifty years, who did much to extend and clarify the ethical implications of Sartre's existentialism. In her analysis of the relationship between the sexes, she was particularly critical of the tendency of men (according to de Beauvoir) to objectify woman as an "other," a tendency that she considered an obstacle to intersubjective communication between the sexes.

DEMOCRITUS, 460–370 B.C., Greek philosopher. As the first major materialist philosopher in the Western world, Democritus theorized that all beings (including human beings) and all the activities of these beings could be explained by hypothesizing that they were constituted from material atoms of various shapes and sizes, interacting in various ways.

DESCARTES, RENÉ, 1596–1650, French mathematician and philosopher, noted for advocating a systematic doubt of all our "certainties" (i.e., in his case, those of scholastic philosophy) until we arrive at some *truly* certain and indubitable truth. For Descartes this basic truth was his own existence, hence his famous dictum, "I think, therefore I exist" (*"Cogito ergo sum"*). From this assumption, Descartes then proceeded to deduce subsidiary conclusions regarding God, the world, and the human condition. Descartes' doctrine is known as Cartesianism. He has been called the "Father of Modern Philosophy," although a great many modern philosophers, especially in the twentieth century, have made a point of calling themselves anti-Cartesian.

DEWEY, JOHN, 1859–1952, American philosopher, psychologist, and educator who contributed to "instrumentalism" (a branch of American pragmatism) and to the extension of child-centered techniques in Anglo-American education. He also helped to develop "functionalism," an empirical biological philosophy in which consciousness and thinking are subservient to action and habit formation.

DIDEROT, DENIS, 1713–84, French philosopher, man of letters, and general editor of the French *Encyclopédie* (35 vols., 1751–1780) during the Enlightenment. Starting from an initial deism, he moved through a form of materialism to a pantheistic naturalism.

DOBZHANSKY, THEODOSIUS, 1900–75, Ukrainian-American biologist, noted for his studies of the social and philosophical implications of genetics and organic evolution.

EINSTEIN, ALBERT, 1879–1955, German theoretical physicist and natural philosopher famous for his special and general theories of relativity.

EMPEDOCLES, 495–435 B.C., pre-Socratic philosopher who taught that all states and changes are brought about by the influence of two cosmic moving principles (love and hate) upon four material elements (earth, air, fire, and water).

ERIKSON, ERIK, 1902– , German-American neo-Freudian psychoanalyst famous for his application of Freud's theories to an environmentally oriented analysis of the stages of normal child, adolescent, and adult development.

EYSENCK, HANS J., 1916– , contemporary English psychologist and behavior therapist known for his research into mental disorders.

FICHTE, JOHANN GOTTLIEB, 1762–1814, German idealist philosopher whose thought centered on an espousal of KANT's moral philosophy. He held that the origin and nature of consciousness is the key to all philosophical problems and that the world has no independent self-existence, but exists only for the purpose of providing man the occasion for realizing the ends of his existence.

FREUD, SIGMUND, 1856–1939, Austrian neurologist and psychologist, originator of psychoanalysis. Freud theorized that a reservoir of erotic energy in the unconscious was both the source of human motivation and (when inhibited or frustrated) an indirect cause of neuroses and psychoses. In his later works, Freud coupled Eros or the Life Instinct with its opposite, Thanatos, the Death Instinct; and also made metapsychological applications of his principles to social philosophy and the philosophy of religion. Freud predicted that a purely physical (physiological, neurological, etc.) basis would be found for all his psychological "poetry." He maintained a keen interest in parapsychology (long before this term was invented) and was a member of the Society for Psychical Research.

FROMM, ERICH, 1900–1980, neo-Freudian psychoanalyst who looks to environmental changes in accord with Marxian theory as a key element in liberating maximum love-energy in the individual psyche.

GEHLEN, ARNOLD, 1904– , German anthropologist and social psychologist who sought to reinterpret the concepts of mind and intelligence in biological and sociological terms.

GESELL, ARNOLD, 1880–1961, American psychologist and pediatrician noted for his use of controlled laboratory methods (one-way screens, moving pictures, etc.) in the study of the stages of normal child and adolescent development.

HANSEL, C.E.M., 1917– , noted critic of parapsychological research who tried to show that SAMUEL G. SOAL's ESP results were fraudulent. Specifically, he postulated cheating by both subjects and agents, and he concluded that the experimenters either lied or were psychotic and hallucinated their data.

HEGEL, G.W.F., 1770–1831, German philosopher noted for his holistic approach to philosophy ("the truth is the totality") and the dialectical unification of traditional opposites, e.g., freedom and necessity, spirit and matter, mind and nature, subject and object.

HEIDEGGER, MARTIN, 1889–1976, German existential phenomenologist who combined a phenomenological concern for uncovering the grounds of experience (being) with a determination (typical of the existentialists) to elucidate not just cognitive experience but concrete and multifaceted human experience of the world. He was initially influenced by the methodology of EDMUND HUSSERL.

HERACLITUS, ca. 536–470 B.C., Greek philosopher who held that fire is the primal substance of the natural world. In opposition to the Milesians, he taught that there is nothing constant or stable in the world and that all things and the universe as a whole are in a constant state of flux and motion.

HOBBES, THOMAS, 1588–1679, English political philosopher who theorized that the political state had evolved as man's response to the insecurity and dangers of some original "state of nature," characterized by Hobbes as "the war of all against all."

HUME, DAVID, 1711–76, British empiricist whose skeptical assaults on traditional philosophical concepts (e.g., causal necessity, the substantiality of the soul, and natural moral obligations) had a profound effect on later philosophy and the questions that have been asked by later philosophers.

HUSSERL, EDMUND, 1859–1938, German philosopher, the founder of contemporary phenomenology. Husserl started with a methodical suspension of consideration (called "bracketing") of the sphere of natural experience, and hoped by doing this to gain access to an understanding of the pivotal subjective forms and ideas that enter into man's peculiar construction of his experiences.

HUXLEY, JULIAN SORELL, 1887–1975, English biologist who thought that it is possible to develop a religion on a naturalistic basis.

ILG, FRANCES LILLIAN, 1902– , American educator and a cofounder (1950) of the Gesell Institute for Child Development.

JAMES, WILLIAM, 1842–1910, American philosopher and psychologist, who advocated a radically empirical, presuppositionless, "pragmatic" approach to the understanding of human consciousness and behavior.

JASPERS, KARL, 1883–1969, German psychiatrist and existential philosopher who analyzed man's possible attitudes toward the world. He thought that man, because of his freedom, is doomed to ultimate "shipwreck."

JENSEN, ARTHUR, 1923– , American educational psychologist whose research on so-called culture-fair IQ tests led him to the highly controversial position that the so-called "IQ lag" of black Americans is due more to genetic than to environmental causes.

JUNG, CARL, 1875–1965, Swiss psychiatrist, the founder of analytical depth psychology. An erstwhile disciple of Freud, Jung broke away to establish a psychological school that deemphasized the role of strictly sexual interpretations of behavior and analyzed the diverse elements of the individual unconscious (repressed events of the individual's life) and the so-called collective unconscious (archetypes). Jung introduced the terms *extroversion* and *introversion* to psychology.

KALLMANN, FRANZ JOSEF, 1897–1965, American psychiatrist noted for his genetic studies and his research into homosexuality and hereditary factors in schizophrenia.

KANT, IMMANUEL, 1724–1804, German philosopher who, in his later years, propounded a "critical" philosophy that would investigate and define the limits of knowledge in the various subdivisions of philosophy. In *Critique of Pure Reason*, Kant defined the valid objects of knowledge in terms of the subjective constructs that give them objectivity. In *Critique of Practical Reason,* Kant defined moral behavior in terms of a concept of universal moral duty that is the basis for man's moral freedom. And in *Critique of Judgment,* he explored the subjective grounds for the experiences of beauty, sublimity, and natural purposiveness.

KIERKEGAARD, SØREN, 1813–55, Danish Christian existentialist. Initially a student of Hegelian philosophy, Kierkegaard finally rejected the Hegelian "system" on the ground that it ignored individual subjectivity. But in his own philosophy, in which he emphasized subjectivity, Kierkegaard employed an Hegelian dialectical methodology and frequently had recourse to Hegelian antitheses, e.g., the "in-itself" and the "for-itself," the eternal self vs. the finite self.

KRETSCHMER, ERNST, 1888–1964, German neurologist and psychiatrist who developed a morphological typology correlating physique and psychosis.

LAMARCK, JEAN BAPTISTE, 1744–1829, French zoologist whose pre-Darwinian theory of evolution conjectured that traits acquired by organisms in response to environmental challenges could be passed on to the offspring of these organisms.

LEIBNIZ, GOTTFRIED, 1646–1716, German Cartesian philosopher who attempted to transcend the Cartesian dualism of mind and matter by postulating units of conscious perception ("monads") as the basic constituents of the world, instead of material atoms. Leibniz seems to indicate in some places that the physical world is a function of the monads and essentially dependent on the monads, and thus does not have reality independent from consciousness.

LEPP, IGNACE, 1909–66, Jungian psychologist and Christian existentialist who attempted to synthesize the Christian concept of love and psychoanalytic theories regarding the dynamics of personal and interpersonal love.

LÉVI-STRAUSS, CLAUDE 1908– , French social anthropologist whose "structuralist" interpretations of the dynamics of cultures are based on his discerning certain basic patterns of thought and communication that are, according to him, replicated in various cultures that are seemingly, but only seemingly, quite different.

LÉVY-BRUHL, LUCIEN, 1857–1939, French positivist philosopher, anthropologist, sociologist, and ethnologist who regarded the thought structures of "primitive" peoples as being determined entirely by their collective representations, characterized by him as "prelogical."

LOCKE, JOHN, 1632–1714, British philosopher and founder of modern empiricism. He denied the existence of innate ideas, holding that all ideas depend on experience. According to Locke, the mind at birth is a blank tablet (*tabula rasa*) whose whole content is derived from sense experience. He distinguished between primary qualities, which inhere in physical objects, and secondary qualities, which are internal to ourselves. Locke defined freedom not as liberty of choice but as liberty of action based upon choices made in accordance with the natural law.

LORENZ, KONRAD ZACHARIAS, 1903– , Austrian zoologist and ethologist who discovered imprinting in young birds. Lorenz views aggression as a general instinct that is highly adaptive to ecological conditions.

MALACHY, ST. (MALACHY O'MORGAIN), 1094–1148, Irish bishop, canonized by the Catholic Church, and famous for his supposedly prophetic descriptions of all popes from 1143 to the destruction of Rome and the papacy.

MARX, KARL, 1818–83, German political economist and theorist of revolution, who sought to apply Hegel's dialectical methodology "scientifically" to socioeconomic realities, and who developed a theory ("dialectical materialism") that would ultimately put an end to man's alienation from nature and his estrangement from his fellow man.

MAY, ROLLO, 1909–66, American existential psychoanalyst noted for his studies of dreams and anxiety.

McDOUGALL, WILLIAM, 1871–1938, Anglo-American philosopher and psychologist, who emphasized future-oriented purposiveness rather than backward-looking causality as the key to understanding psychological functions, including the instincts.

MILL, JOHN STUART, 1806–73, English philosopher, economist, and social and political reformer who reacted against the mechanism of his father, James Mill, and advocated liberty of thought and discussion.

MILTON, JOHN, 1608–74, English poet, author, and political writer with characteristics of Christian humanism and Puritanism.

MONTAIGNE, MICHEL DE, 1533–92, French essayist and novelist who advocated a return to uncorrupted nature and revelation.

MONTESSORI, MARIA, 1870–1952, Italian educator whose method emphasizes educating each child freely in the manner best suited to him or her individually, and without most of the usual pedagogical supervisory apparatus.

NEWTON, ISAAC, 1642–1727, English mathematician and philosopher who discovered the law of universal gravitation.

NIETZSCHE, FRIEDRICH, 1844–1900, German philologist and philosopher, often considered a forerunner of contemporary existentialism, but who is perhaps best characterized as "unclassifiable." One of the most important themes in Nietzsche's philosophy is the idea that the creative individual (not the mass-produced "individual") is the unique source of value and moral progress.

NOSTRADAMUS, MICHEL DE, 1503–66, French physician and astrologer.

ORTEGA Y GASSET, JOSÉ, 1883–1955, Spanish existential philosopher who denied the fundamental presuppositions of European rationalism and held that life consists, not in being, but in coming-to-be.

PASCAL, BLAISE, 1623–62, French philosopher and mathematician who found faith to be superior to reason.

PIAGET, JEAN, 1896–1980, Swiss developmental psychologist who tried to trace the genesis of intelligence organically from lower forms of behavior.

PLATO, 428–348 B.C., Greek philosopher, a pupil of the "philosophical gadfly" Socrates, on whose philosophical utterances Plato's *Dialogues* are the principal source of information (and, possibly, misinformation). Plato also developed his own theories in the *Dialogues,* leading to many disagreements among scholars as to which ideas are Socrates' and which are Plato's. Plato was an "idealist" in that he thought ideas were both prior to and preeminent over mundane realities. In his sociopolitical philosophy Plato favored a strict authoritarian society in which the several classes would function along rigidly defined lines, supported by slaves to do the menial work—a society in which service to the Idea of the Good would be central, and from which such subversive claptrap as the writings of Homer would be banned.

PLESSNER, HELMUTH, 1892– , German philosopher and a founder of modern philosophical anthropology. According to Plessner, man artifically creates his nature and is distinguished from the animals by being "eccentric."

PLOTINUS, A.D. 205–270, Egyptian philosopher who held that all reality consists of a series of emanations from the One.

PRATT, J. GAITHER, 1910– , American professor of psychiatry and researcher in the Division of Parapsychology at the University of Virginia, Charlottesville.

REICH, CHARLES, 1928– , American jurist whose popular book *The Greening of America* interpreted the "hippie" phenomenon and other countercultural movements of the 1960s as symptoms of a transition to a new form of social consciousness that he believed was developing in the United States, and advocated radical changes in America's social structures to accommodate this supposed transition.

RHINE, JOSEPH BANKS, 1895–1980, American parapsychologist noted for his development (at Duke University) of controlled experiments for the verification of so-called psychic phenomena. At the time of his death he was serving as director of the Foundation for Research on the Nature of Man at Duke.

ROSENSTOCK-HUESSY, EUGEN, 1888–1973, German-born American jurist, historian, and existential philosopher who viewed man as essentially "multiform," in opposition to those who consider man as "one-dimensional," categorizable, predictable, or scientifically decipherable.

ROSENZWEIG, FRANZ, 1886–1929, German Jewish existential theologian who advocated a "new thinking" standing between theology and philosophy and beginning not with abstract concepts but with the suffering and anxiety of the individual man.

ROUSSEAU, JEAN JACQUES, 1712–78, French philosopher who characterized man as a "noble savage" and emphasized the corrupting effects of society on man in his natural condition.

RUMBAUGH, DUANE M., 1929– , American psychologist, noted for animal studies at the Yerkes Regional Primate Research Center in Atlanta, Georgia.

RUSSELL, BERTRAND, 1872–1970, British philosopher noted for his magisterial contributions to symbolic logic and for a gallant but ill-omened attempt to establish philosophy as a science.

RYLE, GILBERT, 1900–1976, British philosopher and early protagonist of linguistic philosophy who has criticized Descartes' alleged "ghost-in-the-machine" view of mind and body.

SANTAYANA, GEORGE, 1863–1952, Spanish-born naturalist, essayist, and philosopher whose system includes themes of naturalism, realism, essentialism, idealism, and romanticism.

SARTRE, JEAN-PAUL, 1905–80, French man of letters, philosopher, and supporter of radical and Marxist causes. Sartre was a major figure in the "existentialist" movement that peaked in France after World War II. In his philosophical writings, which show the profound influence of EDMUND HUSSERL and MARTIN HEIDEGGER, Sartre gives absolute priority to individual freedom, which is supposedly attained by the negation of objective being, and which is maintained by the resolute refusal of the free individual to be made into an "object" by any other individual or by society or the state.

SCHELER, MAX, 1874–1928, German philosopher and sociologist who attempted to establish a basis for objectivist values. Scheler also held that emotional experience, especially love, is the key to the disclosure of being.

SCHELLING, FRIEDRICH VON, 1775–1854, German idealist philosopher who held that subject and object coincide in the absolute and that nature and spirit are different aspects of the same reality.

SCHILLER, FERDINAND CANNING SCOTT, 1864–1937, British philosopher whose "personal idealism" or "humanism" is closely related to the pragmatism of WILLIAM JAMES.

SCHOPENHAUER, ARTHUR, 1788–1860, German philosopher who emphasized the role of the will in the world.

SCHWARTZ, OSWALD, 1883–1949, German psychologist who was introduced to Freud's psychology by FREUD's disciple ALFRED ADLER (later apostate), and who eventually specialized in applying Freudian principles to psychosexual relationships.

SHAFTESBURY, ANTHONY ASHLEY-COOPER, THIRD EARL OF, 1671–1713, English moral philosopher and representative of the moral-sense school, which holds that human beings have a natural sense of right and wrong.

SHELDON, WILLIAM HERBERT, 1899– , American psychologist whose theory of bodily types identifies three such types (endomorphic, ectomorphic, and mesomorphic) with three clusters of characteristic temperamental traits.

SIDGWICK, HENRY, 1838–1900, English moral philosopher and cofounder of the Society for Psychical Research in London.

SKINNER, B. F., 1904– , American behavioral psychologist who emphasizes operant conditioning and positive reinforcement as principles of behavior acquisition and control.

SOAL, SAMUEL G., 1889–1975, British mathematician and statistician interested in parapsychology. Initially unsuccessful in card-guessing experiments for clairvoyance, Soal discovered that the very experiments that were inconclusive regarding clairvoyance showed a significant success rate when analyzed for their relevance to precognition. That is, Soal's subjects tended to guess correctly the card just *ahead* of the one being presented. See HANSEL, C.E.M.

SOCRATES, 469–399 B.C., enigmatic Greek philosopher, about whom little or nothing is known directly, but who figures prominently in the writings of one of his students, Plato, who is the principal source of information (or possibly misinformation) about his teacher. As a young man, Socrates engaged in cosmological speculation, but eventually he decided that such speculation was useless and turned his attention to moral philosophy. The "Socratic method," as it comes to us from Plato, involved question-and-answer dialogues about currently accepted values and meanings. Widespread opposition to Socrates' investigations and his evident irreverence resulted in his being condemned to death by the pious citizens of Athens. Socrates' teachings were recorded (no one knows how completely or accurately) and expanded upon in the written *Dialogues* of PLATO— Socrates' most famous but not (as recorded by Plato himself) his favorite or necessarily his best pupil.

SOLOVYEV, VLADIMIR SERGEYEVICH, 1853–1900, Russian philosopher and religious thinker with tendencies toward mysticism and pantheism.

SPINOZA, BENEDICT, 1632–77, Dutch lens grinder and philosopher. Though a devout Jew, Spinoza embraced the philosophy of Descartes and elaborated the two basic Cartesian principles, extension and thought, into a massive cosmic system whose sole underpinning was God. As the only substantial reality in Spinoza's system, God was construed rather pantheistically (or, according to some, panentheistically); this was a serious stumbling block for many later Jewish and Christian philosophers, including Spinoza's coreligionist Moses Mendelssohn.

TEILHARD DE CHARDIN, PIERRE, 1881–1955, French Jesuit paleoanthropologist and philosopher. Teilhard expounded a non-Darwinian, teleological view of evolution that traces the evolution of consciousness from its origins in preliving matter to its summits in a "communal consciousness," in which a final fusion of the divine and the human will be created.

TERMAN, LEWIS MADISON, 1877–1956, American psychologist noted for his investigations into the measurement and development of human intelligence.

TYRELL, G.N.M., 1872–1952, English engineer, mathematician, and psychical researcher, and president of the Society for Psychical Research 1945–46.

UNAMUNO Y JUGO, MIGUEL DE, 1864–1936, Spanish man of letters and educator who epitomized the character of Spain—and of mankind—in his writings on the conflicts between faith and reason, life and thought, culture and civilization.

WEISS, PAUL, 1901– , American philosopher influential in the revival of interest in metaphysics in America.

WILSON, EDWARD OSBORNE, 1929– , American zoologist noted (1) as perhaps the world's foremost authority on the behavior of ants, and (2) for his pioneering studies in the field of sociobiology.

WITTGENSTEIN, LUDWIG, 1889–1951, Austrian philosopher who demonstrated the philosophical importance of the study of language and greatly influenced the development of logical positivism.

GLOSSARY OF TERMS

This glossary is intended to provide students with convenient summary definitions of some of the technical terms used in the text. The definitions given here are not intended to comprehend all usages of the terms listed.

ABSTRACTION: The cognitive process by which the mind leaves behind manifold particular details and focuses on ("abstracts") the general principles or characteristics that are thought to explain, or be relevant to, these details, e.g., the abstraction of "man" as a cluster of certain essential characteristics—rationality, etc.—found in people of all races, religions, nationalities, etc.

AESTHETIC SENSE: The ability to appreciate and/or contribute to the production of beauty in its manifold forms.

AESTIMATIVE POWER: The Aristotelian conception of instinct as that which impels each species of animal to do certain things that are good for the species.

AGNOSTICISM: The thesis that, even if a God exists, there is no convincing evidence that such is the case and one is intellectually justified, therefore, in withholding belief until convincing evidence is forthcoming.

ALTRUISM: Unselfishness; a benevolent or concerned attitude toward others.

ANALYTIC PSYCHOLOGY: A study of the effects of underlying or unconscious drives or instincts on human personality and behavior; also called "depth psychology."

ANDROGYNY: In contemporary usage, the combination of so-called male and female traits to produce a well-balanced personality, as opposed to a one-sided "male" or "female" stereotype.

ANIMA: In Carl Jung's psychology, either (1) the "inner" personality of an individual, in contrast to his or her masklike PERSONA, or (2) the so-called "feminine principle," especially as manifested in the male, and opposed or contrasted with the ANIMUS.

ANIMUS: In Carl Jung's psychology, the "masculine principle," especially as manifested in the female.

A POSTERIORI: In adjectival usage, "derived from experiential sources, or effects external to the mind," in situations where questions arise regarding the source of our conclusions regarding reality. It is opposed to A PRIORI.

A PRIORI: In an adjectival usage, "contributed by the mind itself, and its theories or its logical operations," in situations where questions arise regarding the source of our knowledge of reality. It is opposed to A POSTERIORI.

ARCHETYPE: In Carl Jung's psychology, an innate, inherited, instinctive formation in the human unconscious, which gives a man a predisposition to view the world or organize his experience in a certain way. For example, the Anima (in one sense, the archetype of the ideal female) in a male leads to certain predispositions and expectations in his dealings with females.

ASTRAL BODY: An ethereal or spiritual body, lacking some of the usual material properties such as weight or opacity or destructibility, and present alongside or "within" the ordinary material human body which is identical in appearance to it.

BEHAVIORISM: A school of psychology, currently flourishing in the U. S., which emphasizes: (1) the restriction of the psychologist to observable facts of human and animal behavior; (2) a scientific understanding of the function of stimulus-response mechanisms; and (3) the possibilities of clinical modification of behavior by scientific use of positive and negative reinforcements (rewards and deprivations or punishments) to create conditioned needs or reflexes.

BEING-FOR-ANOTHER: In Hegel's philosophy, a technical term that, if used in reference to a human consciousness, implies that a consciousness is both dependent on another consciousness and is an essential object of knowledge for that other consciousness.

BEING-FOR-SELF: In Hegel's philosophy, a technical term that, when used in reference to human consciousness, implies the power of self-reflection and independent self-possession or "freedom."

CAUSAL RELATIONSHIP: A relationship between A and B such that A is said to be an effect of B, or B an effect of A; or both A and B are effects of each other (reciprocal causality).

COCONSCIOUSNESS: The primitive state of consciousness that emphasizes tribal or group unity and is comparatively unaware of the meaning and importance of individual personality, freedom, and rights.

COENESTHESIS: The peculiar structure of perception in the newly born infant, who would seem to be incognizant of the divisions between "objective" and "subjective," and other derivative divisions, that are taken for granted in mature human perception.

COGITATIVE POWER: A special application of the AESTIMATIVE POWER to human organisms. It is a faculty by which a man knows and judges in a quasi-intuitive way that certain actions will benefit or harm him individually.

COLLECTIVE CONSCIOUSNESS: According to Teilhard de Chardin, a future state of superconsciousness to be created in mankind as a whole, by the spontaneous cooperation of individual consciousnesses on a global level.

COLLECTIVE UNCONSCIOUS: According to Carl Jung, a sphere of consciousness which exists over and above the individual unconscious. The collective unconscious is a repository of the myths and symbols that mankind has found most useful for dealing with reality; and it is transmitted and added to from generation to generation.

COMPLEX INSTINCTS: See INSTINCT.

CONSCIOUSNESS: The sum-total of the things we know, perceive, sense, or intuit.

CONSERVATIVISM: Serious reservations about the basic goodness or trustworthiness of the "average man," combined with an emphasis on traditional sociopolitical structures geared to protecting the interests of, or providing opportunities for, "elite" (specially qualified) individuals and/or groups.

DÉJÀ VU: A person's conviction that he has previously witnessed a scene or event he is presently viewing, even though he has no memory of having done so, and even though it seems impossible or improbable that he could have done so.

DEPTH PSYCHOLOGY: See ANALYTIC PSYCHOLOGY.

DETERMINISM: The thesis that man, like other animals, is completely determined to do what he does because of environmental factors, past training, instinctive drives, etc.—even though he may think he is "free."

DEVELOPMENTAL PSYCHOLOGY: A branch or school of psychology which emphasizes the analysis of the various stages of normal infant, childhood, and/or adult development, on the basis of controlled observations and/or case studies.

DIALECTICS: The logical and/or metaphysical consideration of things or ideas in terms of a relationship to their opposites (e.g., considering "being" in relationship to "nonbeing"); sometimes with an additional attempt to combine or synthesize the opposites (e.g., "potentiality" as a synthesis of "being" and "nonbeing").

DIFFERENCE-IN-DEGREE: A difference between A and B based on a greater predominance of certain characteristics in A that are also found in B.

DIFFERENCE-IN-KIND: A difference of a radical sort between A and B, such that essential characteristics found in A are never found in B and vice versa.

DIFFERENTIAL PSYCHOLOGY: The study of the effect of various natural differences, e.g., sexual differences, racial and national differences, on personality or behavior patterns.

DUALISM: As applied to human existence, an attempt to comprehend, interpret, and explain man in terms of an interrelationship between two principles, e.g., body and soul, mind and body.

EGO: The center of personality, the source of and terminus of the experience of self-identity.

EGO-IDEAL: See SUPER-EGO.

EMPIRICISM: A fundamental philosophical attitude that stresses the need to arrive at knowledge and truth by means of direct experience and observation.

ENVIRONMENTALISM: An emphasis on environmental factors (or "nurture") rather than hereditary factors as determinants conditioning personality, attitudes, aptitudes, and/or behavior. Compare HEREDITARIANISM.

EPIPHENOMENON: A phenomenon that is dependent on and subordinate to some other phenomenon which is considered to have primacy.

EQUIVOCATION: Usage of terms or expressions in apparently similar but really different ways, e.g., (1) "a healthy body" (contrasted with a diseased body), and (2) "a healthy complexion" (contrasted with a pale complexion that may or may not be "healthy" in sense #1).

ESP: See EXTRASENSORY PERCEPTION.

ETHICAL SENSE: The power of discriminating right from wrong, and/or a predisposition to make choices in line with what one judges to be "right."

EVOLUTION: or "organic evolution," a theory claiming that all forms of life have come from previously existing forms and that the known groups of animals and plants have developed from ancestral groups over long periods of earth history through many relatively small individual changes. In Darwin's classic formulation, evolution proceeds by NATURAL SELECTION; i.e., in the struggle for existence, the "fittest" tend to survive and the less fit tend to lose out and to become extinct.

EXISTENCE: In the ordinary physical world, the public accessibility and manifestation of physical objects and qualities, e.g., stones, dogs, sizes; in the mental world, any concept or imaginative construct that is accepted in conventional human communication, e.g., numbers and values and abstract ideas.

EXISTENTIALISM: any of a half-dozen or more schools or systems (or antisystems) of philosophy (and in some cases theology) that differ radically from each other in many respects (some existentialists are, for instance, theistic, while others are atheistic) and yet share a tendency to emphasize the primacy of "existence" over "essence" (hence the familiar existentialist catchwords, "Existence precedes Essence"). (1) In terms of its "schools," existentialism is usually defined as a "modern" development identified first with Søren Kierkegaard and later with such diverse figures as Martin Heidegger, Karl Jaspers, Martin Buber, Gabriel Marcel, Franz Rosenzweig, Eugen Rosenstock-Huessy, Jean-Paul Sartre, Ferdinand Ebner, Simone de Beauvoir, Albert Camus, Reinhold Niebuhr, Rudolf Ehrenberg, and even the neo-Thomist Jacques Maritain—to name just a few so-called existentialists, many of whom, including some of those named here, denied that they were existentialists—just as Freud denied that he was a Freudian, and Marx that he was a Marxist. (2) As a "tendency," existentialism has been traced as far back as the pre-Socratic period in Greek philosophy. Thus Heraclitus, who believed that everything living (including man) was constantly changing, has been called an "existential" thinker in contradistinction to Parmenides of Elea, who believed in the immutability of "being" (identified with the concept of essence) and "proved" that movement (change) was impossible. The whole subsequent history of philosophy, as seen by the existentialists, can be described as a running battle between those for whom "essence precedes existence" (for instance, Plato, with his "world of ideas") and those for whom "existence precedes essence" (including, according to some interpreters, such surprising figures as Socrates, with his "daemon," and St. Thomas Aquinas). Existential thinkers have generally opposed all "idealists" (of whom Plato may be regarded as prototypical) and most "materialists," as well. They have generally given primary emphasis to the situation of the individual person who, willy nilly, forms his "essence" or "being" in the course of the life he chooses to live. The "authentic" individual is constantly changing and has no being, no essence, and indeed no nature (most existentialists deny that there is such a thing as "human nature"); he is unknowable and indefinable except as he may manifest himself at a particular moment—and even in this limited sense, only provisionally. The individual moves through stages on his life's way toward his death, which is his alone and is unshareable. His awareness of his impending death looms large and is the one a priori in all his serious thought and in the decisions and actions he takes. This awareness is the beginning of "authentic" existence, for he knows that he is creating by his life (his "existence") what he will have become in his death (at which time his "essence" or "being" will become knowable).

EXTRASENSORY PERCEPTION: Purportedly, the ability to know or perceive things or events that would be inaccessible by ordinary sensory channels. Forms of ESP include clairvoyance, telepathy, precognition, retrocognition, and mediumship.

EXTROVERSION: A primary interest in, and ability to be affected by, external situations, events, and the values and expectations of the social groups one identifies with. The term was coined by Carl Jung. Compare INTROVERSION.

FIRST-ORDER PHENOMENON: A fact or event which provides the initial experiential basis for the elaboration of scientific or philosophical conclusions.

FORM: In Aristotelian and scholastic philosophies, a term that is used analogously to the way the term is used in everyday life. Just as the form or shape of an object (a vase, a dog, etc.) gives it external characteristics that help us identify it and distinguish it from other objects, so also there is in every being an internal "form" that gives the being its essential characteristics and definition. E.g., the "form" of a man is the rational soul, which endows him with his essential characteristic of rationality; the "form" of a dog is the sentient soul, which endows the dog with the powers of sensation and locomotion.

FREE CHOICE: The supposed ability to do either A or not-A, such that even if one does A, one was not *determined* to do so, but *could* have done not-A ("A" here is used to symbolize a specific line of behavior).

FREE WILL: Self-determination, i.e., having one's actions determined by oneself, either in addition to, or to the exclusion of, determination by factors such as environment and heredity.

GENERAL EXTRASENSORY PERCEPTION (GESP): The possession of more than one ESP ability—abilities that may be activated either simultaneously or successively.

HEREDITARIANISM: An emphasis on heredity (or "nature") rather than environmental conditions in explaining personality, attitudes, and/or behavior. Compare ENVIRONMENTALISM.

ID: In Freud's system, the raw, instinctual side of man, which acts upon the ego through the images and percepts of the preconscious.

IDEALISM: An emphasis on ideal or spiritual existence and values, sometimes to the point of downgrading or even denying material reality.

IMAGINATION: The ability to store images based on perception and memory, make interconnections and reconstructions of these images in sometimes novel ways, and utilize the simple or interconnected or reconstructed images as a basis or stimulus for conceptual thinking and for personal projections of future goals and plans.

INDETERMINATION: The ability of a free agent to resist being determined to a single line of action without any alternative; a denial of DETERMINISM.

INDIVIDUALISM: Emphasis on individual personality, individual rights, and individual freedom.

INSTINCT: An unlearned psychophysical impulse to do certain things or to respond in certain ways, at certain stages in the life cycle of an organism and/or in certain environmental situations. In this book, "Instinct₁" designates instinct in its internal aspect, i.e., the unlearned *impulse* itself, whether or not this impulse actually issues in some form of *external* response or behavior. "Instinct₂" designates instinct as *external*, publicly observable reactions or behavior mechanisms. A relatively simple manifestation of an instinctive activity is designated a "simple" instinct; a relatively complex chain or clustering of instinctive activities is designated a "complex" instinct.

INTROVERSION: A primary interest in and ability to be affected and satisfied by inner "facts" (ideas, personal values, fantasies, etc.). The term was coined by Carl Jung. Compare EXTROVERSION.

INTUITION: Knowledge which is direct, i.e., not a conclusion arrived at only at the end of a chain of reasoning processes.

KIRLIAN PHOTOGRAPHY: A technique developed by Soviet researchers Semyon Kirlian and Valentina Kirlian for photographing the "aura" (a band of colored light) surrounding the human body but invisible to the naked eye. The technique involves placing the subject in an electrical field while he is being photographed.

LIBERALISM: A belief in the basic goodness or trustworthiness of the average person, combined with the belief that sociopolitical and environmental changes will serve best to bring out that goodness or trustworthiness.

LIBERTARIANISM: In contemporary philosophy, the belief that freedom and DETERMINISM *cannot* be reconciled (as opposed to RECONCILIATIONISM); in contemporary politics, the advocacy of minimal government to ensure maximum individual liberty.

LIBERTY: The ability and right to do either (1) whatever one wishes, or (2) what one considers to be one's right *and* duty (moral liberty), without undue interference from others or from natural obstacles. Those who consider liberty in the former sense inadequate sometimes refer to it derogatorily as "license," as distinct from "true" (moral) liberty.

LICENSE: See LIBERTY.

LINGUISTIC ANALYSIS: A philosophical approach, now predominant in English-speaking countries, that emphasizes the analysis of linguistic usages for the purpose of clarifying concepts and issues and eliminating so-called pseudo-problems.

LOGICAL POSSIBILITY (Possibility_L): Any idea or assertion that is not logically self-contradictory. E.g., it is *logically* possible that my spirit could transmigrate to some other world after death, but logically impossible that I should be someone else, if my spirit happened to transmigrate into some new and different living body.

MATERIALISM: An emphasis on material existence and values, sometimes to the extent of reducing "spiritual" realities or values to their implicit material components.

MCE: See MEAN CHANCE EXPECTATION.

MEAN CHANCE EXPECTATION: The probability that anyone would ordinarily have of performing a certain task or achieving a certain result; e.g., anyone throwing a coin would have an MCE of 1/1 for throwing "heads" half the time, or an MCE of 1/2 for throwing "heads" all the time.

MEDIUMSHIP: Purportedly, acting as a mediator between a living person (the "sitter") and a deceased person (the "spirit") with whom the sitter wants to come into contact.

METAPHYSICS: A philosophical investigation of (1) the principles underlying reality, and/or (2) formal or structural attributes of, or elements in, reality, and/or (3) unseen transcendental realities that are at or beyond the boundaries of ordinary experience.

MIND: A term used by DUALISTS to describe the intellectual or spiritual element in human personality, which is involved in a CAUSAL RELATIONSHIP with the body.

MONAD: In Leibnizian philosophy, a kind of immaterial "atom" without extension and with perceptive powers—the basic unit out of which the universe is supposedly constructed, without the necessity for any strictly material "building blocks."

MONISM: As applied to human existence, an attempt to comprehend, interpret, and present man as a unity, avoiding traditional dichotomies between body and soul, etc.

MYSTICAL EXPERIENCE: A nonconceptual, nonsensual, inexpressible, direct experience that seems to transcend ordinary human experiences and is sometimes called, in theistic cultures, an "experience of God" or of the divine.

NATURAL SELECTION: The chance selection of certain species which are best adapted to the environment to pass on their genes to their offspring by a comparatively high reproduction rate, thus producing the "survival of the fittest" in the EVOLUTION of life.

NATURE-NURTURE DEBATE: The controversy between ENVIRONMENTALISTS and HEREDITARIANS.

NEAR-DEATH EXPERIENCES: Purportedly, the "out-of-body" experiences of those who have been declared to be clinically dead but have subsequently been resuscitated, resulting—it is claimed—in the experience of "returning" to the body.

OBJECTIVE NORMS: Generally or widely recognized criteria, promulgated and espoused by those who are competent, or are thought to be competent, to make the relevant judgments.

OEDIPUS COMPLEX: In Freudian psychology, the process in which a young child ordinarily comes into conflict with the parent of the same sex because of mutual rivalry with regard to the parent of the opposite sex. There are homosexual variations of this basic pattern, and as applied to females the process is sometimes called the Electra Complex. According to the theory, the resolution of the complex ordinarily results in the formation of the SUPER-EGO.

ONTOLOGICAL POSSIBILITY (Possibility$_0$): A potentiality or faculty that is thought to be the source for activities or operations, e.g., the faculty of sight as the source for seeing, the faculty of thought as the source of thinking, the SOUL as the ultimate source for all activities and powers in man.

ONTOLOGY: A study of things from the point of view of their essential being, rather than from the point of view of their empirical, phenomenal, external, or peripheral qualities or relationships.

PARADOX: An apparent contradiction, which nonetheless has meaning when taken in a nonliteral sense: e.g., "silence speaks louder than words," "he who is first shall be last," etc.

PARAPSYCHOLOGY: The branch of psychology concerned with the study of purportedly paranormal behavior and abilities, and/or the investigation of claims of such behavior and abilities.

PERCEPTION: The ability to focus on particular objects as clusters or syntheses or sources of various sensory qualities, e.g., color, size, taste, etc.

PERSONA: In Carl Jung's psychology, the specific personality characteristics that an individual takes on and identifies with in response to what he and/or society consider his particular role in society to be, i.e., one's public or "official" personality. See ANIMA.

PERSONALITY: The integration of physical, temperamental, intellectual, and spiritual traits into a unique and manifest totality.

PHENOMENOLOGY: A philosophical movement that emphasizes investigation of the A PRIORI structures that are thought to be at the foundation of ordinary and scientific experience.

PK: See PSYCHOKINESIS.

POSITIVISM: A philosophical movement emphasizing direct description of sensory phenomena, as opposed to theological or metaphysical interpretations of such phenomena.

POSSIBILITY$_L$: See LOGICAL POSSIBILITY.

POSSIBILITY$_O$: See ONTOLOGICAL POSSIBILITY.

PRECOGNITION: Perception or vision of events or states in the future.

PROBABILITY THEORY: Mathematical formulas or procedures for determining the supposed degree of certainty or uncertainty in regard to certain events, e.g., the chances of throwing "heads" when flipping a coin, throwing a "seven" when tossing dice, etc.

PROJECTION: In psychoanalytic literature, dealing with one's subjective states or problems in an external, or objective fashion, e.g., dealing with a quality one does not like in himself by criticizing or persecuting others who are considered to manifest that same quality; or being attracted to a person of the opposite sex because of an unconscious subjective male-ideal or female-ideal that we are "projecting" onto that person.

PROPRIORECEPTION: Perception of one's own emotional reactions, sensations, muscular movements, and the various physiological processes going on in one's body.

PSI: Any form of EXTRASENSORY PERCEPTION or PSYCHOKINESIS.

PSYCHIC: Purportedly, one who significantly exceeds the MEAN CHANCE EXPECTATION in the various forms of EXTRASENSORY PERCEPTION or PSYCHOKINESIS.

PSYCHOKINESIS: Purportedly, moving physical objects or causing physical changes by concentration of the power of will, i.e., without any physical contact or mechanical or instrumental intermediaries.

RATIONALISM: A philosophical stance that emphasizes the importance of mental and/or ideal constructs and/or logical processes or formulations in the cognition of all types of reality.

RECONCILIATIONISM: The thesis that an act that is free may also be in some respects determined (see DETERMINISM); or the stronger theses: (1) a free act is always determined in some respect(s), or (2) the freedom of one's acts is actually enhanced by their having been determined. This position is opposed to LIBERTARIANISM.

REDUCTIONISM: The attempt to explain a thing or phenomenon by reducing it, usually in an oversimplified way, to some single thing or principle or reality; e.g., reducing consciousness to neural mechanisms, or reducing the evils of the world to the imperfect spiritual perspectives of those who view them.

REINCARNATION: Purportedly, the entry of the spirit or soul of a deceased person into another body, human or animal.

REMINISCENCE: The ability not only to remember past experiences, but to reactivate a past memory by systematically "searching through one's mind," retracing one's steps mentally in order, for example, to recall where one left a coat that was lost.

ROMANTIC LOVE: Sexual love that goes beyond infatuation and "exploitation" (if any) to a multileveled potentiation that combines physical, spiritual, intellectual, and emotional components.

SECOND-ORDER PHENOMENON: A "fact" or "event" that is the result of reflection upon some FIRST-ORDER PHENOMENON, and carries that first-order phenomenon into more complex or sophisticated stages. E.g., if love as a first-order phenomenon is manifested as a tendency toward union simultaneously with objects A and B, love as a tendency to unite *these two loves* is a second-order love.

SELF: In Carl Jung's psychology, the unity of opposites in man, e.g., male and female traits, positive and negative traits, conscious and unconscious motivations. See ANIMA; ANIMUS.

SELF-CONSCIOUSNESS: The ability to reflect back on oneself, to understand oneself, and to grow in this understanding.

SENSATION: The reception of sensory data through the five external senses.

SIMPLE INSTINCTS: See INSTINCT.

SOCIOBIOLOGY: The biologically oriented study of the evolution of animal and human groupings with regard to size, age composition, hierarchies, communications systems, differentiation of roles, etc.

SOUL: In the strict classical (Aristotelian) sense, the life principle that gives form, shape, definition, and actuality to any living organism. The sentient-vegetative soul ($Soul_1$) is said to be the source of all the functions, activities, and impulses that men have in common with animals. The rational soul ($Soul_2$), which is central and supreme in human beings, is characterized as endowing man with the ability to engage in rational thought processes, including the formation of SYLLOGISMS.

SPIRIT: As applied to a living human being, the inner source of the individual's life, activated or expressed in some manner.

SUBJECTIVE NORMS: The criteria that an individual adheres to in making evaluative judgments; these may or may not coincide with OBJECTIVE NORMS.

SUPER-EGO: In Freud's system, an unconscious and supraconscious image of law and authority, partly derived as an inheritance from one's ancestors and partly acquired as a resolution of the Oedipus complex in childhood.

SYLLOGISTIC REASONING: The process of arriving at a conclusion (e.g., "John is a

Martian") by connecting elements in the two essential premises that lead to it: (1) the major premise (e.g., "Only Martians have antennas sprouting out of their heads"), and (2) the minor premise (e.g., "John has an antenna sprouting out of his head").

SYNTHESIS: A combination of or fusion of disparate ideas or segments of experience into a unity.

TELEPATHY: Purportedly, reading the thoughts of another person directly, i.e., without the mediation of gestures, words, or other symbols.

TEMPERAMENT: A habitual predisposition to act or react in specific ways. E.g., INTROVERSION is sometimes characterized as a tendency to react to problems or perplexities by personal reflection rather than by swift action or by seeking the guidance or support of others. See EXTROVERSION.

UNCONSCIOUS: That which is considered to be just beyond the boundaries of CONSCIOUSNESS. The unconscious is sometimes portrayed as something "below" consciousness (UC_1), i.e., instinctive drives or emotions that influence consciousness and are at least partly suppressed or repressed; and sometimes portrayed as "above" consciousness (UC_2), e.g., the Freudian Super-Ego as an unconscious assimilation of parental directives and authority, or the Jungian Self-archetype as a symbol of wholeness or holiness.

UNDERSTANDING: The power to form abstract, general concepts (e.g., "humanity," "universality") or categories that may be used to classify particular phenomena (e.g., "mammal" and "marsupial").

VIS AESTIMATIVA: See AESTIMATIVE POWER.

VIS COGITATIVA: See COGITATIVE POWER.

VOLITION: See WILL.

WILL, or VOLITION: The power of evaluating and selecting goals for cognition or action, and making the appropriate efforts for the attainment of these goals.

WÜRZBURG SCHOOL: The school of psychology founded by Oswald Külpe at the University of Würzburg in Germany, and engaged at the turn of the present century in the introspective-experimental study of volition, "imageless" thought, and the effects of attitudes and tasks on perception, recall, and thought.

ZENER CARDS: A deck of twenty-five cards, each marked with one of five different symbols (cross, rectangle, star, circle, wavy lines), that is used in experiments at parapsychological laboratories to test an individual's ESP abilities.

Bibliographical Excursus

The following notes include comments on some of the works cited in footnotes; comparison of these works with some parallel, supplementary, or complementary treatments elsewhere; and remarks tending to show the relationship of some of these representative sources to the general objectives of a philosophical anthropology.

CHAPTER 1

Tom Regan and P. Singer's anthology *Animal Rights and Human Obligations* (Englewood Cliffs, N.J.: Prentice-Hall, 1976) includes analysis of a variety of opinions on the question of the difference between man and animals. Paul Shepard's *Thinking Animals: Animals and the Development of Human Intelligence* (New York: Viking, 1978) is a good source for the investigation of similarities and differences in cognition between human beings and animals. Mortimer Adler's *The Difference of Man and the Difference it Makes* (Cleveland: Meridian, 1967) is by far the most extensive attempt to coordinate a traditional philosophical approach to the "difference" problem with currently available "empirical" data, and Adler's bibliography provides a rather thorough listing of philosophical and scientific works pertaining to the problem. "A Symposium on Language and Communication," edited by Adler et al. for the 1975 edition of *The Great Ideas Today* (Chicago: Encyclopedia Britannica, Inc., 1975), an updated treatment of the same subject, features a discussion by experts from various fields of the pros and cons concerning "difference-in-kind" vs. "difference-in-degree" between man and other animals. Adler's revision of some of his earlier conclusions, set forth in the course of his contribution to this symposium, cannot be taken as his last word on the subject, however, since he clearly (and wisely) makes his latest conclusions contingent on the discovery of further corroboratory scientific evidence.

The greatest threat to Adler's conclusions (e.g., the conclusion that animals cannot use language syntactically) comes, of course, from the currently burgeoning experiments with "talking animals"—experiments such as those described in Maurice Temerlin's *Lucy: Growing up Human, a Chimpanzee Daughter in a Psychotherapist's Family* (Palo Alto, Calif.: Science and Behavior Books, 1975); Duane Rumbaugh and Timothy Gill's report, "Language and the Acquisition of Language-Type Skills by a Chimpanzee," in *The Annals of the New York Academy of Science* 270 (April 28, 1976); and Francine Patterson's article, "Conversations with a Gorilla," in *National Geographic* 154:4 (October 1978).

Speaking of Apes: A Critical Anthology of Two-Way Communication with Man, edited by Thomas A. Sebeok and Donna Jean Umiker-Sebeok (New York: Plenum, 1980), is a compilation of articles on both sides of the question of whether animals are really similar to humans (differing only in degree of sophistication) in their language abilities. For opposing opinions regarding the significance of such research, see *Nim: A Chimpanzee Who Learned Sign Language* (New York: Knopf, 1979), by Herbert S. Terrance, who argues that most apparent cases of sentence-formation by chimpanzees can be explained on the basis of the animals' unconscious imitation of, or the taking of cues from, the researchers who were working with them; and *The Ape's Reflexion* (New York: Dial Press, 1979), by Adrian J. Desmond, who argues that apes have a language of their own that may be misinterpreted as human language by experimenters.

Even if the researchers are successful in responding to these challenges, the thrust of their work would seem to be limited to the claim that the linguistic abilities and corresponding cognitive processes in primates are at least comparable to those of a very young human child. But in response to the critiques of Terrance and others, some researchers are already beginning to reexamine some of the more ambitious conclusions they had reached in the late 1960s and early 1970s. For example, Duane Rumbaugh told a *New York Times* interviewer (Oct. 21, 1979) that he was becoming more "conservative" in the conclusions he was drawing, and that he was returning in a stricter fashion to his earlier objective—to use the chimpanzee "as an animal model to approach the learning problems of mentally retarded children." But attainment of even this limited objective might be hindered by a drastic change in the interpretation of the chimpanzee's language abilities, since the value of the chimpanzee as a model depends on there being a basic similarity between its linguistic abilities and the abilities of the children to which extrapolations are being made by this research.

CHAPTER 2

A good summary of the more widely accepted findings of anthropology and psychology concerning the simple instincts occurring in man is Ronald Fletcher's *Instinct in Man* (London: Allen & Unwin, 1957). Even in Aristotelian-Thomistic circles one hardly hears any more of the *vis cogitativa*, but for a reexamination of this remarkable notion of a semiinstinctive human faculty (reincarnated temporarily in the "moral sense" theories that predominated in eighteenth-century European ethics), one may consult Julien Peghaire, "A Forgotten Sense, the Cogitative According to St. Thomas," *The Modern Schoolman* 20 (November 1924), and Thomas Flynn, O.P., "The Cogitative Power," *Thomist* 16 (October 1953). Flynn takes pains to point out that the "cogitative" is not an instinct in the strict sense but is only analogous to what is found in animals. Henri Bergson's *Introduction to Metaphysics* (New York: Liberal Arts Press, 1949) is a good source for his intuition-as-instinct doctrine.

On Jung's archetype-as-instinct concept, consult the chapter on archetypes in his *Modern Man in Search of a Soul* (New York: Vintage, 1965). Ira Progroff's *The Power of Archetypes in Modern Civilization* (New York: The Julian Press, 1969) is a pro-Jungian application of Jung's archetype theory to problems of contemporary culture. For McDougall's theory of instinct-constellations, see his *An Introduction to Social Psychology* (London: Methuen, 1936). Sigmund Freud gives a clear and brief exposition of his theory of the Life Instinct (Eros) and the aggression-related Death Instinct (Thanatos) in *The Ego and the Id*, translated by James Strachey (New York: Norton, 1960); and applies this theory to society at large in *Civilization and Its Discontents*, translated by James Strachey (New York: Norton, 1961). Konrad Lorenz, in his *On Aggression* (New York: Harcourt Brace & World, 1966), explains what we have called the "instinct for hierarchical social rankings" in terms of a general instinct of aggression operative in both man and animals. A book with a similar interpretative stance is Robert Ardrey's widely debated *The Territorial*

Imperative (New York: Atheneum, 1970), which theorized an essential continuity between the instinctive assertion of rights of territoriality found (according to ethologists) throughout the animal kingdoms and in the systems of legal and moral "boundaries" constructed by human individuals and communities.

If the assertions by Jung, Bergson, Chomsky, et al. on the possibility of a specifically *human* instinct mark a kind of "rightist" departure from the mainstream of science (which prefers to downplay the presence of instinct in human behavior), the tendency of Freud, Lorenz, Ardrey et al. to ascribe much or most human behavior to an instinctive genetic programming possessed in common with animals marks an equally severe and disturbing "leftist" departure from the current scientific orthodoxy concerning the determinants of human behavior. Another "leftist" departure, sociobiology, is discussed in Chapter 3.

CHAPTER 3

Those who wish to read further in sociobiology should consult Edward O. Wilson's *Sociobiology: The New Synthesis* (Cambridge: Harvard University Press, 1975) and his *On Human Nature* (Cambridge: Harvard University Press, 1978), which maintain that many "instinctive" attributes of animals, e.g., territoriality and tribalism and mating rituals, have their counterparts in human beings in all eras and cultures; and Richard Dawkins' *The Selfish Gene* (Oxford: Oxford University Press, 1976), which asserts that humans, like all animals, have an "Evolutionary Stable Strategy" (ESS) that dictates their domination over other species, although human consciousness can override its own ESS intermittently, sometimes producing the typically human pastime of war as a by-product. Two anthologies dealing with the sociobiology controversy are: Arthur L. Caplan (ed.), *The Sociobiology Debate: Readings on Ethical and Scientific Issues* (New York: Harper Colophon, 1978), and *Sociobiology and Human Nature: An Interdisciplinary Critique and Defense* (San Francisco: Jossey-Bass, 1978). Mary Midgley's *Beast and Man—the Roots of Human Nature* (Ithaca: Cornell University Press, 1978) and Irenaus Eibl-Eibesfeldt's *The Biology of Peace and War* (New York: Viking, 1979) offer sympathetic and sustained philosophical defenses of the findings of the sociobiologists, but also take pains to argue that the "instinctive" elements of human nature recognized by the sociobiologists are modified and sublimated by cultural evolution, and are checked or redirected by free choice.

For a rebuttal of some of the main contentions of sociobiology, see Marshall Sahlins' *The Use and Abuse of Biology* (Ann Arbor: University of Michigan Press, 1976). Shortly before his death, the noted philosopher Charles Frankel published some interesting reflections on the causes of the sociobiology debate: "Why Has Sociobiology Caused an Uproar?," *Commentary* 68:12 (July 1976). A more general rebuttal of innatism, or hereditarianism, is to be found in Erich Fromm's *The Anatomy of Human Destructiveness* (New York: Fawcett Crest, 1973), which lashes out against the theories of innate human aggression (i.e., the theories of Sigmund Freud, Konrad Lorenz, Robert Ardrey, and Desmond Morris) and argues that environmental (societal) factors are chiefly responsible for mankind's aggressiveness and violence. Another noted environmentalist is Ashley Montagu, whose *The Nature of Human Aggression* (New York: Oxford University Press, 1977) challenges the views of those who think aggressivity is inherited.

Considering the recurring, almost cyclical nature of environment-heredity debates, it was perhaps inevitable that someone should eventually perceive the debate not as something to be resolved one way or the other but as a kind of constant in the evolution of mankind. Such a thesis is proposed in C.D. Darlington's *The Evolution of Man and Society* (New York: Simon & Schuster, 1969), a monumental chronicle of human genetic evolution, which explains the development of the migrations, the emergence of nations, classes, and social structures, and human history as a whole in terms of the interplay of clannish hereditarianism (inbreeding) and abandonment to the selectivity of the environment (outbreeding). Less of a tour de force than Darlington's book, but very useful for understanding the dimensions of contemporary anthropological-psychological debates about environment and heredity, is A. H. Halsey's anthology, *Heredity and Environment* (New York: The Free Press, 1977), which gives particular attention to issues such as population control, social class, and the effect of race on IQ scores.

Earlier twentieth-century antecedents of the race-and-IQ debate are explored in *Cyril Burt, Psychologist,* by L. S. Hearnshaw (Ithaca, N.Y.: Cornell University Press, 1979). The contemporary currents in this debate have been recapitulated in a series of articles published between 1968 and 1973 by the magazine *Psychology Today* and collected under the title *Index of the I.Q. Controversy.* The contemporary controversy emerging out of Jensen's assertions regarding race and IQ is discussed by Antony Flew in "The Jensen Uproar," *Philosophy* 48:3 (1973): 63–69.

The shock waves from this controversy have led to flurries of negative reactions challenging Jensen's conclusions, such as the article by Scarr and Weinberg, "IQ Test Performance of Black Children Adopted by White Families," in *American Psychologist* 31 (1976), which offers evidence that there is no significant difference in the elevation of IQ scores of adopted white and black children, respectively, after both whites and blacks are placed in similar, favorable environments. But Sandra Scarr, Harold Grotevant, and Richard Weinberg, in their article "Patterns of Interest Similarity in Adoptive and Biological Families" in the *Journal of Personality and Social Psychology* 35 (1977), have tipped the scales back again in favor of heredity. They show that there is a significant correlation of the *interests* of natural children, but not of adopted children, with the parents by whom they are raised. The article has no racial overtones, but this does not guarantee that it will not elicit controversy and reaction from those who are more environmentally inclined.

One of the few books available that explores the reasons why heredity-environment debates elicit such strong and emotional reactions is Nicholas Pastore's *The Nature-Nurture Controversy* (New York: King's Crown Press, 1942). To date, Pastore's thesis that there is a correlation between one's stance on heredity-environment issues and one's sociopolitical outlook has not been systematically and extensively tested by means of procedures now standard in studies in social psychology, perhaps because of natural differences in opinion that must emerge among researchers when it comes to defining traits like "conservatism," "authoritarianism," etc. Although the combined European-American research venture that led to the publication of *The Authoritarian Personality,* by T. W. Adorno et al. (New York: Norton, 1950), laid some groundwork for the investigation of such correlations, the possibilities suggested by Pastore have simply not yet been taken seriously enough to elicit direct and concerted investigations.

At present, it seems that one's opinions on these matters must be almost hopelessly influenced by one's disciplinary biases. For example, the geneticist C. D.

Darlington tends to interpret even periods of environmentalist "outbreeding" as genetically determined; the social psychologist Erich Fromm interprets even the conservatism of privileged classes whose members take such pride in their genes as an attitude determined by their favored social position; and the Adlerian psychologist William Toman, in *Family Constellations* (New York: Springer, 1969), traces attitudes such as "autocratic conservatism" to one's relative sibling position in the family (e.g., oldest sisters tend to be more "conservative" than younger sisters), thus giving evidence of his Freudian-Adlerian training. (Adler's revision of Freud strongly emphasizes sibling relationships.)

CHAPTER 4

A useful starting place for acquainting oneself with the current state of affairs in psychology regarding the question of male-female differences is Eleanor Maccoby and Carol Jacklin's *The Psychology of Sex Differences* (Stanford: Stanford University Press, 1974). The authors state that they lean towards a "feminist" position. Another fairly comprehensive and feminist-oriented treatment of the differential status quo is to be found in Carol Tavris and Carole Offir's *The Longest War: Sex Differences in Perspective* (New York: Harcourt Brace Jovanovich, 1977), a book that sides with Maccoby and Jacklin's conclusion that the only bona fide psychological differences between men and women are: (1) the greater aggressivity of males, (2) male superiority in solving visual-spatial problems (a superiority that seems to be the only genetically conditioned sex-related personality trait), (3) differences in mathematical abilities, and (4) the superiority of females in verbal ability. After the publication of the books by Jacklin, Tavris, and Offir, further studies were published offering evidence that differential development of the right and left lobes of the brain in males and females is responsible for certain cognitive differences between the sexes, such as the relative inability of boys to respond to the "look-say" method of teaching words (see, e.g., Sandra F. Witelson's article, "Sex and the Single Hemisphere Specialization of the Right Hemisphere for Spatial Processing," *Science* 193:4251 [1976]).

For more specifically philosophical treatments of this age-old issue, see Martha Lee Osborne's anthology, *Women in Western Philosophy* (New York: Random House, 1979); Mary B. Mahowald's anthology, *Philosophy of Woman* (Indianapolis: Hackett, 1977); a symposium edited by Adler et al. on "The Difference of Woman, and the Difference it Makes," in the 1968 edition of *The Great Ideas Today* (Chicago: Encyclopedia Britannica, 1968); and the following articles by Christine Allen (née Garside): "Can a Woman Be Good in the Same Way as a Man?" in *Dialogue* 10:3 (1971), a critique of the positions of Aristotle and Kierkegaard; "Plato on Women," in *Feminist Studies* 2:213 (1975); and "Sex-Identity," in Volume 1 of the Contemporary Canadian Philosophy series, *Philosophy and the Quality of Life*, edited by W. Shea, J. King-Farlow, and Neal Watson (Montreal: Academic Publications, Inc., 1976).

The case against traditional sex-role stereotyping is argued by Ashley Montagu in *The Natural Superiority of Women* (New York: Collier, 1974), which sets forth anthropological evidence proving that women are both physically and psychologically superior to men. The case for natural (innate) differences between men and women that cannot be obliterated by any amount of "consciousness-raising" is provocatively made by Samuel Florman in his essay, "Engineering and the Female Mind: Why Women Will Not Become Engineers," in *Harper's* 257:1533 (February 1978); and by Steven Goldberg, who maintains, in *The Inevitability of Patriarchy* (New York: William Morrow & Co., 1973), that if we accept the fact (as even many feminists do) that males are naturally more aggressive, various forms of patriarchal male dominance are inevitable. One of the most thought-provoking arguments along more moderate lines is that of Alice Rossi, a noted feminist of the 1950s who more recently has done some moderate backtracking; in "The Biosocial Side of Parenthood," in *Human Nature* 1:5 (May, 1978), she suggests that there is a natural, biological "link-up" of the erotic and the reproductive aspects of sexuality through the hormone oxytocin, which acts as a kind of "chemical bridge" connecting these two aspects—a connection that most feminists would deny. J. R. Lucas, in "Because You Are a Woman," *Philosophy* 48:4 (1973), argues that the tendency of feminists to deny sex differences could lead to an egalitarianism that would accentuate the very depersonalization that feminists so deplore.

Finally, although there is a movement afoot to reinterpret human personality as "androgynous," it is not likely that June Singer, author of *Androgyny: Towards a New Theory of Sexuality* (Garden City, N.Y.: Anchor, 1977), will become the spokesperson for that movement, since her approach is heavily Jungian and to most feminists minimally conversant with Jung's thought this means it is unscientific if not "sexist."

CHAPTER 5

The philosophy of evolution and consciousness that is developed at length in Teilhard de Chardin's *The Phenomenon of Man* (New York: Harper Torchbooks, 1959) is also developed in several posthumously published collections of essays, including those published under the titles *The Future of Man* (New York: Harper & Row, 1964) and *Human Energy* (New York: Harcourt Brace Jovanovich, 1969). To understand the philosophical background of Teilhard's approach, one should consult Henri Bergson's *Creative Evolution,* translated by Arthur Mitchell (Westport, Conn.: Greenwood Press, 1975), which was the source of the initial insights that would later be fully explicated in *The Phenomenon of Man.* Teilhard's idea of a collective consciousness finds striking contemporary parallels not only in Reich's *The Greening of America* and Thomas' *The Lives of a Cell* (both of which are discussed in Chapter 5), but also in Fritjof Capra's *The Tao of Physics* (New York: Bantam, 1977), which draws an extended parallel between contemporary developments in atomic physics (in which the subsistence of individual material particles is being questioned) and the views of Oriental philosophies, which emphasize the universal prevalence of spirit, energy, and consciousness.

The idea of progress through distinguishable stages in the development of consciousness can be developed from either a spiritualistic or a materialistic point of view. Raimundo Panikkar's essay, "The New Innocence," in *Cross Currents* 27:1 (Spring, 1977), offers a spiritual interpretation of the development of consciousness from primal innocence, to guilt-laden and limitation-conscious knowledge, and thence to a "new innocence," a "cosmotheandric vision" in which the human, divine, and cosmic are synthesized. Julian Jaynes, on the other hand, in *The Origins of Consciousness in the Breakdown of the Bicameral Mind* (Boston: Houghton Mifflin,

1976), relies on theories based on our knowledge of the functions of the right and left hemispheres of the brain in presenting a materialistic explanation of the breakup of primitive coconsciousness and the processes that began to lead to the emergence of "individual" consciousness in the modern sense.

One of the distinctive aspects of Teilhard de Chardin's theory of the evolution of consciousness is his version of a paradoxical enhancement of individual consciousness not only in spite of, but because of, the final development of a "collective" consciousness, an enhancement that assures increasing human control of evolution as evolution progresses. The noted geneticist Theodosius Dobzhansky, who in *Mankind Evolving* (New Haven: Yale University Press, 1962) expresses great sympathy for the Teilhardian vision, has developed his own insights regarding the same basic paradox in *The Biological Basis of Human Freedom* (New York: Columbia University Press, 1956). The Teilhardian, "neo-Lamarckian" revolt against evolution interpreted solely in terms of "natural selection" is reflected also in Jean Piaget's *Behavior and Evolution* (New York: Pantheon, 1978), which develops the thesis that, whereas we are indeed determined by our evolutionary environment, we also *select* that environment.

CHAPTER 6

The problem of a monistic vs. dualistic interpretation of human personality may be viewed as but one aspect of a larger problem, the problem of a monistic vs. dualistic interpretation of man's world and his life in that world. Octavio Paz, in *Conjunctions and Disjunctions* (New York: Viking, 1953), offers a philosophico-poetic view of man's ambiguous monism-dualism as reflected in various aspects of Western and Eastern civilizations. Hannah Arendt, in a posthumously published book on *Thinking* (New York: Harcourt Brace Jovanovich, 1977), analyzes the relation of man's thought processes to the objective state of the world and vice versa and shows how the mind-body problem emerges out of some of these very complex relationships. Eugen Rosenstock-Huessy, in *The Multiformity of Man* (Norwich, Vt.: Argo Books, 1973), considers the transition of man in the technological world through a succession of aspects—unity, duality, and plurality.

For a specific treatment of the mind-body problem as the subject of a centuries-old debate among philosophers, one may consult Sidney Hook's anthology *Dimensions of Mind: A Symposium* (New York: New York University Press, 1960), which includes discussions of the mind-body problem from representatives of both monistic and dualistic viewpoints. A more recent contribution to the same debate is *The Self and its Brain,* by Karl Popper and John Eccles (New York: Springer-Verlag, 1977), which is divided into three major sections. In the first section Popper presents the philosophical issues related to the mind-body problem from both a historical and a systematic viewpoint; in the second section, Eccles, a scientist, develops the main neurological issues related to the problem; and in the last part of the book, their recorded conversations, which amount to a concerted defense of dualism and a rebuttal of materialism, are reproduced.

One's position on the mind-body problem is of great practical consequence in the field of medicine. A recent issue of the *Journal of Medicine and Philosophy* 2:2 (1977), edited by H. Tristam Engelhardt, Jr., is given over to the topic of "mind-body quandaries," the quandaries being philosophical problems that have emerged in connection with certain medical procedures. Pedro Entralgo, in *Mind and Body: Psychosomatic Pathology: A Short History of the Evolution of Medical Thought* (New York: P. J. Kennedy and Sons, 1936), critically contrasts the one-sided physical approach of Western medicine and the psychosomatic approach of Hippocratic medicine and ancient Greek medicine generally. A more recent book, C. Alberto Sequin's *Introduction to Psychosomatic Medicine* (New York: Indiana University Press, 1970), proposes from a medical point of view a theory similar to the one proposed toward the end of this chapter, namely, that both dualism and monism are one-sided and must be eschewed; i e., that both dualistic and monistic aspects must be consciously recognized and inte: ... lated in the human totality.

CHAPTER 7

Mortimer Adler's *The Idea of Freedom: A Dialectical Examination of the Conceptions of Freedom* (New York: Doubleday, 1958) is an encyclopedic examination of the quite varied ideas of freedom that have developed in Western philosophy. This book also contains an exhaustive bibliography of writings on freedom. (So does Paul Edwards and Arthur Paps' anthology, *A Modern Introduction to Philosophy* [New York: Free Press, 1966].) For a pamphlet-length summation of Adler's analysis of freedom, see his *Freedom: A Study of the Development of the Concept in the English and American Traditions of Philosophy* (Albany: Magi Books, 1968). Systematic treatments of various aspects of freedom, with thorough historically oriented bibliographies, are also included in Adler's *Syntopicon* (volumes 2 and 3 of the *Great Books of the Western World* [Chicago: Encyclopedia Britannica, 1952]), under the headings "Cause," "Liberty," "Necessity and Contingency," and "Will."

Since the notion of will is intimately linked with the notions of free choice and free will, one may find it useful to consult Vernon J. Bourke's *Will in Western Thought* (New York: Sheed & Ward, 1964), a critical-historical survey of the concept of will. The major issues in traditional and contemporary debates on determinism vs. free will are discussed in several representative anthologies, including Sidney Hook's *Determinism and Freedom in the Age of Modern Science* (New York: Collier, 1961), Sidney Morgenbesser and James Walsh's *Free Will* (Englewood Cliffs, N.J.: Prentice-Hall, 1962), and Bernard Berofsky's *Free Will and Determinism* (New York: Harper & Row, 1966).

The *locus classicus* for the distinction between free choice, free will, and liberty that is emphasized in the present work is the introduction to Hegel's *Philosophy of Right* (§§1–33). A summary of this highly abstruse analysis, in the context of Hegel's political philosophy, is included in H. Kainz, *Hegel's Philosophy of Right, with Marx's Commentary* (The Hague: Nijhoff, 1974), pp. 14–17. A very readable contemporary analysis of freedom, which is similar in tone and spirit to Hegel's, is Fritjof Bergmann's *On Being Free* (Notre Dame: University of Notre Dame Press, 1977), which argues for a theory of freedom that is compatible with causal "determination," shows the untenability of the arguments for "pure" freedom, and differentiates the notion of freedom from the notions of indetermination, lack of restraint, and free choice, with which it is often equated and/or confused. (Bergmann agrees with my contention that any choice can be "free" if it is accompanied by free will, but traces our idea of free will to our varying experiences of self-identity rather than to experiences of effort-expenditure.)

CHAPTER 8

Basic and relevant factual studies of infant development are *The First Twelve Months of Life,* edited by Frank Caplan (New York: Bantam, 1978), and "Rhythmic Habit Patterns in Infancy: Their Sequence, Age of Onset and Frequency," in *Child Development* 42:2, (June 1971). For the period from birth through age ten, see *Child Behavior,* by Frances Ilg and Louise Bates (New York: Harper & Row, 1955), which shows how the psychological growth of the child follows a regular but pulsating pattern of equilibrium and disequilibrium until a synthesis of the various extremes is reached.

The dean of developmental psychologists is Jean Piaget, whose early books—*The Origins of Intelligence in Children* (New York: International Universities Press, 1966), *The Construction of Reality in the Child* (New York: Basic Books, 1954), and *Play, Dreams and Imitation in Childhood* (New York: Norton, 1962)—are classic examples of systematic observation and interpretation of young children. Many of Piaget's later works, however, end up in interpretations of a highly cerebral and specula- tive sort, based on a minimum of observation, and seem to have edged away from what is now called "developmental psychology." An extraordinary encounter between Piaget and Noam Chomsky, at a three-day symposium held in France, forms the centerpiece of *Language and Learning: The Debate between Jean Piaget and Noam Chomsky,* edited by Massimo Piattelli-Palmarini (Cambridge: Harvard Uni- versity Press, 1980), a volume in which a number of the problems dealt with in the present work are touched upon in significant ways. Of particular interest is Chomsky's defense of the study of man's linguistic ability as a species-specific "organ of the mind," a view that is attacked by another participant in the sym- posium (not Piaget) with evidence from "language-using" chimpanzees—evidence that is no longer thought to be quite so convincing as it was, to many, in the late 1970s.

A specifically Freudian interpretation of developmental stages that has had a great influence on discussion of early psychological development is Erik Erikson's *Childhood and Society,* revised edition (New York: Norton, 1964). Erikson gives a short and readable summary of the stages of "trust," "autonomy," "identity," etc., in a 1959 paper, "Identity and the Life Cycle," which appeared in the first issue of *Psychological Issues.*

James Feibleman's *The Stages of Human Life* (The Hague: Nijhoff, 1975) is a highly speculative account of child development, including an interpretation of certain stages as symbolic of philosophical positions. (Readers should be forewarned that Feibleman sees the stage of "adult maturity" epitomized in Aris- totelianism and Hegelianism!) From a philosophical-anthropological perspective, the best extensive study now available is Bernard Boelen's *Personal Maturity: The Existential Dimension* (New York: Seabury, 1978), a unique interpretive sifting and synthesis of the data of developmental psychology from the vantage point of existential phenomenology.

CHAPTER 9

In recent years developmental psychologists have given increased emphasis to the study of postadolescent development. One of the most comprehensive studies of mature development is Roger Gould's *Transformations* (New York: Simon & Schuster, 1978), which is the result of a long series of studies designed to pinpoint major recognizable stages and transitions in the mature years with a reliability comparable to that with which Arnold Gesell, Jean Piaget, Erik Erikson, and others have charted such stages and transitions in the earlier years. Daniel Levinson's *The Seasons of a Man's Life* (New York: Knopf, 1978) is a further contribution to this trend, with specific emphasis on male development. Gail Sheehy's *Passages* (New York: Bantam, 1977), which was published before Gould's and Levinson's works, and which quickly attained best-seller status, drew heavily on the research of Gould, Levinson, and others, and applied their concepts to a great number of case studies. Published just prior to all of these, Theodore Lidz's *The Person: His and Her Development Throughout the Life Cycle* (New York: Basic Books, 1976) is a truly comprehensive treatment of all stages of development from birth to old age.

Erik Erikson, whose studies of development were cited elsewhere, has also published two psychobiographical studies that follow some selected paradigmatic individual through life stages into maturity, e.g., *Young Man Luther* (New York: Norton, 1962), which reconstructs and relives Martin Luther's efforts to attain a sense of identity, and *Ghandhi's Truth or the Origin of Militant Non-Violence* (New York: Norton, 1969), a psychoanalytic reflection on Gandhi's attempt to maintain his extraordinary personal composure and integrity amid fierce and shattering extremes of experience. Finally, Bernard Boelen's *Personal Maturity*, cited elsewhere, includes detailed, systematic, and empirically based sections examining the exigencies and criteria of maturity from an existential-phenomenological viewpoint; of all the studies mentioned here, this is the only one that explicitly strives for, and to a certain extent achieves, a philosophical-anthropological synthesis.

CHAPTER 10

Although more than two thousand years have elapsed since the writing of Plato's *Symposium*, its discussion of love remains one of the most thought-provoking (and entertaining) discussions of this topic—or, indeed, of any topic—ever written. Another very readable dialogue of Plato, the *Lysis*, takes up the problem of the source of love between and among friends, an aspect of the general problem of love that is too often neglected. This dialogue seems to have provided the basis for Aristotle's famous discussion of friendship in Books 8 and 9 of his *Nicomachean Ethics*.

Denis de Rougemont's *Love in the Western World* (New York: Harcourt Brace, 1940) traces the concept of love in its many guises and vicissitudes—divine love, courtly love, romantic love, etc.—in the evolution of Western thought since the days of Plato. Douglas Morgan's *Love: Plato, the Bible and Freud* (Englewood Cliffs, N.J.: Prentice-Hall, 1964) compares and contrasts three monumental and influential conceptions of love in Western thought. Martin d'Arcy's *The Mind and the Heart of Love* (London: Faber & Faber, 1954), a speculative reflection on the metatheories of de Rougemont and others, includes an abstruse but interesting attempt to synthesize various opposites in love—the "lion" and the "unicorn," centripetal love and centrifugal love, self-regard and altruism, and love-as-essence and love-as-existence. Ralph Waldo Emerson's 1843 essay on love is strikingly similar in tenor to Socrates' discourse on love in Plato's *Symposium*.

The Meaning of Love, Vol. I of Isidor Schneider's two-volume anthology *The World of Love* (New York: George Braziller, 1964), is the most comprehensive collection available of representative philosophical writings on the meaning of love, the stages of love, love and maturity, love and friendship, love and sex, love and community, and other aspects of love.

In twentieth-century philosophy, extensive philosophical theses on love have been contributed by Vladimir Solovyev, Max Scheler, and José Ortega y Gasset. Solovyev's *The Meaning of Love* (New York: International Universities Press, 1947) emphasizes the altruistic-sacrificing qualities of true love ("The meaning of human love . . . is the justification and deliverance of individuality through the sacrifice of egoism"). Scheler's *The Nature of Sympathy* (London: Routledge & Kegan Paul, 1954) distinguishes human love as an active regard for others from "fellow-feeling" as a more passive sense of unity, and emphasizes the relation of love to interpersonal progress in the consciousness of values. Ortega's *On Love: Aspects of a Single Theme* (New York: Meridian, 1957) also emphasizes the active nature of love (as contrasted with "desire," a passive appetite), and defines love summarily as "a centrifugal act of the soul in constant flux that goes toward the object and envelops it in warm corroboration, uniting us with it and positively affirming its being."

Erich Fromm's *The Art of Loving* (New York: Bantam, 1956) develops a similar theme—the essentially active rather than passive nature of love—from the perspective of neo-Freudian psychology. Freud's own major metapsychological commentary on love (or Eros) in *Civilization and its Discontents* (New York: Norton, 1962) goes beyond the analysis of the dynamics of individual love encounters to theorize about love in its cosmic and sociohistoric development. One of the most interesting anthropological studies on love relevant to philosophical inquiry is Robert Brain's *Friends and Lovers* (New York: Basic Books, 1976), an analysis of friendship customs throughout the world, which poses questions concerning the very un-Platonic neglect of friendship rituals among those of the same sex in the West (particularly in so-called Anglo-Saxon cultures), and a corresponding and compensating modern tendency to overemphasize married love as the supreme source and exemplar of friendship.

CHAPTER 11

Bibliographical information on books and articles on parapsychology is abundant. In addition to Ashby's Guide Book, mentioned in Chapter 11, one may consult *Parapsychology: Sources of Information,* compiled by Rhea A. White and Laura A. Dale (Meluchen, N.J.: Scarecrow Press, 1973), and *Bibliography of Parapsychology,* compiled by George Zorab (New York: Garrett-Helix, 1957), which lists European as well as Anglo-American studies.

Good introductions to controlled studies performed on the various forms of Psi are Benjamin Wolman's anthology, *The Handbook of Parapsychology* (New York: Van Nostrand, Reinhold, 1977), and J.B. Rhine's *Parapsychology Today* (Secaucus, N.J.: Citadel Press, 1968). Adam Smith's *The Powers of Mind* (New York: Random House, 1975) is an overview by a popular author of all the "fringe" areas of human consciousness, and of the attempts of both "straight" scientists and adventurous laymen to explore the uncharted areas. To understand the dilemmas encountered by scientists trying to verify or account for paranormal phenomena in conventional scientific terms, one should consult J.R. Smythie's anthology, *Science and ESP*

(London: Routledge & Kegan Paul, 1967) and Philip Slater's *The Wayward Gate: Science and the Supernatural* (Boston: Beacon Press, 1977).

A wide range of philosophical problems emerging from or otherwise related to current research in parapsychology—e.g., questions as to what the "Basic Limiting Factors" of experience are, and the revolutionary effects acceptance of the paranormal would have on contemporary science—are discussed in James Wheatley's and Hoyt Edge's anthology, *The Philosophical Dimensions of Parapsychology* (Springfield, Ill.: Charles C. Thomas, 1976), Jan Ludwig's anthology, *Philosophy and Parapsychology* (Buffalo: Prometheus, 1978), and Gardner Murphy's anthology of William James' writings on parapsychology, *William James on Physical Research* (New York: Viking, 1960).

For a specific treatment of philosophy from the time of Plato and the issue of precognition, see *Precognition and Philosophy of Science: An Essay on Backward Causation* by Bob Brier, (Atlantic Highlands, N.J.: Humanities Press, 1974). Although F. W. H. Myers' *Human Personality and its Survival of Bodily Death* (New York: Arno Press, 1975), a reprint of Myers' turn-of-the-century case studies in psychic phenomena (London: Green & Co., 1902), consists mostly of anecdotal information with little direct relevance to philosophy, Myers does offer a thesis that is perhaps worthy of further development. Myers contends that there is (a) a state of "normal" body-mind (or body-soul) composition; (b) the possibility of extreme severance or disintegration of this composition, leading to "mental disease"; and finally (c) the equal and opposite and hitherto unrecognized possibility of extraordinary integration or unity in the composition, leading to what (to the normal composite personality) seems to be paranormal phenomena. Thus, according to Myers' thesis, Psi would be the precise obverse of neurotic and psychotic mental states.

CHAPTER 12

Many traditional debates regarding "survival" after "death" have hinged on interpretation of the nature of the "soul"; hence some understanding of the traditional concept of "soul" is a prerequisite to understanding these debates. For a detailed analysis of the various interpretations of this concept in Thomistic and Western philosophy, see Gerald F. Kreyché's "The Soul-Body Problem in St. Thomas," in *The New Scholasticism* 46:4 (Autumn 1972). It is also helpful to have some understanding of what death is, or is thought to be, as a preamble to speculation or research on the possibility of human survival *after* death. The physical and societal aspects of death are discussed in *Brain Death: Interrelated Medical and Social Issues,* edited by Julius Korein (New York: New York Academy of Sciences, 1978).

Howard K. Congdon, in *The Pursuit of Death* (Nashville: Abingdon, 1977), shows how many philosophical problems develop in man's attempt to interpret the meaning of death. Jacques Choron, in *Death and Western Thought* (New York: Collier, 1963), chronicles the history of Western philosophical attempts to come to grips with death by disbelievers in human survival (e.g., Nietzsche and Sartre), believers (e.g., Leibniz and Kant), and ambiguous cases (e.g., Hegel). Arnold Toynbee's anthology *Life After Death* (New York: McGraw-Hill, 1976) brings together a wide variety of viewpoints—historical, anthropological, biological, physical, theological—geared to the interpretation of human attitudes towards death, the clarification of the possibility of survival after death, or both. An exploration of the evolution of Judaeo-Christian attitudes towards death is offered in Paul Badham's *Christian Beliefs in Life After Death* (New York: Barnes and Noble, 1976), which concludes with an apologetic for the logical possibility of human immortality. Antony Flew's anthology *Body, Mind, and Death* (New York: Macmillan, 1964) includes selections representative of some of the most important philosophical positions regarding immortality; and Terrence Penelhum's anthology *Immortality* (Belmont, Calif.: Wadsworth, 1973) features traditional and contemporary writings on the subject. John Perry's *A Dialogue on Personal Identity and Immortality* (Indianapolis: Hackett, 1978) is an imaginary conversation taking place at the deathbed of a skeptical but open-minded professor of philosophy; as the dialogue proceeds, it focuses mainly on problems of personal identity connected with the idea of personal immortality. Hywel D. Lewis' *Persons and Life After Death* (New York: Harper & Row, 1978) features dialogues with Antony Flew, Anthony Quinton, and other critics of the immortality theory, in addition to essays by Lewis on various aspects of the topic (in this volume Flew offers a sustained and interesting defense of the "astral body" hypothesis discussed in Chapter 12).

Raymond Moody's *Life After Life*, cited in Chapter 12, has been followed by his *Reflections on Life After Life* (New York: Bantam, 1978) which adds little except additional anecdotal "confirmation." In Chapter 10 of his *Memories, Dreams, and Reflections* (New York: Vintage, 1961) the psychoanalyst Carl Jung relates a near-death experience that bears many similarities to the composite experience outlined by Moody, and follows this account with personal and mythological reflections on the idea of life after death. Toward the end of Plutarch's essay "Concerning Those Whom God is Slow to Punish," in the *Moralia* (first-century), there is an interesting account of a soldier's near-death experience that is similar in some respects to Moody's "composite." It seems that such experiences are not just the product of late twentieth-century interest in death and dying, fanned by best-selling paperbacks and radio-and-TV talk-show interviews.

While the present study was in press, information on 102 near-death experiences became available in Kenneth Ring's *Life at Death* (New York: Coward, McCann & Geoghegan, 1980). Scientific, standardized techniques were used in studying the 102 subjects, all of whom had narrowly escaped death from sickness, accident, or attempted suicide. Ring found that about half these subjects underwent the basic near-death experience described by Moody. Little evidence turned up, however, for the following elements of Moody's "composite": the initial loud buzzing or other noise, the "tunnel" phenomenon, the "being of light," and the final vision of a "threshold" or "barrier."

For the development of "astral body" theories in ancient and medieval philosophy, see E.R. Dodds' translation of the fifth-century neo-Platonic thinker Proclus' *Elements of Theology*, second edition (Oxford: Oxford University Press, 1963), Appendix II. The "astral-body" theory discussed in Chapter 12 is closest in conception to the theories propounded by Proclus (see *Elements of Theology*, Props. 196, 207, 208) and the third-century Christian philosopher Origen (see his *De principiis*), both of whom argue for the absolute inseparability of the astral body and the rational soul.

Indexes

Index of Authors

Acts of the Apostles, 105
Adler, Alfred, 154, 177
Adler, Mortimer, 136 (n. 6), 136 (n. 7), 154, 173, 180
  The Difference of Man and the Difference it Makes, 13–14, 136 (n. 3), 173
Adorno, T. W., 154, 176
  The Authoritarian Personality, 37–38, 176
Allen, Christine, 177
Ames, L. B., 79, 154
Anastasi, Anne, 30, 137 (n. 1), 138 (n. 1), 154
Anaxagoras, 100–01, 154
Anaximander, 2, 154
Anaximines, 2, 154
Apocalypse, book of, 149 (n. 22)
Apostle. *See* names of individual apostles
Aquinas, St. Thomas. *See* Thomas Aquinas, St.
Ardrey, Robert, 174–75
Arendt, Hannah, 57, 143 (n. 11), 155, 179
Aristotle, 1, 13, 87, 94, 114, 139 (n. 11), 145 (chap. 9, n. 1), 152 (n. 23), 155, 177, 182
  ancient concept of evolution, 2
  bridging soul/body dualism, 2
  classifying man, 9–10
  concept of human maturity, 2
  De Anima, 140 (n. 15), 142 (n. 3)
  development of consciousness, 2
  form and matter dualism, 59
  Nichomachean Ethics, 182; freedom, 2; happiness, 87; intuitive reason, 17; maturity, 145 (n. 5)
  On Memory and Reminiscence, 9
  treatises on dreams and divination, 3
Ashby, Robert H., 147–48 (n. 5), 183
Augustine, Aurelius, 94, 155
Aurobindo Ghose, Sri, 48, 141 (n. 14)
Averroes, 149 (n. 26), 155

Bacon, Francis, 140 (n. 15), 155
Badham, Paul, 185
Bates, Louise, 181
Beauvoir, Simone de, 45, 139 (n. 9), 156, 166
  The Second Sex, 45, 141 (n. 5)
Bergmann, Fritjof, 180

Bergson, Henri, 4, 141 (n. 11), 155, 174, 175, 178
  Creative Evolution, 57
  future of evolution, 2
  instinct and intuition, 21–22
  philosophy of evolution, 53
  Society for Psychical Research, 103
Berkeley, George (Bishop Berkeley), 62, 110, 155
Berofsky, Bernard, 180
Boelen, Bernard, 181, 182
Bonhoeffer, Dietrich, 4, 155
Bourke, Vernon J., 180
Brain, Robert, 183
Brier, Bob, 184
Broad, C. D., 155
  Society for Psychical Research, 103
Brooks, Jeanne, 144–45 (n. 5)
Brooks, Michael, 144–45 (n. 5)
Browning, Robert, 9
Buber, Martin, 4, 12, 155–56, 166

Camus, Albert, 166
Caplan, Arthur L., 175
Caplan, Frank, 181
Capra, Fritjof, 178
Carnap, Rudolf, 58, 156
Carrington, Hereward, 102
Cassirer, Ernst, 156
  classifying man, 10
Cayce, Edgar, 104
Chomsky, Noam, 27, 29, 137 (n. 5), 156, 175, 181
  Reflections on Language, 17–18
Choron, Jacques, 184
Chuang-Tzu, 156
Clemens, S. L. *See* Twain, Mark
Congdon, Howard K., 184
Corinthians, book of, 113

Dale, Laura A., 148 (n. 11), 183
Daly, Mary, 139 (n. 11)
d'Arcy, Martin, 182
Darlington, C. D., 176, 176–77
Darwin, Charles, 166
Dawkins, Richard, 175
Democritus, 2, 58, 61, 156
de Rougemont, Denis, 182
Descartes, René, 60, 114, 156
  dualistic view of man, 2, 59
Desmond, Adrian J., 174
Dewey, John, 1, 156
Diderot, Denis, 4, 156
Dixon, Jeanne, 104
Dobzhansky, Theodosius, 40, 138 (n. 9), 157, 179

Evolving Man, 56
  Indian caste system as self-defeating,
    38–39
Dodds, E. R., 185

Ebner, Ferdinand, 166
Eccles, John, 179
Edge, Hoyt, 184
Edwards, Paul, 180
Ehrenberg, Rudolf, 12, 166
Eibl-Eibesfeldt, Irenaus, 175
Einstein, Albert, 133, 157
Emerson, Ralph Waldo, 182
Empedocles, 93, 97, 157
  love and hate, 96
  love as attraction of similars, 2–3
Engelhardt, H. Tristam, Jr., 179
Entralgo, Pedro, 180
Erikson, Erik, 78, 157, 181, 182
Eysenck, H. J., 138 (n. 8), 157

Feibleman, James, 181
Fichte, J. G., 60, 157
  development of consciousness, 2
Fletcher, Ronald, 174
Flew, Anthony, 176, 185
Florman, Samuel, 178
Flynn, Thomas, O.P., 174
Fox, H. Munroe, 11–12, 136 (chap. 1, n. 1),
  136 (n. 2), 136 (chap. 2, n. 1), 137 (n. 2)
Frankel, Charles, 175
Freud, Sigmund, 70, 84, 94, 97, 102, 138
  (n. 1), 139 (n. 4), 139–40 (n. 14), 149 (n.
  1), 154, 157, 158, 166, 171, 174, 175, 177,
  182, 183
  Analysis Terminable and Interminable, 93
  Civilization and its Discontents, 44, 93, 174,
    183
  Society for Psychical Research, 103
  The Ego and the Id, 96, 146 (n. 7), 146 (n.
    8), 174
  Three Essays on Sexuality, 41
Fromm, Erich, 4, 35, 94, 97, 97–98, 143 (n.
  6), 157, 175, 177, 183
  The Art of Loving, 95, 146 (n. 4), 146 (n.
    10), 183

Garside, Christine, 139 (n. 11)
  See also Allen, Christine
Gehlen, Arnold, 4, 157
Geller, Uri, 148 (n. 15)
Genesis, book of, 12, 74, 139 (n. 11)
Gesell, Arnold, 78, 157, 182

Gill, Timothy V., 136 (n. 4), 173
Goldberg, Steven, 178
Goldenberg, American Academy of Pediat-
  rics, 144 (n. 2)
Gould, Roger, 182
Greer, Germaine, 140–41 (n. 15)
Grotevant, Harold, 176

Hansel, C. E. M., 157
  ESP: A Scientific Evaluation, 104
Hasley, A. H., 176
Hearnshaw, L. S., 176
Hegel, Georg Wilhelm Friedrich, 1, 11, 45,
  75, 76, 91, 94, 114, 157, 160, 180, 184
  concept of human maturity, 2
  development of consciousness, 2
  discussions of hypnotism, clairvoyance,
    telepathy, and precognition, and
    paranormal, 3
  instinct in man, 23–24
  Phenomenology of Spirit, 23–24, 78
  Philosophy of Right, 180; classifying man,
    10; paranormal and, 3
  The Philosophy of Mind, 77
  unity-duality problem, 60
Heidegger, Martin, 4, 157–58, 161, 166
  dualisms, 60–61
Heraclitus, 158, 166
  love as conflict of opposites, 2
Hobbes, Thomas, 2, 12, 144 (n. 13), 158
  on liberty, 75, 76
Homer, Plato's view of, 160
Hook, Sidney, 179, 180
Hume, David, 4, 17, 18, 59–60, 158
Husserl, Edmund, 4, 157–58, 161
  dualisms, 60–61
Hutcheson, Francis, *An Inquiry into the Orig-
  inal of our Ideas of Beauty and Virtue,* 93
Huxley, Julian, 158
  future of evolution, 2
  introduction to Teilhard de Chardin's
    The Phenomenon of Man, 55

Ilg, Frances L., 79, 158, 181

Jacklin, Carol, 177
James, William, 10, 13, 35, 36, 37, 80, 110,
  138 (n. 5), 142 (n. 7), 143 (n. 5), 144 (n.
  3), 149 (n. 25), 158, 184
  content over form, 63
  Essays on Faith and Morals, 102
  free will, 72
  Human Immortality, 102

Pragmatism, 68
Principles of Psychology, 10, 102
Society for Psychical Research, 103
Jaspers, Karl, 4, 158, 166
Jaynes, Julian, 178
Jensen, Arthur, 32, 33, 137 (chap. 3, n. 3),
   137–38 (chap. 3, n. 4), 158, 176
Jesus, 74, 106, 126, 127, 130, 132
Joel, book of, 85
John, St., gospel of, 90
Johnson, Miss G. M., 149 (n. 20)
Joseph, Rabbi Samuel K., 152–53 (n. 24)
Jung, Carl, 50, 53, 65, 85, 110–11, 115, 141
   (n. 3), 145 (n. 4), 158, 167, 168, 170, 171,
   174, 175, 178, 185
   archetypes and human instincts, 21, 174
   *Flying Saucers: A Modern Myth of Things
      Seen in the Skies,* 29
   introversion and extroversion, 36
   Memories, Dreams, and Reflections, 113, 185
   Psychological Types, archetype and instinct,
      17
   syzygy, 139–40 (n. 14)
   temperament, 37

Kainz, Howard P., 139 (n. 8), 139 (n. 9), 139
   (n. 10), 139 (n. 13), 143 (n. 6), 143 (n. 8),
   144 (n. 12), 144 (chap. 8, n. 1), 149–50 (n.
   3), 150 (n. 10), 180
Kallmann, F. J., 31, 137 (chap. 3, n. 2), 158
Kant, Immanuel, 114, 139 (n. 6), 142 (n. 8),
   157, 158–59, 184
   distinguishes two sexes, 44–45
   dualistic view of man, 2, 60, 61
   form over content, 63
   free will, 72–73
   freedom, 2, 143 (n. 9)
Kierkegaard, Søren, 1, 75, 139 (n. 7), 139
   (n. 8), 142 (n. 5), 159, 166, 177
   as dualist, 61
   differentiation of sexes, 45
   self, soul, and body, 60
King-Farlow, J., 177
Kirlian, Semyon, 168
Kirlian, Valentina, 168
Korein, Julius, 184
Kravitz, Harvey, 79, 144 (n. 2)
Kretschmer, Ernst, 65, 159
Kreyché, Gerald F., vii–viii, 184
Külpe, Oswald, 172
Kunz, Hans, 12
Kurtz, Paul, 147–48 (n. 5)

Lamark, J. B., 159
Leibniz, Gottfried, 159, 184
   monads, 59
Lepp, Ignace, 94, 97, 159
   The Psychology of Loving, 95–96, 146 (n. 6)
Letwin, Shirley, 146 (n. 9)
Levinson, Daniel, 182
Lévi-Strauss, Claude, 51, 159
Lévy-Bruhl, Lucien, 141 (n. 3), 159
Lewis, Hywel D., 185
Lidz, Theodore, 182
Locke, John, 4, 114, 159
   freedom, 2
Lorenz, Konrad, 31, 159, 174, 175
Lucas, J. R., 178
Ludwig, Jan, 184

Maccoby, Eleanor, 177
McDougall, William, 22, 160, 174
   Society for Psychical Research, 103
McLuhan, Marshall, 53, 141 (n. 10)
Mahowald, Mary B., 177
Malachy, St., 104, 159
Marcel, Gabriel, 166
Margolese, M. Sidney, 31, 137 (chap. 3, n.
   2)
Maritain, Jacques, 166
Martin, D. R., 106
Marx, Karl, 1, 11, 52, 160, 166
   *Economic and Philosophic Manuscripts of
      1844,* 46, 139 (n. 12)
May, Rollo, 4, 160
Mendelssohn, Moses, 163
Midgley, Mary, 175
Miles, Catherine C., 43, 139 (n. 3)
Mill, John Stuart, 160
   freedom, 2
Miller, Robert, 149 (n. 24)
Milton, John, 12, 160
Montagu, Ashley, 175, 177
Montaigne, Michel de, 4, 57, 160
Montessori, Maria, 137 (chap. 2, n. 4), 160
Moody, Raymond A., 151–52 (n. 19), 185
Morgan, Douglas, 182
Morgenbesser, Sidney, 180
Morris, Desmond, 175
Moses, 106
Murphy, Gardner, 184
Myers, F. W. H., 184
Myers, Gerald, 151 (n. 16)

New Testament, 74, 130
Newton, Isaac, 160

Neyhus, American Academy of Pediatrics, 144 (n. 2)
Niebuhr, Reinhold, 166
Nietzsche, Friedrich, 1, 11, 160, 184
  classifying man, 10
  concept of human maturity, 2
  Genealogy of Morals, 10
Nostradamus, Michel de, 104, 148 (n. 7), 148 (n. 8), 148 (n. 9), 148 (n. 10), 160

Offir, Carole, 177
Old Testament, 104
  Jews, 84
Origen, 185
Ortega y Gasset, José, 94, 160, 183
Osborne, Martha L., 139 (n. 8), 177

Panikkar, Raimundo, 178
Paps, Arthur, 180
Parmenides of Elea, 166
Pascal, Blaise, 12, 160
  Pensées, 17
Pastore, Nicholas, 138 (n. 6), 176
  The Nature-Nurture Controversy, 36, 176
Patterson, Francine, 173
Paul, St., 56, 130
Paz, Octavio, 179
Pearce (Zener card subject), 103, 106
Peghaire, Julien, 174
Penelhum, Terrence, 185
Perry, John, 185
Piaget, Jean, 144–45 (n. 5), 160, 181, 182
Piattelli-Palmarini, Massimo, 181
Pike, James, 149 (n. 22)
Pines, Maya, 145 (chap. 2, n. 6)
Plato, 1, 36, 109, 113, 143–44 (n. 10), 155, 160, 162, 166, 167, 177, 182, 184
  ancient concept of evolution, 2
  concept of human maturity, 2
  development of consciousness, 2
  Meno: freedom, 2; instinct, 17, 23
  Phaedo: immortality, 3
  radical dualism, 58–59, 61
  Republic, 1, 139 (n. 11)
  Statesman, 10
  Symposium, 1, 46, 94, 139 (n. 11), 182
  Timaeus, 1, 29, 70, 143 (n. 3)
Plessner, Helmut, 12, 161
Plotinus, 161
  ancient concept of evolution, 2
Plutarch, 185
Popper, Karl, 179
Pratt, J. Gaither, 103, 106, 161

Proclus, 185
Progroff, Ira, 174

Quinton, Anthony, 185

Regan, Tom, 173
Reich, Charles, 53, 141 (n. 9), 161, 178
Reinhart, Philip, 149 (n. 24)
Revelation, book of, 149 (n. 22)
Rhine, J. B., 103, 106, 107, 147–48 (n. 5), 148 (n. 11), 161, 183
Ring, Kenneth, 185
Roberts, Jane, 149 (n. 22)
Rosenstock-Huessy, Eugen, 161, 166, 179
Rosenzweig, Franz, 12, 161, 166
Rossi, Alice, 178
Rousseau, J. J., 12, 161
Rumbaugh, Duane M., 13, 136 (n. 4), 161, 173, 174
Russell, Bertrand, 161
  freedom, 2
Ryle, Gilbert, 58, 161

Sahlins, Marshall, 175
Samuel, book of, 107
Santayana, George, 161
Sartre, Jean-Paul, 4, 94, 144 (n. 11), 146 (n. 2), 156, 161, 166, 184
  dualisms, 60–61
  freedom, 2
Saul, King, 107
Scarr, Sandra, 176
Scheler, Max, 12, 94, 162, 183
  Man's Place in Nature, 9
Schelling, Friedrich von, 60, 162
Schiller, F. C. S., 162
  Society for Psychical Research, 103
Schneider, Isidor, 183
Schopenhauer, Arthur, 1, 94, 162
Schwartz, Oswald, 44, 50, 53, 94, 97, 139 (n. 5), 141 (n. 2), 141 (n. 6), 162
  The Psychology of Sex, 95, 146 (n. 5)
Sebeok, Thomas A., 173
Seguin, Alberto, 180
Shaftesbury, A., 4, 162
Shea, W., 177
Sheehy, Gail, 182
Sheldon, W. H., 65, 138 (n. 7), 139–40 (n. 14), 162
  temperament, 37
Shephard, Paul, 173
Sherfey, Mary, 138 (n. 1)
Shockley, William B., 32

Sidgwick, Henry, 103, 104, 162
Singer, June, 178
Singer, P., 173
Skinner, B. F., 162
    Beyond Freedom and Dignity, 70
Slater, Philip, 184
Smith, Adam, 183
Smythie, J. R., 183–84
Soal, S. G., 103, 106, 108, 157, 162
Socrates, 1, 17, 23, 74, 94, 113, 143–44 (n. 10), 160, 162, 167, 182
    knowledge needed for moral freedom, 73, 74
Solovyev, V. S., 94, 162, 183
Spinoza, Benedict, 94, 114, 162–63
    monistic view of man, 2, 59, 61
Stassinopoulos, A., 140–41 (n. 15)
Stewart, Mrs. Gloria, 103, 106
Stribic, F. P., 106
Struik, D. J., 139 (n. 12)

Tavris, Carol, 177
Teilhard de Chardin, Pierre, 4, 14–15, 48, 51, 53, 56, 141 (n. 4), 141 (n. 8), 149 (n. 26), 163, 178, 179
    convergent consciousness, 54–55
    critical threshold, 52
    evolution and biology, 54; analogies, 54–55
    fundamental option, 52
    future of evolution, 2
    radial energy, 133
    The Phenomenon of Man, 14, 49–50, 55, 141 (n. 1), 141 (n. 7), 141 (n. 13), 152 (n. 22)
Tennyson, Alfred, 72
Temerlin, Maurice, 173
Terman, Lewis M., 43, 139 (n. 3), 163

Terrance, Herbert S., 173
Thomas, Apostle, 130–31
Thomas Aquinas, St., 1, 94, 95, 97, 114, 143 (n. 9), 150 (n. 8), 154, 155, 167
    discussion of occult, and paranormal, 3
    instinct in man, 23
    love vs. knowledge, 146 (n. 3)
Thomas, Lewis, 141 (n. 13), 178
Tibetan Book of the Dead, 113
Tolstoy, L., *War and Peace,* 68
Toman, William, 177
Toynbee, Arnold, 184
    Surviving the Future, 93
Tuckachinsky, Rabbi Y. M., 152–53 (n. 24)
Twain, Mark, *Huckleberry Finn,* 42–43
Tyrell, G. N. M., 149 (n. 20), 163

Umiker-Sebeok, Donna Jean, 173
Unamuno, Miguel de, 94, 163

Walsh, James, 180
Watson, Neal, 177
Weinberg, Richard, 176
Weiss, Paul, 163
    "What is Man?" in *This Week,* 9
Wheatley, James, 184
White, Rhea A., 183
Wilson, Edward O., 163, 175
    Sociobiology: The New Synthesis, 33, 175
Witelson, Sandra F., 177
Wittgenstein, Ludwig, 58, 145–46 (chap. 10, n. 1), 163
Wolman, Benjamin, 183
Worrall, Olga, 149 (n. 24)

Yogananda, 149 (n. 22)

Zorab, George, 183

Index of Subjects

a posteriori, 164
a priori, 164
Abstract concepts, man's ability to, 13
Abstraction, 163
Action vs. knowledge, 74
Adlerian(s), 7, 177
Aesthetic sense, 163
    human consciousness and, 83–84

Aestimative power, 1, 163, 172
Afterlife, 73, 109, 118, 129–30, 149 (n. 22)
    See also Immortality
Aggression, 34, 35
Agnosticism, 163
Altruism, 163
Analogies, biology and evolution: Teilhard de Chardin, 54–55
Analytical psychology, 164
androgyny, 139–40 (n. 14), 164
Anima (Jung), 139–40 (n. 14), 164, 170, 171
Animus (Jung), 139–40 (n. 14), 164, 171

Anthropologists:
  distinguishing human characteristics, 13
  distinguishing human instincts, 22–23
Anthropology, 7
  as source of philosophical interest, 7–8
  dualism vs. monism, 2
  See Philosophical anthropology
Archetypal images, 110–11
Archetype(s), 164, 174
  human instincts and, 21, 24, 174
Astral body, 129–30f, 151 (n. 17), 151 (n. 19), 164, 185
Attitudinal traits, 37–38
Automatic-writing mediums, 107

Baconian, 46, 140 (n. 15)
Beavers and instinct, 20
Bee(s), 11, 12, 19
  and man's symbol-making ability, 12
  instinct and, 19
  use of symbols, 11–12
Behaviorism, 164
Being-for-another, 164
  and being-for-self, Kierkegaard's differentiation of sexes, 45
Being-for-self, 164
  and being-for-another, 45
Belief and existence of human soul, 122
Bible, 104, 148 (n. 6), 182
  See also under names of specific books, apostles, saints, etc., in Index of Authors
Biology and evolution, analysis: Teilhard de Chardin, 54–55
Bisexuality, 45, 46, 139–40 (n. 14)
  and male/female predominances, 45–46
Blacks and intelligence, 32–33, 34–35
Body/mind dualism, 6, 7, 57–67 (chap. 6), 142 (n. 1), 179–80
  vs. body/soul relationship, 66–67
Buddhism, 113

Caste system (India), 35
  as self-defeating, 38–39
Categorization and human consciousness, 81–82
Causal relationship, 164, 169
Causality, 65, 66, 69
  and body/mind interaction, 65–66
  and freedom, 69
  and prime analogate, 66, 142–43 (n. 10), 151 (n. 15)
Cause, ultimate, 119–20, 150 (n. 11)
Chauvinism, 1, 95

metaphysical, 45
Chimpanzee, Lana, 13–14
Choice, free. See Free choice
Christian point of view in philosophical inquiry, 3
Clairvoyance, 105–06
  Hegel's discussion of, and the paranormal, 3
Cockayne's syndrome, 91
Coconsciousness, 164
Coenesthesis, 24, 164–65
Cognitive power, 1, 165, 172, 174
  in Aquinas, and instinct, 23–24
Collective consciousness, 165
  Teilhard de Chardin, 132, 149 (n. 26)
Collective intellect, Averroes, 149 (n. 26)
Collective unconsciousness, 165
Communism and proper mutuality between sexes (Marx), 46
Community, love for, 147 (n. 13)
Concept of human maturity, 6, 87–92 (chap. 9), 181–82
  and philosophical analysis, 2
Concepts, man's ability to abstract, 13
Consciousness:
  collective (Teilhard de Chardin), 149 (n. 26)
  convergent (Teilhard de Chardin), 54–55
  development of, 2, 48–56 (chap. 5), 77–86 (chap. 8), 178–79; 181, Hegel and Fichte, 2; Plato and Aristotle, 2
  human, and aesthetic sense, 83–84; ethical sense, 84–85; evolution, 6, 7, 48–56 (chap. 5), 178–79; imagination, 81; irony, 85; memory, 81; paradox, 85; perception, 80; religious sense, 85; self-awareness, 82–83; sensation, 79–80; social extensivity, 83; understanding, 81–82; volition, 82; will, 82
  stages, 79–86
  primitive and modern, 50
  term defined, 115, 149 (n. 2), 165, 172
Conservatism, 165
Conservatives as hereditarians, 36
Content and form, 63–64
  human soul, 122–23
Convergent consciousness (Teilhard de Chardin), 54–55
Critical threshold (Teilhard de Chardin), 52
Cupid, 147 (n. 14)
  See also Eros

Darwinian, 51

Death:
  as experience, 118, 126–27f
  astral-body and, 129–30, 151 (n. 17)
  awareness of, 15
  individual survival after, 3, 6, 7, 113–34
    (chap. 12), 151–52 (n. 19), 184–85
  instinct (Freud), 96
  near-, experiences, 169
  purging Christian notion of, 131
Déjà vu, 165
Democracy as example of ideal unity, 62–63
Depth psychology. See Analytical psychology
Desires and love, 99–100
Determinism, 165, 170
Development:
  human. See Human development
  of consciousness, 2, 77–86 (chap. 8), 181;
    Plato, Aristotle, Hegel, and Fichte, 2
Developmental psychology, 165
Diabetes, 30
Dialectics, 165
Difference-in-:
  degree, 165
  kind, 165
Differences:
  between man and woman, 1, 6, 41–47
    (chap. 4), 177–78
  specific, between man and other animals,
    1, 5–6, 9–16 (chap. 1), 173–74
Differential psychology, 165
Differentiation, subject/object, and instinct,
  23–24
Direct-voice medium, 107
Disembodied:
  entity, 127–28
  soul, 130
Divination and dreams, Aristotle's treatises
  on, paranormal and, 3
Divine instinct in man, 1
Down Through (DT), 108, 148 (n. 12)
Dreaming and soul, 126
Dreams and divination, Aristotle's treatises
  on, paranormal and, 3
Drosophila fruit flies, 30
DT (Down Through), 108, 148 (n. 12)
Dualism, 165
  vs. monism, 6, 7, 57–67 (chap. 6), 179–80
  and Psi, 109–10, 112
  in anthropology, 2
Dualistic:
  views of man, 2; Descartes, 2; Kant, 2
  vs. monist, 142 (n. 1)

Dualists, 169
Duality:
  three meanings of, 64–67
  -unity problem, 57–67 (chap. 6), 179–80

Ego, 114–15, 149 (n. 1), 165
  -Ideal. See Super-Ego
"Ego," 83, 115
Einsteinian perception, 51
Empirical, multiple connotations and
  philosophical anthropology, 4–5
Empiricism, 165
Energy, radial, and spirit, 133
England, research on telepathy, 103–04
Environment vs.:
  genetic variables, 140 (n. 15)
  heredity, 1, 6, 29–40 (chap. 3), 175–77;
    and liberal vs. conservative, 36; educa-
    tion and, 1; real test, 39–40
Environmentalism, 165, 167
Environmentalists, 169
Epistemology, 148 (n. 18)
  and paranormal, 108f
Equivocation, 166
Eros, 93ff, 101, 147 (n. 14), 157, 174
  See also Love
ESP, 102ff, 166, 167, 172
  See also Telepathy, Paranormal Phe-
  nomena, Extrasensory perception
Eternity, 123
Ethical sense, 166
  and human consciousness, 84–85
Evolution, 166, 169
  diminution of instinct in man, 20–21
  human consciousness, 6, 48–56 (chap. 5),
    178–79
  future of, 2; Teilhard de Chardin on,
    49ff; and biology, analogies, 54–55
  highest stages of, 2
  human society and, 48ff
  theories of, 2
Existence, 166
  implied fulfillment of, 88–89
  meanings of term, 88, 150 (n. 10)
  of soul, 119–21
Existential maturity, attempt to define,
  91–92
Existentialism, 4, 166–67
Existentialist:
  Kierkegaard as, 45
  monistic views of man, 2
Extrasensory perception, 102ff, 167, 170

See also ESP, Paranormal phenomena, Telepathy
Extroversion, 167, 168, 172
  and introversion (Jung), 36

Faith, leap of, 134
Felicity, 145 (chap. 9, n. 1)
Female/male:
  differentiation, 43–44
  predominances, 46
  See also Woman, Man
Feminine, three meanings from Freud, 41
  See also Woman
First-order phenomena, 167, 171
Flies, fruit, 30
Form, 167
  and content, 63–64; human soul, 122–23
Free:
  choice, 69–72, 167
  will, 69, 72–75, 167; as self-determination, 72, 73–75
Freedom(s), 2, 6, 51, 57f, 68–76 (chap. 7), 180
  Aristotle's (*Nichomachean Ethics*), 2
  development of idea, 69–76
  moral, and knowledge, 73–74
  Plato's (*Meno*), 2
  requirements for, 76
  sociopolitical, 69, 75–76
Freudian(s), 7, 31, 35, 50, 84, 88, 115, 149–50 (n. 3), 169, 172, 177, 181; neo-Freudians, 44, 183
Fruit flies, 30
Fulfillment, 145 (chap. 9, n. 1)
  as substitute for happiness, 87
  See also Maturity, human
Fundamental option (Teilhard de Chardin), 52
Future:
  evolution of man, and Teilhard de Chardin, 49ff
  of evolution, 2

General Extrasensory Perception (GESP), 108, 109, 167
Genetic:
  mutations, 30–31
  science, 30
  vs. environmental variables, 140 (n. 14)
GESP. *See* General Extrasensory Perception
"Glossalalia" as complex nonuniversal human instinct, 25–26
God, 59, 110, 123, 133, 149–150 (n. 3)

grace of, 75
love of, 146–47 (n. 12)
Spinoza's, 162–63
union with, 89
Gospels, 106
"Great Chain of Being," 2
  See also Evolution
Greek:
  culture, 139 (n. 11)
  philosophy, 1
"Gynandrophenia" (Sheldon), 139–40 (n. 14)

Happiness, 87f, 145 (chap. 9, n. 1)
Hate vs. love, 96
Heaven, 132
Hegelian, 45
  "system" and Kierkegaard, 159
Hell, 132
Hereditarianism, 167
Hereditarians, 169
Heredity:
  -environment problem, 1
  vs. environment, 1, 6, 29–40 (chap. 3), 175–77; conservative vs. liberal, 36; real test, 39–40
Hermaphrodite, 42
Hierarchical social rankings as complex, nonuniversally recognized human instincts, 26–27, 174
"Highest stages" of:
  evolution. *See* Evolution
  consciousness. *See* Paranormal phenomena
Hindu, 56, 130, 133, 149 (n. 26)
  maya, 56
Homosexuality, "causes" of, 31
Hormones, sex, and personality, 42
Hostility, 145 (n. 2)
Human:
  consciousness, 78; and aesthetic sense, 84–85; evolution, 6, 48–56 (chap. 5), 178–79; imagination, 81; irony, 85; memory, 81; paradox, 85; perception, 80; religious sense, 85; self-awareness, 82–83; sensation, 79–80; social extensivity, 83; understanding, 81–82; volition, 82; will, 82; *see also* Consciousness
  development, stages, 89–90; of consciousness, 79–86
  happiness, 87f
  instinct(s), 1, 7; *see* Instincts; Instincts, human

maturity, concept of, 6, 87–92 (chap. 9),
    181–82; and philosophical analysis, 2
nature, 15–16
society, evolution, 48ff
soul, 58f
Hypnotism:
    as complex, nonuniversal human instinct,
        25–26
    Hegel's discussions of, paranormal and, 3

"Id," 115, 149–50 (n. 3), 167
Ideal or mental:
    duality, 64–65
    unity, 62–63
Idealism, 167
Identity as person vs. sex identity, 46
Imagination, 167–68
    and human consciousness, 77, 81
Immortality, 3, 109f, 132
Indetermination, 168
India, caste system, 35
    as self-defeating, 38–39
Individual survival after death, 3, 6, 113–34
    (chap. 12), 151–52 (n. 19), 184–85
Individualism, 168
Individuality, 57f
Infinity, 123
Instinct(s), 17–28 (chap. 2), 168, 174–75
    by analogy of attribution (Instinct₂), 19
    human, 1, 7, 20; Bergson's intuition and,
        21–22, 24; complex, nonuniversal,
        25–26, 26–28; Jung's archetypes and,
        21, 24, 174
    in man vs. animals, 18
    primary sense (Instinct₁), 19
    simple vs. complex, 19–20ff
    used equivocally, 18
    vs. learning, 23, 24
    vs. reason, 5–6
Intellect, collective, Averroes, 149 (n. 26)
Intelligence, 31–32
    and race, 32–33
    measuring, problems, 33
    See also IQ
Intentionality and knowledge, 146 (n. 2)
Introversion, 167, 168, 172
    and extroversion (Jung), 36
Intuition, 168
    and instinct, 21–22, 24
IQ, 31–32, 34–35, 39, 137 (chap. 3, n. 3),
    137–38 (chap. 3, n. 4), 176
    and androgyny, 139–40 (n. 14)
    scores of blacks, 32–33, 34–35, 137–38
        (chap. 3, n. 4)

Irony and human consciousness, 85

Jungian(s), 7, 31, 88, 115, 116, 149–50 (n.
    3), 172, 178

Kirlian photography, 132, 168
Knowledge:
    as unity-in-distinction, 98
    compared to love, 94–95, 97–98, 145–46
        (chap. 10, n. 1), 146 (n. 3), 146 (n. 11)
    intentionality and, 146 (n. 2)
    needed for moral freedom, Socrates, 73
    self-determination and, 73–74
    vs. action, 74

Language and syntactical structures as
    complex, nonuniversally recognized
    human instinct, 27–28
Last Judgment, 128, 131
Law of Talion, 84
Leap of faith, 134
Learning vs. instinct, 23, 24
Liberalism, 168
Liberals as environmentalists, 36
Libertarianism, 168, 171
Liberty, 69, 75–76, 168
    and Thomas Hobbes, 75, 76
License, 168
Life after death, 113–34 (chap. 12), 184–85
    See also Survival after death, individual;
        Death
Linguistic:
    analysis, 168
    philosophy, 4
Logical possibility, 168, 170
Love, 2–3, 6, 93–101 (chap. 10), 144 (n. 14),
    182–83
    as attraction of similars (Empedocles),
        2–3; conflict of opposites (Heraclitus),
        2; a kind of perfection, 6; mature aes-
        thetic sense, 84; unity-in-distinction, 98
    cosmic, 100–01
    compared to knowledge, 94–95, 97–98,
        145–46 (chap. 10, n. 1), 146 (n. 3), 146
        (n. 11)
    for community, 147 (n. 13)
    romantic, 144 (n. 14), 145 (chap. 8, n. 6),
        146 (n. 9)
    throughout history of Western philoso-
        phy, 94–97ff
    types and ordering, 97–101, 146–47 (n.
        12), 147 (n. 13)
    vs. desires, 99–100; hate, 96; needs,
        99–100

what it is, 97; and is *not*, 95–97

Male/female:
  differentiation, 43–44; *see also* Man, Woman
  predominances, 46
Man:
  and other animals, specific differences, 1, 5–6, 9–16 (chap. 1), 173–74
  as political animal, 9, 11; rational animal, 9, 10; user/maker of symbols, 10, 11–12
  classified by Aristotle, 9–10
  final definition (epilogue), 135
  /woman differences, 1, 6, 41–47 (chap. 4), 177–78
Manic-depressive psychoses, 31
Marxian, 35, 48
Masculine, three meanings from Freud, 41
  See also Man
Materialism, 169
Materialistic:
  explanations: extreme position, 62; of universe, 58–61
  reductionist point of view in philosophical inquiry, 3–4
Maturity, 82
  existential, attempt to define, 91–92
  human: concept of, 6, 7, 87–92 (chap. 9), 181–82; Aristotle and, 145 (n. 5); philosophical analysis and, 2; defining, 87–88
maya (Hindu sages and mystics), 56
MCE (mean chance expectation), 147 (n. 2), 169
  See also Mean chance expectation
me. See Ego
Mean chance expectation, 147 (n. 2), 169, 170
Measuring intelligence, problems, 33
Medieval(s), 51
  scholastics and human instinct, 1
Mediums, 107, 108–09
  See also specific types of mediums
Mediumship, 107, 108–09, 169
  and life after death, 114
Memory and human consciousness, 81
Mental:
  and personality traits, 31
  explanation: extreme position, 61–62; of universe, 58–61
  or ideal: duality, 64–65; unity, 62–63
  -physical: duality, 65–66; unity, 63–64
Metaphysics and paranormal, 108f

Methodology and objectivity in philosophical inquiry, 3–5
Middle Ages, 51, 59, 104
Mind:
  /body: as prime analogate of causality, 66, 142–43 (n. 10); dualism, 6, 57–67 (chap. 6), 83, 142 (n. 1), 179–80; vs. soul-body relationship, 66–67
  -reading, 105-06
  term, 115, 142 (n. 4), 149–50 (n. 3), 169
  See also Consciousness
Miracles, 106, 148 (n. 6)
Monad, 169
Monism, 169
  vs. dualism, 6, 57–67 (chap. 6), 179–80; and Psi, 109–10, 112; in anthropology, 2
Monistic:
  views of man, 2; and freedom, 69; existentialists, 2; Spinoza, 2
  vs. dualist, 142 (n. 1)
Moral freedom and knowledge, 73–74
Myopia, 30–31
Mystical experience, 169

Naked thought (Würzburg school), 129
Natural selection, 166, 169
Nature:
  -nurture: and human consciousness, 86; debate, 169; problem, 1, 176
  of man, 15–16
Near-death experiences, 169, 185
Needs and love, 99–100
"Neonate," 80
Netherlands, research on telepathy, 103–04
New Testament, 74, 130
  See also entries on specific New Testament books in Index of Authors
Nonmaterialist:
  explanation: extreme position, 61–62; of universe, 58–61
  term, 142 (n. 2)
Norms:
  objective, 169, 171
  subjective, 171
Nurture, Nature-. *See* Nature-nurture

Object/subject. *See* Subject/object
Objective norms, 169, 171
Objectivity and methodology in philosophical inquiry, 3–5
Occult:
  Aquinas' discussion of, paranormal and, 3

as field of study (Freud), 102
See also Paranormal phenomena
Occultism, 131
Oedipus complex, 84, 169, 171
Old Testament, 104
Jews, 84
See also entries on specific Old Testament
books in Index of Authors
Ontological:
differences between man and woman, 1
possibility, 169–70, 170; soul as, 122
Ontology, 170
Opposites, love as conflict of, 2
Oriental philosophies, 149 (n. 26), 178
See also entries on individual philosophies
(Existentialism, et al.)

Paradox, 170
and human consciousness, 85
Paranormal phenomena, 3, 6, 102–12
(chap. 11), 128, 183–84
See also Parapsychological, Parapsychol-
ogy
Parapsychological phenomena, 3
See Paranormal
Parapsychology, 7, 103f, 170
as source of philosophical interest, 8
journals, 147–48 (n. 5)
Perception, 170
and human consciousness, 80
Person, 151 (n. 19)
identity as, vs. sex-identity, 46
Persona, 170
Personality, 57f, 116, 170
and mental traits, 31; sex hormones, 42
as self, 115–16
Phenomenology, 4, 170
Philosophical anthropology, 173
and Renaissance times, 4–5
generalization, 4
Philosophy of science and paranormal,
108f
Photography, Kirlian, 132, 168
Physical:
duality, 64
mediums, 107, 148 (n. 16)
-mental: duality, 65–66; unity, 63–64
unity, 62
PK (psychokinesis), 106–07, 110, 149 (n. 23),
149 (n. 24), 170
Platonist point of view in philosophical inquiry, 3
Political freedom. See Liberty
Positivism, 170

Possibility:
logical, 168, 170
ontological, 122, 169–70, 170
soul, 122, 124–25f, 170
term, 151 (n. 13)
Precognition, 104–05, 109, 170
Hegel's discussions of, paranormal and, 3
Predominances, male/female, 46
Premonitions, 104
Probability of soul's possibility, 126ff
Projection, 170
Proprioreception, 170
Psi, 104ff, 147 (n. 4), 148 (n. 6), 170, 183,
184
Psyche, 147 (n. 14)
Psychic(s), 104, 128, 170
Psychokinesis (PK), 106–07, 110, 149 (n.
23), 149 (n. 24), 170
Psychologists, and distinguishing human
characteristics, 12
Psychology:
as source of philosophical interest, 7
contemporary developmental, and de-
velopment of consciousness, 2
Psychoses, manic-depressive, 31

Race and intelligence, 32–33
Radial energy and spirits, 133
Rankings, hierarchical social, as complex,
nonuniversally recognized human in-
stinct, 26–27, 174
Rationalism, 170–71
Reason:
in man, 10; Aristotle, 9
vs. instinct, 5–6, 17–28 (chap. 2), 174–75
Reasoning, syllogistic, 171–72
Reconciliationism, 168, 171
Reductionism, 171
Reductionist, materialistic point of view in
philosophical inquiry, 3–4
Reflection in man, 14–15
Reincarnation, 171
Religious sense and human consciousness,
85
Reminiscence, 171
in man, 10–11; Aristotle, 9
Renaissance, 51, 94
and philosophical anthropology, 4–5
Resurrection, 126, 151 (n. 17)
Jesus, 130
Romantic love, 144 (n. 14), 145 (chap. 8, n.
6), 146 (n. 9), 171

Salmon and instinct, 19

Schizophrenia, 31
Science, philosophy of, paranormal and, 108f
Second-order phenomenon, 171
Secondary sex characteristics, 33–34
Self, 83
    as archetype, 172; concept, beginnings, 51
    -awareness and human consciousness, 82–83
    -concept, 83
    consciousness in man, 14–15, 57f, 171
    -determination, free will as, 72, 73–75
    -reflection, 15
    term defined, 115–16, 171
Sensation, 171
    and human consciousness, 77, 79–80
Sex:
    characteristics, secondary, 33–34
    hormones and personality, 42
    -identity vs. identity as person, 46
    organs, development of, 41–42
Sickle-cell anemia, 30
Similars, love as attraction of, 2–3
Simple instincts. See Instincts
Sleep and soul, 126–27, 128
Social:
    extensivity and human consciousness, 83
    rankings, hierarchical, as complex, nonuniversally recognized human instinct, 26–27, 174
Society:
    for Psychical Research (SPR), 103
    human, evolution, 48ff
Sociobiology, 33, 171
Sociopolitical freedom. See Freedom, Liberty
Sophists, 36
Soul (human), 57–61f, 114, 115, 116, 117, 118, 170, 171, 184–85
    as ground for existence, 119–21; ontological possibility, 122
    -body vs. mind-body relationship, 66–67
    dialogue over, 121–34
    form vs. content, 122–23
    possibility, 122, 124–25f
    probability, 126ff
    question of existence, 119
    term, 116, 142 (n. 4), 149–50 (n. 3), 150 (n. 4)
    vs. spirit, 117–18, 118, 131, 150 (n. 9), 151 (n. 19)
Soviet Union, 48, 103
Space, 64, 142 (n. 9)

Speaking in tongues. See Glossalalia
Spiders and instinct, 19
Spirit, 171
    term, 150 (n. 7)
    vs. soul, 117–18, 118, 131, 150 (n. 9), 151 (n. 19)
Spiritualist religion, 107
Structures, syntactical, and language as complex, nonuniversally recognized human instinct, 27–28
Subject/object differentiation and instinct, 23–24
Subjective norms, 171
Suicide, 12, 15
"Super-Ego," 84, 115, 169, 171, 172
Survival after death, individual, 3, 6, 113–34 (chap. 12), 151–52 (n. 19), 184–85
Syllogisms, 171
Syllogistic reasoning, 171–72
Symbols:
    and man, 11–12; Cassirer, 10
    used by bees, 11–12
Syntactical structures and language as complex, nonuniversally recognized human instinct, 27–28
Synthesis, 172
Syzygy (Jung), 139–40 (n. 14)

Talion, law of, 84
Taoism, 149 (n. 26)
Taoist philosopher, 156
Telepathy, 102, 106, 110, 149 (n. 25), 172
    analogy, 111–12
    Hegel's discussions of, paranormal and, 3
    research, 103–04
    See also Paranormal phenomena
Temperament, 172
    and Jung and Sheldon, 37
Temperamental types, James', 35–36
Temporality and future of evolution, 2
Thanatos, 93, 157, 174
Time and intellectual operations of soul, 123
Tongues, speaking in. See Glossalalia
Trance mediums, 107
    control, 148 (n. 17)
Transcendence. See Paranormal, Survival
Transcendent. See Paranormal, Survival
Types, temperamental (William James), 35–36

Ultimate cause, 119–20, 150 (n. 11)
Unconscious:

collective, Jung, 110–11
  term defined, 115, 172
Understanding, 172
  and human consciousness, 77, 81–82
Unisex, 46, 139–40 (n. 14)
Unity:
  -duality problem, 57–67 (chap. 6),
    179–80
  three meanings of, 62–64

Vis aestimativa, 1, 163, 172
Vis cogitativa, 1, 165, 172, 174
Volition:
  and human consciousness, 82
  See also Will

Will, 172
  and body, 6, 68–76 (chap. 7), 180
  and human consciousness, 77, 82
  free. *See* Free will
  See also Freedom
Woman and man, differences, 1, 6, 41–47
  (chap. 4), 177–78
World, other than our own, 118–19
Würzburg school, 129, 172

Zener:
  cards, 103, 172
  symbols, 103, 106, 147 (n. 1)